The Critic's
Notebook

The critic possesses a dual personality. He is at once an 'artist' and a 'thinker,' the 'man of feeling' and the 'intellectual.' He has a speculative mind and is interested in ideas. It is not enough to see and feel; he wants to know why he sees and feels as he does, why certain forms of seeing and feeling are more important than others. He is an artist, but a special kind of artist.

MARTIN TURNELL, "An Essay on Criticism," *Dublin Review*, 444 (Last Quarter 1948), 73.

Damn your taste, I would like if possible to sharpen your perceptions, after which your taste can take care of itself.

EZRA POUND, *Polite Essays*, p. 136. Copyright 1937 by Faber and Faber, Ltd., and by New Directions Books. Reprinted by permission of the publishers.

The Critic's Notebook

EDITED BY

Robert Wooster Stallman

THE UNIVERSITY OF MINNESOTA PRESS · Minneapolis

LONDON · GEOFFREY CUMBERLEGE · OXFORD UNIVERSITY PRESS

TO THE RICARDO QUINTANAS

Foreword

The Critic's Notebook consists of notes which I collected in trying to search out the ways in which a literary work can be viewed and theory criticized. I was concerned with finding out—to quote F. R. Leavis' phrase—"how to talk to the point about poems, novels, and plays, and how to promote intelligent and profitable discussion of them."

Theoretical discussion should be cross-checked by textual analysis; theory and opinion specifically applied to literary examples. To talk to the point about the literary text requires both theoretical and technical thinking. Technical thinking begins in scrutinizing the poem in terms of the critical questions it raises, or conversely, in demonstrating the critical answers in terms of the poem. Though my quotations have to do principally with poetic and critical theory, they include some specimens of "practical" criticism.

For example, the text and an interpretation of Allen Tate's poem "The Subway" are presented to illustrate John Crowe Ransom's discussion of the problem of intentions. The problem is discussed by Paul Valéry in commenting on the interpretation a critic made of his poem "Le Cimetière Marin," and it is raised by Hart Crane's statement of his intended meaning in "At Melville's Tomb." T. S. Eliot wrote: "I do not believe that an author is more qualified to elucidate the esoteric significance of his own work than is any other person of training and sensibility and at least equal intelligence." The other side of this matter is posed by A. E. Housman's pronouncement that he intended no irony in his poem "1887," a pronouncement of author's intentions of which the test lies in an examination of his poem. The reprinting of such documents should provide a useful strategy for the study and teaching of criticism.

Three hundred quotations are organized into eight chapters dealing systematically with central concepts and problems of modern criticism. They are the problems which the literary work raises and which confront the critic in his job of elucidating the work of art. Each chapter deals with one of these constant factors in critical theory or practice: the Nature and Function of Criticism, Life and Art, Form, Poetic Meaning, the "Objective Correlative," the Personal Element, Poetic Belief, the Problem of Intentions. An Index provides cross-references to the miscellany of topics discussed: the creative process, symbolism and realism, myth, et cetera. The scope of my source material is indicated by the Bibliography, which supplements this selection. The Bibliography looks forward to the growing interests of the scholar concerned with tracing the history of these root ideas and key problems of criticism — for instance, the problem of belief, which is generally considered "the chief problem of poetic criticism."

Each chapter — except Chapter 1, "The Nature and Function of Criticism," which treats the relation of poem to reader or critic — is divided into sections illustrating the three main categories of criticism. The opening sequence of quotations in each chapter presents insights on the creative process; the middle section defines the nature of a work of art; the final section attends to the critic's job of interpretation. Each chapter is thus ordered into these three categories: the poem in relation to the poet (poetic creation); the poem as a thing in itself (poetic meaning and form); and the poem in relation to the reader or critic (poetic appreciation). These three aspects are implied, for example, in the idea of the "Objective Correlative" (Chapter V), which, viewed thus, becomes something more than simply a principle of composition. The Problem of Intentions (Chapter VIII) falls into the same three divisions and must be similarly discriminated — in terms of the poet-to-poem and poem-to-reader relationships. All critical writings, in fact, can be classified under one or another of these three dimensions of criticism.

What I aimed at was to create a fresh synthesis. Drawing from the whole body of British and American criticism from 1920 to 1950, I have attempted to bring together for the first time the best critical thought on the basic critical issues. The quotations are unified by internal kinship apart from authorship or school. They are not meant to be "representative" of their authors, or exclusively of any single school. And they are ordered so as to conduce to an over-all design. Thus, some of them serve to define or demonstrate the designated problem; some serve solely as echoes or parallelisms, whereby the development of these ideas is traced; others, representing the point of view of the opposition, serve as counter-allegations to the dominating critical stand.

What this criticism has achieved, both in elucidation of texts and in establishment of doctrine, has come about by the collaborative contributions of *many* critics, all of them dealing with the same family of themes and problems. Insights and critical discriminations proposed by one member of the group evolve from, and in turn furnish, the germinal hints of others. No one critic formulates all the principles. The richest possible critical achievement is the collective one. This book demonstrates that criticism is a collaborative enterprise. It should prove a useful aid in furthering this collective process.

ROBERT WOOSTER STALLMAN

Acknowledgments

To the members of my course in Modern Criticism at the University of Kansas (1947–48–49) who discussed these critical ideas with me and helped me compile some of these chapters, I wish to express my deep appreciation. For work done in assembling these notes I have to thank Laurel Crabb, Mary Faulders, Barbara Haffner, Herbert Kauffman, and Robert Taylor. I want also to thank Albert Blair and Betty Henderson for their valued assistance; Mrs. Marvin Gregory for the typing of the manuscript; the Graduate School of the University of Kansas and its dean, John H. Nelson, for grants-in-aid; the librarians of the University of Kansas for friendly service; and my wife, Virginia Stallman, for her assistance in cataloguing a vast collection of notes and preparing the manuscript for the press.

I am indebted most of all to Robert Penn Warren, who sponsored this book from the start, guided its development, and helped me in every possible way. Mr. Warren went over the manuscript several times and offered many valuable suggestions. This book has benefited greatly from his expert criticisms.

I am obliged to my numerous authors and publishers for allowing me to quote from works to which they hold copyright; their names are cited in the reference notes. Grateful acknowledgment is made also to the editors of the journals in which parts of this book have appeared: *American Literature*; *American Review*; *College English*; *Critique*; *Dial*; *Dublin Review*; *English Literary History*; *Explicator*; *Hound and Horn*; *Hudson Review*; *International Literature*; *New Mexico Quarterly Review*; *Partisan Review*; *Poetry*; *Rice Institute Pamphlets*; *Southern Review*; *Times Literary Supplement*; *University of Kansas City Review*; *University of Toronto Quarterly*; and *Western Review*.

My thanks are due also to John Middleton Murry, editor of the *Adelphi*; Joseph T. Shipley, editor of the *American Bookman*; Edgell Rickword, editor of the *Calendar of Modern Letters*; T. S. Eliot, editor of *Criterion*; John Crowe Ransom, editor of the *Kenyon Review*; F. R. Leavis, editor of *Scrutiny*; John Palmer, editor of the *Sewanee Review*; and Philip Wheelwright, editor of *Symposium*.

Of the authors contributing to this book, more than fifty have contributed one or more passages of their writings which have not appeared elsewhere in book form. I wish to acknowledge the special debt I owe to T. S. Eliot for his generous grant of permission to draw freely upon his periodical publications; to Mrs. W. A. Bradley for kind permission to reprint from essays of the late Paul Valéry which appear in book form here for the first time; to Pearn, Pollinger, and Higham, Ltd., authors' agents, for permission to quote from the writings of D. H. Lawrence and from Ezra Pound's *Polite Essays*; to F. R. Leavis, John Middleton Murry, and Mario Praz for allowing me to quote large amounts of their writings from essays which have not received previous book publication. And, finally, I wish here to express my gratitude to Philip Wheelwright for the gift of his collection of little magazines made several years ago; his gift provided me with some of the source material for this book.

R. W. S.

Storrs, Connecticut
May, 1950

Table of Contents

xiii

I

The Nature and Function of Criticism

My opinion of critics is that:
*The best are those who actually cause an amelioration in the
art which they criticize.*

*The next best are those who most focus attention on the best
that is written (or painted or composed or cut in stone).*

*And the pestilential vermin are those who distract attention
from the best, either to the second rate, or to hokum, or to their
own critical writings.*

The Critic's Job

. . . it becomes the critic's job first to discriminate between different kinds of literary experience, then to show how the best kind, the kind that is richest and deepest, can be obtained, and only later to explain how an individual work, such as *Paradise Lost*, is related to the society that produced it, or how its effect on the reader is related to the society that produced *him*. The critic's job is to boost or jack up the individual reader to as high as possible a level of enjoyment, to move him from the cellar to the pent-house, where he can get a better view. "Society" is only a part of the prospect.

The main function of criticism, Matthew Arnold said, is "to see the object in itself as it really is." He added to that the necessity of seeing the object as a *whole*. And it is in trying to achieve that essential vision that the double, if secondary, relation between literature and society plays a part.

. . .

The critic's first job, then, in trying to see the work as fully as possible, becomes almost at once a technical one. To isolate, to analyse, to compare, and to evaluate — his four-fold function —

this will first be performed on the level of technique. And if he does this well, if he discusses the use of words, the rhythms, the relation of one part to another and of the parts to the whole, in a properly professional manner, he will be performing a considerable service to criticism. But he cannot happily think of this as an isolated function. While he performs it the modern critic (in a way that would never have troubled Dr. Johnson) becomes aware of the implications, the relationships, behind his act, and he soon comes to the conclusion that technique in any art includes not merely the use of given material but also the choice of what materials to use, and when he reaches this point, a new set of relationships begins to appear. The question changes from "what?" to "why?" and the various historical explanations raise their seductive and delusive heads. The most delusive, and often the least fruitful of these is the hunt for source material; Mr. Sinclair Lewis has himself best illustrated this fact. He was once asked what he thought of a work which traced the sources of his novels to Zola and the French realists. "Nothing," he replied. "The only source for *Main Street* that I am aware of was Malory's *Morte D'Arthur*; I wrote *Main Street* because there was nothing like Malory in the Middle West." THEODORE SPENCER [1]

All men crave forms and standards. We take delight in recognition. The individual work of art has precision in itself; the critic must make equally precise the relations, as he sees them, between the work of art and its various elements, its milieu, its history, its creator, its reader, its critic, and all standards used in judging it.

The critic keeps a perilous balance between awareness of the individual work of art and awareness of its communal audience. Unique, extrarational in many of its elements, and immediate as a poem is and must, after criticism, remain, the critic must nevertheless proceed in method to find in it common elements which may make it more intelligible after deliberate survey and analysis. And finally, no man is a literary critic, excellent though he be

[1] "The Critic's Function," *Sewanee Review*, 47 (October–December 1939), 553, 555–56.

as esthetician, scholar, or creative artist, in whose writings our primary pleasure does not spring from seeing specific works of art more clearly, easily or completely. DONALD A. STAUFFER [2]

I assume that criticism is that department of thought which either seeks to find out what poetry is, what its use is, what desires it satisfies, why it is written and why read, or recited; or which, making some conscious or unconscious assumption that we do know these things, assesses actual poetry. We may find that good criticism has other designs than these; but these are the ones which it is allowed to profess. Criticism, of course, never does find out what poetry is, in the sense of arriving at an adequate definition; but I do not know of what use such a definition would be if it were found. Nor can criticism ever arrive at any final appraisal of poetry. But there are these two theoretical limits of criticism: at one of which we attempt to answer the question "what is poetry?" and at the other "is this a good poem?" No theoretic ingenuity will suffice to answer the second question, because no theory can amount to much which is not founded upon a direct experience of poetry; but on the other hand our direct experience of poetry involves a good deal of generalising activity.

The two questions, which represent the most abstract formulation of what is far from being an abstract activity, imply each other. The critic who remains worth reading has asked, if he has only imperfectly answered, both questions. T. S. ELIOT [3]

Criticism, as Pope observed, is an invidious task: for while it requires for its practice taste, judgement, learning, candour and truth, and the exercise of a genius second only to that of the poet. it carries with it a greater probability of error than any other

[2] Introduction, pp. 24-25 in *The Intent of the Critic*, edited by Donald A. Stauffer. Copyright 1941 by Princeton University Press. Reprinted by permission of the publisher.
[3] *The Use of Poetry and the Use of Criticism*, p. 16. Copyright 1933 by Faber and Faber, Ltd., and by Harvard University Press. Reprinted by permission of the publishers.

theoretical activity of comparable distinction. For unlike a scientific hypothesis or a mathematical proposition, an aesthetic judgement is incapable of proof and can never therefore be conclusive in the same way. But this does not invalidate the principles on which it is based, nor does it lessen the importance of the critical faculty which is not only allied to the creative, but, as such, to that which Giambattista Vico, the founder of modern aesthetics, regarded as primitive and fundamental — the power of imaginative expression. On the contrary, if, as Croce contends in his exposition and development of this theory, the creative and critical faculties differ not in kind but only in degree, it may even be said that the fallibility of the judgement is a proof that it belongs, like other vital and formative processes, to the perpetual "becoming" of life, of which finality, in one sense, must always be a negation. Moreover, in so far as the exact sciences are tending increasingly towards the acceptance of "the principle of indeterminacy," the fact that aesthetics must likewise be "satisfied with probabilities" may be regarded as significant.

If, then, the theory of art is progressive, no judgement of taste can be absolute, though it may remain true within limits of its statement, which is perhaps the most that can be required of it — as of the critic, who must, nevertheless, be held responsible for his opinions, whether they be valid or otherwise. At the same time, when he has once determined the principles of his aesthetic creed he cannot be expected to justify his conclusions, since "what is wrong with criticism today," as Herbert Read, himself, has pointed out, "is not too much dogma, but too little" — a statement that is not only true on the face of it, but one which indicates that criticism is no enviable task nor lightly to be undertaken. E. H. RAMSDEN [4]

The critic can justify his choice of method in three ways: (1) by theoretical arguments defining its nature and the grounds of ·

[4] "Herbert Read's Philosophy of Art," p. 42 in *Herbert Read*, edited by Henry Treece. Copyright 1944 by Faber and Faber, Ltd. Reprinted by permission of the publisher.

his choice; (2) by practical demonstrations of the method in operation; (3) by claims for it as a moral contribution over and above its value as a specialty (that is, he may argue for it as a cultural amenity, equipment for living, means of political betterment, etc.). Often the third class of justifications is non-descript, deriving vitality from true or false promises of individual reward (social, occupational, financial, sexual, etc.), interests which are not recognized formally. KENNETH BURKE [5]

Good critical writing is always more or less empirical in method, which means that the critic looks first and last at the poem, while he tries to determine what poetic theory will be the one to accomplish its analysis. Each poem is a new poem, and each analysis is probably the occasion of a new extension of theory in order to cope with it. Poetic theory will never become final and complete in that sort which is the aspiration of most sciences, and often their realized achievement. JOHN CROWE RANSOM [6]

The critic's first duty is neither to condemn nor to praise, but to elucidate technique and meaning. Ethical judgment at this stage is irrelevant. MICHAEL ROBERTS [7]

There must, that is to say, be standards and feelings in common. In other words, unless you believe that a work of art exists to produce an identical effect in all its spectators, and that its proper appreciation consists in appreciation of that effect, you cannot believe in criticism. For what is criticism? All definitions of the type, "The adventures of a soul among masterpieces," may be dismissed as inane rhetoric. The critic, I take it, exercises a two-

[5] "Kinds of Criticism," Poetry, 68 (August 1946), 272.
[6] Editorial in the Kenyon Review, 3 (Winter 1941), 96.
". . . Eliot has nothing like a formula ready in advance; he looks at the poem against its nearest background to see what sort of criticism it needs; he comes up presently with a set of judgments which are comparative in the first instance, but critical in the end." J. C. Ransom, The New Criticism (New Directions Books, 1941), p. 141.
[7] Critique of Poetry, p. 79. Copyright 1934 by Jonathan Cape, Ltd. Reprinted by permission of the publisher.

fold function. He addresses both the artist and the spectator. He tells the artist whether the latter has succeeded in producing the effect intended, and he tells the spectator, i.e. the spectator less expert than himself, what the effect is. Further, the critic tells both artist and spectator how the effect ranks, i.e. he correctly classifies it. And unless the correct classifying is an utter waste of time, it must bear on appreciation.

If it does not bear, then you cannot be undergoing the work of art's effect, you cannot be properly appreciating the work, if you "respond" to that work independently, in ignorance or defiance of its classification. You cannot fully enjoy art according to your own sweet fancy. Either you must yourself be a critic, or you must accept the guidance of critics. MONTGOMERY BELGION [8]

Literary criticism is not the contemplation of general principles. It is a practice: the responsible application of principles to specific art. DONALD A. STAUFFER [9]

Criticism, on the other hand, must always profess an end in view, which, roughly speaking, appears to be the elucidation of works of art and the correction of taste. T. S. ELIOT [10]

The art of criticism, as I see it, begins with an act of interest, either of attraction or of passionate repulsion in relationship to a work of art. Once that sense of being moved has been aroused critical processes can follow. Coleridge in defining poetry writes "that not the poem which we have read, but that to which we return, with greatest pleasure, possesses the genuine power and claims the name of essential poetry."* The definition might be extended to include other forms of literature. The emotion may not always be pleasure in its simpler forms but some "strange ne-

[8] "What Is Criticism?" *Criterion*, 10 (October 1930–July 1931), 132.
[9] "A Letter from the Critical Front," *Kenyon Review*, 4 (Winter 1942), 133.
[10] *Selected Essays 1917–1932*, p. 13. Copyright 1932 by Harcourt, Brace and Co., and by Faber and Faber, Ltd. Reprinted by permission of the publishers.

cessity" that calls us back to the work that has attracted us. Without such attraction there can be no criticism of a definitely literary character. B. IFOR EVANS [11]

* S. T. Coleridge. *Biographia Literaria* (London, 1847).

Criticism seeks, legitimately, to perform several functions: it tries to guide and improve public taste, to disclose the relations of art, considered purely as art, to non-aesthetic activities and values, to determine the comparative worth of the aesthetic qualities embodied in objects which may compete for our attention, and to enlighten the artist on the true nature and meaning of his created object, since the artist may do better or worse or quite differently than he intends. ELISEO VIVAS [12]

A good critic is one who helps the creative situation. The most valuable criticism of the past has been that which, directly or by implication, limited the contemporary writer's freedom of choice in form or subject-matter. Certain modes of expression, expansions of a certain nature, certain states of being, even, may be shown up by the critic as false developments of a preceding tradition, and taboo, therefore, to writers who might otherwise waste energy in experimental blind-alleys. That is all the critic can contribute to the constructive movement of literature, and, apart from this possibility, he is only an educationalist, having no part in the dynamic of the art he writes about. In this, his ordinary capacity, he can be tested by all sorts of standards, moral, social, criminal, personal. Perhaps the most useful are those which judge the critic by his ability to prepare the public beforehand to appreciate the ascendant writers. BERTRAM HIGGINS [13]

[11] "The Limits of Literary Criticism," p. 43 in *Essays and Studies by Members of the English Association,* Vol. XVIII, edited by Hugh Walpole. Copyright 1933 by the Clarendon Press. Reprinted by permission of the publisher.
[12] "The Objective Basis of Criticism," *Western Review,* 12 (Summer 1948), 197.
[13] "Euthanasia: Or the Future of Criticism," p. 160 in *Towards Standards of Criticism,* edited by F. R. Leavis. Copyright 1933 by Lawrence and Wishart, Ltd. Reprinted by permission of the publisher.

The point may be made by means of two simple propositions about the business of the critic. He endeavours to see the poetry of the present as continuation and development; that is, as the decisive, the most significant, contemporary life of tradition. He endeavours, where the poetry of the past is concerned, to realize to the full the implications of the truism that its life is in the present or nowhere; it is alive in so far as it is alive for us. His aim, to offer a third proposition, is to define, and to order in terms of its own implicit organization, a kind of ideal and impersonal living memory.

. . .

But no treatment of poetry is worth much that does not keep very close to the concrete: there lies the problem of method. The only acceptable solution, it seemed to me, lay in the extension and adaptation of the method appropriate in dealing with individual poets as such. In dealing with individual poets the rule of the critic is, or should (I think) be, to work as much as possible in terms of particular analysis — analysis of poems or passages, and to say nothing that cannot be related immediately to judgments about producible texts. Observing this rule and practising this self-denial the critic limits, of course, his freedom; but there are kinds of freedom he should not aspire to, and the discipline, while not preventing his saying anything that he should in the end find himself needing to say, enables him to say it with a force of relevance and an edged economy not otherwise attainable. F. R. LEAVIS [14]

"Criticism" to me suggests a certain process of deliberately objectifying the work under consideration; the comparison of it with other similar works in order especially to show in what respects it surpasses, or falls short of, those works; the dividing its "good" from its "bad"; and, finally, a formal judgement as to its lasting validity. "Interpretation," on the contrary, tends to

[14] *Revaluation*, pp. 1-2, 2-3. Copyright 1936 by Chatto and Windus, Ltd., and 1946 by George W. Stewart, Inc. Reprinted by permission of the publishers.

merge into the work it analyses; it attempts, as far as possible, to understand its subject in the light of its own nature, employing external reference, if at all, only as a preliminary to understanding; it avoids discussion of merits, and, since its existence depends entirely on an original acceptance of the validity of the poetic unit which it claims, in some measure, to translate into discursive reasoning, it can recognize no division of "good" from "bad." G. WILSON KNIGHT [15]

The assertion of the possibility of objectivity of aesthetic judgments does not mean that such judgments are absolutely correct but merely that they are corrigible. The correction of judgments involves greater difficulties in art than it does in science, where techniques of abstraction, isolation, quantification, and controlled experiments enable the inquirer to confine his attention to the precise phenomena to which the judgment refers and to exclude idiosyncratic irrelevancies. In art, in the absence of such instrumentalities, corrigibility takes place through the give and take of criticism of the object. In such give and take the criteria of criticism are themselves open to criticism. And only by means of a criticism of such criticism is the presence of a value in an object isolated and related to its structure. ELISEO VIVAS [16]

Evaluation is truly the ultimate function of criticism, one which it cannot subordinate to any other or, in a pseudo-scientific effort toward the scientific, replace by mere description; to eliminate judgment is to eliminate criticism. But critical judgment is not the direct and spontaneous evaluation in which all reading naturally culminates. It is a reflex operation by which this evaluation, or any other proposition about a literary work or process, is itself evaluated, in the light ideally of everything that can be known about it and about its occasion. (In practise the primary

[15] *The Wheel of Fire*, p. 1. Copyright 1930 by Oxford University Press, and 1949 by Methuen and Co., Ltd. Reprinted by permission of the publishers.
[16] "The Objective Basis of Criticism," *Western Review*, 12 (Summer 1948), 201–2.

and the reflex operations may be concomitant, the latter controlling the former as it proceeds; the complete critical process is usually not a separate recapitulation of the normal process of reading but simply an expansion and deepening of it by addition of concurrent cognitive acts, so that when the final evaluation emerges its critique is provided with it. A given criticism, however, may and usually does involve only a part of this full process, and may evaluate not the final judgment but only prior incidental evaluations or propositions not evaluatory at all but simply descriptive or classifying.) The specifically differentiating operation of criticism is thus not evaluation but discrimination among evaluations, actual or possible, explicit or implied; *"krinein"* meant "to discriminate" before it meant "to judge." And the principle of this discrimination is cognitive; for the only criterion by which evaluations can in any sense be tested is that of relative consistency with all the relevant reality that is securely known. Criticism thus adds to lay reading a greater cognitive curiosity and more relevant knowledge, and its work is to bring this knowledge methodically to bear upon judgment. But it is evidently absurd to use for discrimination means selected and applied without discrimination; the knowledge and the method used by the critic must themselves be critically evaluated by the criteria appropriate to them. This is to say that they must be scientific. Criticism is not a science, because its concern is with the particular, thing or value, whereas science is by definition concerned only with what is general; but it realizes itself and achieves its own ideal only in the degree to which it appropriates and assimilates science and scientific method. Criticism is simply the application to a particular judgment of as much science and as scientific a method as possible.

. . .

Scientific method in criticism means simply bringing to bear upon literary judgment every item of relevant knowledge (conversely excluding from consideration everything that is not relevant knowledge) and restricting judgment to what is warranted or permitted by the sum of this relevant knowledge. The knowledge required for criticism, though all susceptible of scientific scrutiny, is not all science, for much of it is particular (of the particular data immediately concerned, and of other similar or related particulars and their relations, *i. e.*, of literary history); but a large part of it is or should be science, for continuous discourse in terms of the particular alone is impossible and the critic's determinations concerning the particular must rest upon some systematic generalized knowledge of the nature and categories of literary phenomena. The ideal of such a science or general literary theory is to provide accurate observation of the literary object and the processes of its production and reception (including evaluation), analysis of these into their elements, and exact description and classification of them in terms of these elements and their combinations.

In the practise of criticism, to be scientific or truly critical is to say nothing that is not somehow grounded in strictly relevant knowledge, and to make this grounding clear. This means in general to avoid merely affective or volitional exclamation, which, though legitimate in itself and for the lay reader often a convenient means of summarily indicating an unanalysed reaction, is not criticism; in criticism feeling should appear only as a datum for cognition, object of analysis or item of evidence. It means to avoid also multiplication of purely evaluatory propositions on the way to the final judgment; for these, unless only parenthetical, interrupt and embarrass the progress of logical argument and create rather than dispose of critical problems. In constructing the descriptive and classifying propositions that should preponderate in critical discourse, to be scientific is to be careful of one's terms, using them as exactly and as univocally as possible and choosing those with plain denotations and without compromising connotations; it is to make all crucial statements as obviously verifiable as possible, presenting or suggesting the means used or the sources relied upon by the critic himself for verification. . . . But to be scientific is above all to accept the established fact always, whatever its character or one's disposition toward it; and it is sometimes to acknowledge that the fact cannot be established. The critic must not shrink from noting the subjective and the relative as such where they occur, or from confessing that a given object of his attempted scrutiny eludes it, or that in a given case the inadequacy, perhaps the inaccessibility, of reliable knowledge makes evaluation of a judgment impossible. What is unscientific and uncritical is not to observe and report subjectivity, relativity, and ignorance, but to mistake these for or to pretend that they are their opposites.

The ideal suggested by this account of method is not often realized. Most criticism is, perhaps all criticism must always be, partial and imperfect. But it is something to recognize the ideal, to see that it is the only possible ideal, and to understand that we are truly critical only in so far as we approach its realization. CRAIG LA DRIERE [17]

To criticise is to appreciate, to appropriate, to take intellectual possession, to establish in fine a relation with the criticised thing and make it one's own. HENRY JAMES [18]

It consists, first, in being willing to concentrate your maximum attention upon the work which the words and motions of the words — and by motions, I mean all the technical devices of literature — perform upon each other. Secondly, it consists in submitting, at least provisionally, to whatever authority your attention brings to light in the words. In doing this you will be following in pretty close parallel the procedure which the writer followed. Whether your submission is permanent or must be withdrawn will be determined by the judgement of all the standards and all the interests you can bring to bear. These will differ with the work

[17] "Scientific Method in Criticism," pp. 509–11 in *Dictionary of World Literature*, edited by Joseph T. Shipley. Copyright 1943 by the Philosophical Library. Reprinted by permission of the publisher.
[18] Preface to *What Masie Knew*, p. 155 in *The Art of the Novel*, edited by R. P. Blackmur. Copyright 1941 by Charles Scribner's Sons. Reprinted by permission of the publisher.

in hand. But the act of submission must be made before you can tell; it is an act of imagination, not of will; and it is the enabling act of criticism. R. P. BLACKMUR[19]

It can hardly be too often repeated that the first aim of literary criticism is, by means of a supple and disciplined attention to the use of words, to explore and assess the sensibility of each particular writer, to discover, that is, the range and quality of that perceptiveness, physical and moral, which nourishes and is nourished by the life of the emotions. Any discussion of literature not informed and controlled by this purpose is bound to be peripheral — at best — or irrelevant and misleading. In the light of this simple truth Mr. Lewis's account of Milton's aims and achievement [C. S. Lewis, *A Preface to Paradise Lost*] is seen to be built up from the outside; it does not strike to the centre. L. C. KNIGHTS[20]

I have certainly tried to make my judgment as objective as possible, but the critic must work with the only instrument he possesses — namely, his own sensibility with all its personal equations. All that he can consciously endeavor is to perfect that tool to its utmost by studying the traditional verdicts of men of aesthetic sensibility in the past, and by constant comparison of his own reactions with those of his contemporaries who are specially gifted in this way. When he has done all that he can in this direction — and I would allow him a slight bias in favour of agreement with tradition — he is bound to accept the verdict of his own feelings as honestly as he can. ROGER FRY[21]

[19] "The Enabling Act of Criticism," p. 879 in *American Issues*, II, edited by Willard Thorp, Merle Curti, and Carlos Baker. Copyright 1941 by J. B. Lippincott Co. Reprinted by permission of the author and the publisher. This essay is reprinted in *Critiques and Essays in Criticism*, edited by R. W. Stallman. Copyright 1949 by Ronald Press.
[20] "Milton Again," *Scrutiny*, 11 (December 1942), 146.
[21] *Vision and Design*, pp. 285-86. Copyright 1920 by Chatto and Windus, Ltd. Reprinted by permission of the publisher.

Kinds of Criticism

Literary criticism plays two rôles; it reviews and describes the work of the past, and, by deciding which practices are good and which are bad, it dictates the practice of the future. Aristotle, reviewing the work of the Greek tragic poets, not only arranges and classifies, he also, by passing judgment, tacitly creates the criterion according to which other work may best be accomplished. This double rôle of criticism is responsible for the irregularities in its history; for when it becomes too dictatorial, over-emphasizing its second function, it produces rules, and a lifeless literature, and when it becomes too much of a parasite it produces pedantry and no literature at all. THEODORE SPENCER [22]

Contemporary critics appear ultimately divisible into two groups: the first, which may claim the Aristotle of the Poetics as its sponsor, addresses itself to the study of the artifact, – the poem, the play, the novel – with reference to its internal relationships, its formal structure, the interplay and interpenetration, as parts of its total meaning, of rhythms, phonetic sequences, images, conceptual statement, and dramatic counterpoint. It would be presumptuously absurd – especially for men of letters – to dismiss this theory of criticism, since as specialists their obvious and unique business is the analysis and evaluation not of the *ideas* conveyed in and through literature (which would be the job of the scientist, the economist, the theologian, or the philosopher) but of the craftsmanship discoverable in the artist's working or shaping of his materials, his methods of handling ideas imaginatively, his symbolic or mythic or dramatic incarnation of them. And in England and America, both moralistic lands, we have never had enough of informed, patient, and exact aesthetic analysis and need rather to urge forward than discourage such few qualified practitioners as exist.

The second group of critics regards the values of art as instrumental to other values, – economic, political, ethical, religious.

[22] Review in *Hound and Horn*, 2 (July–September 1929), 447.

Its ultimate sponsor is Plato; and, concerned as it is with the relation of literary to other values, it may be called extrinsic criticism. In general, the first group characterizes the aesthetic attitude as cathartic, detached, contemplative; the second holds art to be incitory, an invitation to action. These opposed emphases may be stated more strongly, and regarded as hostile to one another, — mutually exclusive, as at the last ditch, they probably are. But we are not yet forced to the last ditch; and present strategy for criticism would rather indicate a popular front.

As a matter of fact, the more sensitive and ranging minds in both groups feel the necessity for avoiding exclusion, and seek rather for arrangement or proportion.

We can, with Aristotle and Maritain, reconcile by separation — that is, deal with the arts twice, now as poetics, now as politics; we can, with that modified and scrupulous Platonist, T. S. Eliot, urge that, though extrinsic criteria determine whether or not literature is "great," only aesthetic criteria can determine whether or not it is "literature." AUSTIN WARREN [23]

The more we study the criticism of the past, the more obvious it becomes that critics can be divided broadly into two main groups — those whose interest is purely "historical," and those whose work remains "actual" and can still help to form taste. Many of the critics in the first group have been men of outstanding ability; their work is still good reading; it provides us with useful information about the development of critical theory and the condition of taste at a particular period; but there its utility ends. The first group includes Dryden and Johnson in England, Boileau and Voltaire in France, and it is coming more and more to include Sainte-Beuve and Taine. The second group includes Coleridge, and Arnold as well as Baudelaire and Gourmont.

What is not perhaps so obvious is that, though the life of a critic is necessarily shorter than that of an imaginative writer, the time factor is not decisive. Boileau's interest is purely historical,

[23] "Literature and Society," pp. 304-5 in *Twentieth Century English*, edited by William S. Knickerbocker. Copyright 1946 by the Philosophical Library. Reprinted by permission of the publisher.

but parts of Saint-Évremond's work can still be read with profit; and though they were contemporaries, Baudelaire's criticism is more actual than Taine's. Nor is it simply a matter of being "right" about an author. Dryden was right in his placing of Shakespeare and Boileau in his placing of Villon; but though this was of great importance at the time, it has not prolonged the life of their criticism. A critic's value depends in the last resort on the quality of his sensibility and on his ability to stand aloof from the more ephemeral theories of his time. MARTIN TURNELL [24]

Apart from aesthetics, which includes the general discussion of how works of art produce any effect at all, there are two branches of criticism: elucidatory criticism, or the removal of technical difficulties, and judgment or evaluation of the attitudes communicated by a work. Technical criticism is so difficult that most reviewers confine their attention to the second aspect of criticism, and even then they often reveal neither the poet's attitude nor their own. They merely praise or condemn, and their work is useless unless the reader happens to know their attitude already. In sound criticism the reader, shown the agreement or conflict between the values of the critic and those of the artist, is left to choose for himself. If the critic's work has been well done his judgment is obvious.

Every reader is necessarily a critic, good or bad; to neglect careful technical criticism is to deny the poem a fair hearing; hasty decision often produces sentimental judgment, and sometimes the hasty reader even accuses the poet of sentimentality, whereas the fault lies in his own inadequate response. The fullest appreciation of poetry or of any art may require as much training and effort as the appreciation of mathematics, and the effort is justified by the additional delight. MICHAEL ROBERTS [25]

[24] "Literary Criticism in France," *Scrutiny*, 8 (December 1939), 281. This essay is reprinted in *Critiques and Essays in Criticism*, edited by R. W. Stallman. Copyright 1949 by Ronald Press.
[25] *Critique of Poetry*, pp. 58, 59. Copyright 1934 by Jonathan Cape, Ltd. Reprinted by permission of the publisher.
EDITOR'S NOTE. Roberts lists as technical critics Eliot, Sitwell, Graves,

The Boundaries of Criticism

No criticism that is not a criticism of form in its relation to matter has ever advanced any of the arts a single step. The virtue of any art wholly inheres in its appeal to the senses and the "imaginative reason," and all other criteria, whether moral or sociological, are *aesthetically* irrelevant. HERBERT READ [26]

You can never draw the line between aesthetic criticism and moral and social criticism . . . you start with literary criticism, and however rigorous an aesthete you may be, you are over the frontier into something else sooner or later. The best you can do is to accept these conditions and know what you are doing when you do it. T. S. ELIOT [27]

Clearly the work of criticism is not a specialized department of knowledge and judgment which can operate in disregard of any part of experience; on the contrary it demands for itself the best and most inclusive reflections on human experience in its entirety as a condition for assessment of the place and significance of creative imaginative work. Whatever value we may attach to that aspect of literary criticism which is virtually a part of history, the tracing of facts relating to the creation of literature and of

Empson; as critics of dogma and judgment (the second branch of criticism), Herbert Read and J. M. Murry. "The *Poetics* of Aristotle, Coleridge's *Biographia Literaria,* and Mr. Richards' *Principles of Literary Criticism* are examples of a third type of writing related to criticism: that which attempts to relate literature to other aspects of life and criticism to other sciences. Such works do not elucidate or judge particular poems, they are studies in theoretical poetics, and their value depends upon the degree or order they impose upon their chosen subject-matter. Much of the confusion which clouds discussion of the status of the literary critic disappears when we remember the distinctions between critics of technique, critics of value, and students of the theory of aesthetics. These latter are philosophers rather than critics; their object is to arrive at concepts (categories) which shall be of service to the practical critic." *Critique of Poetry,* pp. 59–60.

[26] *In Defence of Shelley and Other Essays,* p. 213. Copyright 1936 by William Heinemann, Ltd. Reprinted by permission of the publisher.

[27] *Selected Essays 1917–1932,* p. 42. Copyright 1932 by Harcourt, Brace and Co., and by Faber and Faber, Ltd. Reprinted by permission of the publishers.

THE NATURE AND FUNCTION OF CRITICISM

literary form, there remains, as the final labour of criticism, the judgment of literary work, not as a historical occurrence, but as an imaginative apprehension which is complete in itself, and which the historical judgment does not affect. D. G. JAMES [28]

No matter how thorough and complete our explanations of works of literature may be from the historical and biographical points of view, we must be ready to try to estimate the relative degrees of success attained by the products of the various periods and the various personalities in some such way as Eliot and Saintsbury do. We must be able to tell good from bad, the first-rate from the second-rate. We shall not otherwise write literary criticism at all, but merely social or political history as reflected in literary texts, or psychological case histories from past eras, or, to take the historical point of view in its simplest and most academic form, merely chronologies of books that have been published. EDMUND WILSON [29]

Criticism should be partial, passionate and political, that is to say, written from an exclusive point of view, but from the point of view which opens up the widest horizons. CHARLES BAUDELAIRE [30]

Criticism, in the literary process, should become the agent that makes for the understanding and evaluation of works of literature. It should create the atmosphere through which a maximum of value and effect, rather than a minimum, is produced by our living literature. It should strive to make the meanings of books clear, to draw out these essential meanings and refer and assimilate them in a wider social area. In performing these functions, criticism will evidently be making judgments, and on the basis of analysis; the criteria for these judgments being not alone internal to the literary process, and not alone external. Like the books to

[28] *Scepticism and Poetry*, pp. 242-43. Copyright 1937 by Allen and Unwin, Ltd. Reprinted by permission of the publisher.
[29] *The Triple Thinkers*, p. 267. Copyright 1948 by Oxford University Press. Reprinted by permission of the publisher.
[30] *Oeuvres* (Paris: Bibliothèque de la Pléiade, 1932), p. 64.

which they are applied they have both a subjective or aesthetic side and an objective or functional side. These criteria must be rationally established, tested by reference to experience, and used flexibly. In other words, they cannot be absolutized and fixed; they cannot be invented. They must have applicability to the literary work that is being judged. This is my conception of ideal criticism. JAMES T. FARRELL [31]

The "greatness" of literature cannot be determined solely by literary standards; though we must remember that whether it is literature or not can be determined only by literary standards. T. S. ELIOT [32]

. . . the question [is] whether, really, we can accept or reject a literary work by the application of literary standards alone. Here the answer is double; partly yes and partly no, only good sense — the taste of practice — determining which. T. S. Eliot's remark is initially in order, that while we can only tell that a work is literature by literary standards, we cannot tell whether it is great literature except by other than literary standards. A first qualifying reflection is that there is not very much great literature; and a second is that, even when a critic is concerned with great literature, most of the problems he handles will not directly affect his estimate of its greatness. Greatness is come up to, felt, discovered; not handled. A critic who tried to handle merely the greatness of Shakespeare or Dante would see it disappear before his eyes. And a critic who attempted to establish the greatness of Joyce or Eliot or Yeats would be largely wasting his time; for greatness is established by custom, by time, by the apprehension in the minds of many men of inexhaustibility, and even so greatness is transitory and variable. Milton is not so great today as a century ago. Dante is greater. And I use the copulative

[31] *A Note on Literary Criticism*, p. 216. Copyright 1936 by Vanguard Press, Inc. Reprinted by permission of the publisher.
[32] *Essays Ancient and Modern*, p. 92. Copyright 1932 and 1936 by Harcourt, Brace and Co., Inc., and by Faber and Faber, Ltd. Reprinted by permission of the publishers.

deliberately, for greatness is an act of estimation, not an assertion of fact, and hence may be expected to vary, but not, once estimated, ever to disappear irrecoverably. It would be intolerable as well as impossible for us today to look at Milton either with our own full mind and sensibility or with those of his own generation, or with those of the eighteenth century. We use of our own what will bear, of the others only what will elucidate – and then only putatively. On the other hand . . . it would be intolerable if we did not bring the full force of our literary standards to bear in order to determine what of Milton is literature and what is not. Equally, the other way around, we should bring as much as possible of Milton's literary achievement to bear on the products of our own time; and the extent to which this can be done will constitute a literary judgment on both Milton and our own time. Those other, extra-literary standards, the standards of the convictions of our whole culture, will thus tend to disappear or to be transformed into the literary standards. R. P. BLACKMUR [33]

Any rational approach is valid to literature and may properly be called critical which fastens at any point upon the work itself. The utility of a given approach depends partly upon the strength of the mind making it and partly upon the recognition of the limits appropriate to it. Limits may be of scope, degree, or relevance, and may be either plainly laid out by the critic himself, or may be determined by his readers; and it is, by our argument, the latter case that commonly fails, since an active mind tends to overestimate the scope of its tools and to take as necessary those doctrinal considerations which habit has made seem instinctive. No critic is required to limit himself to a single approach, nor is he likely to be able to do so; facts cannot be exhibited without comment, and comment involves the generality of the mind. Furthermore, a consciously complex approach like that of Kenneth Burke or T. S. Eliot, by setting up parallels of reference, affords

[33] "The Enabling Act of Criticism," p. 877 in *American Issues*, II, edited by Willard Thorp, Merle Curti, and Carlos Baker. Copyright 1941 by J. B. Lippincott Co. Reprinted by permission of the author and the publisher.

a more flexible, more available, more stimulating standard of judgment — though of course at a greater risk of prejudice — than a single approach. What produces the evil of stultification and the malice of controversy is the confused approach, when the limits are not seen because they tend to cancel each other out, and the driving power becomes emotional. R. P. BLACKMUR [34]

Scholarship and Literary Criticism

The Arraignment

Since the time of Brunetière, and before him since Taine, Frenchmen who have professed literature have been almost exclusively preoccupied with history, evolution, movements, developments; with a "scientific" approach to ideological content at the expense of judgment; with the rigorous separation of ingredients to the neglect of synthesis; above all with the relations between works — sources, influences, comparisons, *confrontations* — rather than with the works themselves as literature. There have been sound textual critics among them; but few, if any, have been concerned with taste.

Who, moreover, among Frenchmen of the nineteenth century, or so far of the twentieth, could qualify strictly as a literary critic? The genius of the nineteenth century in France as in England lay definitely in Irrelevance. Sainte-Beuve, for instance, was as sensitive as any of us are to the encroachments of philosophy and science; but the thing for him was the man not the book. For the modern university critic the thing is not the book or the man but the background. P. MANSELL JONES [35]

Today the academic and nonacademic servants of letters are in derisive conflict, the public itself, with substantial common sense,

[34] *The Double Agent*, pp. 277–78. Copyright 1935 by Arrow Editions. Reprinted by permission of the author.
[35] "A French Critic," *Scrutiny*, 6 (June 1937), 116.

siding with the authors and critics against the professors. We have a sharp divorce between the journalist critics, who despise learning yet need it, and the men of learning, who despise criticism yet need it. We have a divorce between the creative authors, unhappily indifferent to the letters of the past, and the scholars, unhappily indifferent to the letters of the present. Patently, the result of these artificial divisions has been nothing less than the impoverishment of our national literature and culture. NORMAN FOERSTER [36]

One of the few entertaining spectacles in this last depressing decade has been that of the academics who had shown themselves most hostile to modern literary criticism, recognizing that Eliot had achieved a lasting position in spite of them; but while desiring a place on the platform alongside him they couldn't afford to show too glaring an inconsistency. . . . Mr. Eliot has accordingly become incorporated into the canon of accepted Literature — which must be accepted and may not be criticized; and those critics who only recently were outlawed for daring to insist that *The Sacred Wood* and *The Waste Land* were important are now rebuked by the same pens for venturing to disagree with later critical pronouncements of his. The academics, that is, have not changed their skins at all, merely camouflaged them. They still object, as they always have objected, to the practice of real literary criticism, which necessarily menaces their self-esteem and professional reputation. Q. D. LEAVIS [37]

. . . the historical scholars, once the carriers of the humane tradition, have now merely the genteel tradition; the independence of judgment, the belief in intelligence, the confidence in literature, that informed the humane tradition, have disappeared; under

[36] "The Study of Letters," p. 29 in *Literary Scholarship*. Copyright 1941 by the University of North Carolina Press. Reprinted by permission of the publisher.
[37] "The Discipline of Letters," *Scrutiny*, 12 (Winter 1943), 21. This essay is reprinted in *The Importance of Scrutiny*, edited by Eric Bentley. Copyright 1949 by George W. Stewart, Inc. Reprinted by permission of the publisher.

the genteel tradition the scholars exhibit timidity of judgment, disbelief in intelligence, and suspicion of the value of literature. These attitudes of scholarship are the attitudes of the *haute bourgeoisie* that support it in the great universities; it is now commonplace to observe that the uncreative money-culture of modern times tolerates the historical routine of the scholars. The routine is "safe," and it shares with the predatory social process at large a naturalistic basis. And this naturalism easily bridges the thin gap between the teachers' college and the graduate school, between the sociologist and the literary source-hunter, between the comptometrist of literary "reactions" and the enumerator of influences.

The naturalism of the literary scholar is too obvious to need demonstration here; his substitution of "method" for intelligence takes its definite place in the positivistic movement which, from my point of view, has been clearing the way for the slave state; and the scholar must bear his part of the responsibility for the hypocrisy that will blind us to the reality of its existence, when it arrives.

The function of criticism should have been, in our time, as in all times, to maintain and to demonstrate the special, unique, and complete knowledge which the great forms of literature afford us. And I mean quite simply *knowledge*, not historical documentation and information. But our literary critics have been obsessed by politics, and when they have been convinced of the social determinism of literature, they have been in principle indistinguishable from the academic scholars, who have demonstrated that literature does not exist, that it is merely history, which must be studied as history is studied, through certain scientific analogies. The scholars have not maintained the tradition of literature as a form of knowledge. ALLEN TATE [38]

H. V. Routh's *Toward the 20th Century* is in some ways the most satisfactory history of 19th Century literature I know

[38] *On the Limits of Poetry: Selected Essays 1928-1948*, pp. 7-8. Copyright 1941 and 1948 by Allen Tate. Reprinted by permission of the Swallow Press and William Morrow and Co., Inc.

of. Its scholarship is wide and sound; it is brilliantly aware of the difficulties to which the writers of the time responded; it is critically very sensitive. Yet, because of one assumption that it makes, Mr. Routh's book has an odd invalidity. Mr. Routh believes that literature has a spiritual function — namely, to respond effectively to the spiritual troubles of its age. It must, according to this view, make a synthesis of life, resolve the cultural contradictions which make the good life difficult. It is with this assumption that Mr. Routh judges the literature of the last century. He finds — could he find anything else? — that none of it does what it should have done. Some works do some things, some do others, but none does all or enough. In short, the literature of the 19th Century was a noble failure. But how can it be otherwise when it is required to serve, if not as dogma, at least as a gospel?

The result is that Mr. Routh is committed to the teaching of a subject-matter which he considers inadequate and mistaken. And whoever proceeds on Mr. Routh's basically religious view of literature will, if he is equally honest and intelligent, come to this same unfortunate position. A man like V. L. Parrington, whose large and sympathetic figure has had so great an influence on ideas about American literature, was less concerned than Mr. Routh with spiritual matters, but Parrington's political preoccupation yielded very similar results. For him, two such commanding personages in American literature as Hawthorne and Henry James are not much more than interesting failures because they did not offer effective answers to the problems of their time.

. . .

It is in this way that the frankly religious-political attitude to literature works itself out. But there are two other attitudes which, like this one, express our culture's exclusive concern with knowledge for the purpose of control. One of these is the belief that literature is primarily a material for scientific investigation. The other is the belief that literature is primarily a material for the historical imagination. LIONEL TRILLING [89]

[89] "Literature and Power," *Kenyon Review*, 2 (Autumn 1940), 436-37, 437-38.

Literary history, as a matter of "facts about" and accepted critical (or quasi-critical) description and commentary, is a worthless acquisition; worthless for the student who cannot as a critic — that is, as an intelligent and discerning reader — make a personal approach to the essential data of the literary historian, the works of literature (an approach is personal or it is nothing: you cannot take over the appreciation of a poem, and unappreciated, the poem isn't "there"). The only acquisition of literary history having any educational value is that made in the exercise of critical intelligence to the ends of the literary critic. Does this need arguing? F. R. LEAVIS [40]

Toward a Reconciliation

It would certainly be a disservice to criticism to make the aesthetic method and the ideological divide the work between them by assuming that the business of the one is with *form* in the sense of external technique, of the other with *content* as political or moral doctrine completely separable from the mode of embodiment. We must rather take these two methods as complementary emphases. Formal criticism will then study the total structure of a literary work, including conceptual statements as parts of the structure; ideological criticism will concern itself with the explication and judgment of a work's philosophical attitude, explicit and implicit, including the expressive character of its structure and its tone. Properly conducted, the two will interpenetrate.

. . .

Between literary history in its strict sense and criticism, the relation appears to be this: That which is at once *history* and *of literature* must take form as a chronologically arranged study of an aesthetic sequence (as distinct from the biographical or social references of literature or its ideological content); it must concern

[40] *Education and the University*, p. 68. Copyright 1943 by Chatto and Windus, Ltd., and 1948 by George W. Stewart, Inc. Reprinted by permission of the publishers.

itself with the cycle — the rise, equilibrium, and fall of a genre or style. But this involves, at every moment, the use of critical criteria — in the definition of the genre (and what belongs or does not belong within it), in the estimate of what elements (added or enhanced or better arranged) are to constitute "progress," and of what constitutes the norm or height of the genre toward which it advances, from which it falls away. It is thus a serious error to speak of literary history as concerned only with facts, for only a system of values can determine what facts are relevant. The literary historian must either be a critic as well, or borrow his standards from traditional estimates or from practising critics.

Criticism is not historical in its ultimate method. Characteristically, its comparisons and contrasts (like Arnold's touch-stones or Eliot's juxtapositions of plays and passages from poems) propose significant relationships, ideological or aesthetic, between works composed in widely separated periods. Criticism ideally assumes a system of values which, if not à priori, is at least timeless. It may include within its total judgment the "historic estimate," the assignment of value relative to a closed past sequence; but it does not stop with such appraisal. Its final judgment, taking into account all that has been written up to the present, and, granting favoritism neither to past nor to present, proposes a hierarchic arrangement. AUSTIN WARREN [41]

There is apparent difference of opinion as to whether being historical and being critical coincide: some writers imply that uncriticalness is the product only of a mistaken historical method; Mr. [Cleanth] Brooks says that we can get history without criticism, but he does not indicate whether he considers this to be good history, or real history; Mr. Ransom alone takes the extreme position: "A critical discourse and a historical are qualitatively distinct." *Discourse*, indeed, is elusive; no doubt there can be an

[41] "Literary Criticism," pp. 151, 169–70 in *Literary Scholarship*. Copyright 1941 by the University of North Carolina Press. Reprinted by permission of the publisher.

essay so brief that it must of necessity be restricted to matters of structure or chronology; but how a discourse of book-length, for instance, can be truly historical without being critical is hard to see. It is pseudo-history which is uncritical. The critical attitude is "tough, scientific, and aloof." But must not the historical also be "tough, scientific, and aloof"? . . .

Though one might adjust the minute events of literary history in a flat and neutral fashion, it is impossible to see how a full, meaningful history can fail to be essentially critical. How can one take the sonnet from Tottel to Milton without an examination of stylistic differences, structures, uses of words, the different kinds of imagery in Sidney, Shakespeare, and Milton; without judgments on the kinds of achievement? Or how can one talk about the "Age of Prose" without inquiring into the kind of prose written, the varying vocabularies and rhythms and their respective functions; or the different means by which Swift's prose and Browne's achieve different effects; or the extent of statement in some of the characteristic poetry of the age, or the peculiar possibilities and limitations of couplet structure? Or in turn the Romantic Movement without investigating the value of some of the new pretensions in poetry, or the methodic distinctions among Romantics, or the relation between belief and method? It is doubtful whether there can be "*mere* training in literary history," whether uncriticalness can arise from historical studies; for the observation of change is a mode of understanding literature; one can hardly exaggerate the critical value of studying change and continuity, the permanent excellence underlying different forms and formulations.

. . .

To repeat: history which is history is criticism. There is no theoretical ground for surrendering the chronological patterns that determine the order of procedure in many of our [university] courses. ROBERT BECHTOLD HEILMAN [42]

[42] "Footnotes on Literary History," *Southern Review*, 6 (Spring 1941), 763–64, 765.

[*On the function of literary training in education*:] This is, to start with, a training in the use of words for any and every purpose, of words as "the tools of thought"—the means by which one mind can influence another; and training in the ways that words are used not only equips the individual for dealing with the modern environment (newspapers, propaganda, etc.), it is the necessary foundation for *all* education. It is, it seems necessary to add, the starting point for the study of literature. But even in elementary exercises in "practical criticism," analysis of what certain words are *doing* is — as I. A. Richards has made plain — inseparable from judgment concerning the *quality* of thought, feeling, or perception that the words express. The reading of literature, in so far as it is anything more than a pastime, involves the continuous development of the power of intelligent discrimination. Literature, moreover, is simply the exact expression of realized values — and these values are never purely personal: even when they conflict with accepted modes they are conditioned by them, and it is part of the artist's function . . . to give precise meaning to ideas and sentiments that are only obscurely perceived by his contemporaries. The discipline of strict literary criticism is the only means we have of apprehending those embodied values with sureness and subtlety. L. C. KNIGHTS [43]

I believe that the scholar and the practitioner in the field of literary criticism should supplement each other's work. The criticism of the practitioner will be all the better, certainly, if he is not wholly destitute of scholarship; and the criticism of the scholar will be all the better if he has some appreciation of the difficulties of writing good English. But the orientation of the two critics is different. The scholar is more concerned with the understanding of the masterpiece in the environment of its author: with the world in which the author lived, the temper of his age, his intellectual formation, the books which he had read, and the influences which had moulded him. The practitioner is

[43] *Explorations*, p. 193. Copyright 1946 by Chatto and Windus, Ltd., and 1948 by George W. Stewart, Inc. Reprinted by permission of the publishers.

concerned less with the author than with the poem; and with the poem in relation to his own age. He asks: Of what *use* is the poetry of this poet to poets writing today? Is it, or can it become a living force in English poetry still unwritten? So we may say that the scholar's interest is in the permanent, the practitioner's in the immediate. T. S. ELIOT [44]

All scholars, whether they deal with history or sociology or philosophy or language or, in the narrower use of the word, literature, are servants of the critical spirit, in so far as they transmit and interpret and mould the sum of experience from man to man and from generation to generation. Might not one even say that at a certain point criticism becomes almost identical with education, and that by this standard we may judge the value of any study as an instrument of education, and may estimate the merit of any special presentation of that study? It is at least, in the existing chaos of pedagogical theories, a question worthy of consideration. PAUL ELMER MORE [45]

There are encouraging signs that it is no longer so difficult as it was, in the last generation, for men of such distinction as Spingarn and Sherman, to reconcile a literary life with a professional career. It is time for a truce between those two opposing camps which may be characterized, with invidious impartiality, as pedants and aesthetes. They have much to learn from each other. There is some danger that reaction may swing us away from scholarly excesses toward less moderate extremes. Rash generalizations can do no more harm than trivial data, and journalistic irresponsibility is much more sinister than academic. To award a doctoral degree for a piece of imaginative writing is a *mélange des genres*, if not a more serious confusion. A more acute perception of the relations between creative talent and literary study envisions the poet's soul under the tutelage of the Byzantine sages:

[44] "Milton," *Sewanee Review*, 56 (Spring 1948), 186.
[45] *Selected Shelburne Essays*, p. 24. Copyright 1935 by Oxford University Press. Reprinted by permission of the publisher.

> Nor is there singing-school, but studying
> Monuments of its own magnificence.

Our immediate problem is the choice and care of monuments. HARRY LEVIN [46]

The critic is ideally a scholar that does not stop at knowing, but goes on to judgment in the light of his knowledge. (The scholar likewise must ideally be a critic, for knowing demands discrimination, and all selection implies evaluation.) Logically, therefore, there can be no conflict between philology or scholarship and criticism. The assertion of such conflict in recent controversy between partisans of "criticism" and of "literary history" has been due partly to confusion concerning the real issues contested, which are not reducible to the simplicity implied by the unfortunate opposition of these two terms, and partly to wayward and uncritical use of the terms chosen to designate the contending ideals. If the literary departments in the universities, the function of which is to provide society and the practising critic with an adequate philology, have neglected the theoretical part of their work in a (historically intelligible) temporary excess of emphasis upon the historical, and especially if they have in this allowed other kinds of history to usurp the place of literary history, any other exclusive emphasis would equally jeopardize the satisfactory performance of their total function. The fact that neither history nor criticism can ever actually appear in isolation suggests that the only satisfactory ideal is the common and equal development of both, in an ordered general system that relates them to each other and to the whole of which they are parts. CRAIG LA DRIERE [47]

[46] "Pseudodoxia Academica," *Southern Review*, 6 (Autumn 1940), 267–68.
[47] "Philology," p. 433 in *Dictionary of World Literature*, edited by Joseph T. Shipley. Copyright 1943 by the Philosophical Library. Reprinted by permission of the publisher.

The Contemporaneousness of Criticism

To be contemporary in the right sense means to find the peculiar emotional tension of the time and to mould language to its expression. [So was Donne in his age and so is Eliot today — their idioms are contagious; they taught us how to be "contemporary."] GEORGE WILLIAMSON [48]

. . . all poetry is contemporary. Any element that depends for its value upon a convention no longer operative is *ipso facto* a defect. The logical conclusion of such a principle is that each generation must rewrite its history of poetry, determining the new aesthetic validity of its past. MORRIS U. SCHAPPES [49]

The critical mind operating *in* poetry, the critical effort which goes to the writing of it, may always be in advance of the critical mind operating *upon* poetry, whether it be one's own or someone else's. I only affirm that there is a significant relation between the best poetry and the best criticism of the same period. The age of criticism is also the age of critical poetry. And when I speak of modern poetry as being extremely critical, I mean that the contemporary poet, who is not merely a composer of graceful verses, is forced to ask himself such questions as "what is poetry for?"; not merely "what am I to say?" but rather "how and to whom am I to say it?" T. S. ELIOT [50]

It is, I suggest, the function of the critic to establish such relationships between the work of art and present values as may seem to him significant. His success will be due in part to his fidel-

[48] "Donne and the Poetry of Today," p. 165 in *A Garland for John Donne*, edited by Theodore Spencer. Copyright 1931 by Harvard University Press. Reprinted by permission of the publisher.
[49] "Notes on the Concrete as Method in Criticism," *Symposium*, 2 (July 1931), 316.
[50] *The Use of Poetry and the Use of Criticism*, p. 30. Copyright 1933 by Faber and Faber, Ltd., and by Harvard University Press. Reprinted by permission of the publishers.

ity to the spirit of the author, but even more to his response to those new insights and richer associations that are the contributions of time and the sensitivity of men. For if the past has made the present, the present no less modifies the past and thus prepares the future. Louis Teeter [51]

It is part of the business of the critic to preserve tradition – where a tradition exists. It is part of his business to see literature steadily and to see it whole; and this is eminently to see it *not* as consecrated by time, but to see it beyond time; to see the best work of our time and the best work of twenty-five hundred years ago with the same eyes. T. S. Eliot [52]

. . . a critic's taste is always based upon the art of his day. . . . He can look at the art of the past with the eyes of the past, but he judges it with the experience of the present, which contains, and makes present, the whole of the past. Therefore his aim, even if he studies the art of the past, is always to make suggestions for, to take a stand in relation to, contemporary artists. Lionello Venturi [53]

The discipline of the critic is to learn on what grounds *not* to admire the poets whom he primarily loves, and to learn to love a little those poets whom he only frigidly admires. T. S. Eliot [54]

No poet, no artist of any art, has his complete meaning alone. His significance, his appreciation is the appreciation of his relation

[51] "Scholarship and the Art of Criticism," *English Literary History*, 5 (September 1938), 192.
[52] *The Sacred Wood*, pp. xv–xvi. Copyright 1920 and 1928 by Methuen and Co., Ltd., and 1921 and 1930 by Alfred A. Knopf, Inc. Reprinted by permission of the author and the publishers.
Cf. Eliot in *Essays Ancient and Modern* (Harcourt, Brace and Co., 1936), p. 111: "For literary judgement we need to be acutely aware of two things at once: of 'what we like,' and of 'what we *ought* to like.'"
[53] *Art Criticism Now*, pp. 1–2. Copyright 1941 by Johns Hopkins University Press. Reprinted by permission of the publisher.
[54] "Donne in Our Time," p. 7 in *A Garland for John Donne*, edited by Theodore Spencer. Copyright 1931 by Harvard University Press. Reprinted by permission of the publisher.

to the dead poets and artists. You cannot value him alone; you must set him, for contrast and comparison, among the dead. I mean this as a principle of aesthetic, not merely historical criticism. T. S. ELIOT [55]

From time to time, every hundred years or so, it is desirable that some critic shall appear to review the past of our literature, and set the poets and the poems in a new order. This task is not one of revolution but of readjustment. What we observe is partly the same scene, but in a different and more distant perspective; there are new and strange objects in the foreground, to be drawn accurately in proportion to the more familiar ones which now approach the horizon, where all but the most eminent become invisible to the naked eye. The exhaustive critic, armed with a powerful glass, will be able to sweep the distance and gain an acquaintance with minute objects close at hand; he will be able to gauge nicely the position and proportion of the objects surrounding us, in the whole of the vast panorama. This metaphorical fancy only represents the ideal; but Dryden, Johnson and Arnold have each performed the task as well as human frailty will allow. The majority of critics can be expected only to parrot the opinions of the last master of criticism; among more independent minds a period of destruction, of preposterous over-estimation, and of successive fashions takes place, until a new authority comes to introduce some order.

. . .

The rudiment of criticism is the ability to select a good poem and reject a bad poem; and its most severe test is of its ability to select a good *new* poem, to respond properly to a new situation. T. S. ELIOT [56]

If we are ever to have the beneficent presence of art, it is surely time for a criticism to arise which is content to make the art in art its dominant concern. EDWIN BERRY BURGUM [57]

[57] Review in *Symposium*, 4 (January 1933), 114.

II

Life and Art

The artist ought to be in his work like God in Creation, invisible and all-powerful; let him be felt everywhere but not seen.

GUSTAVE FLAUBERT, Letter to Mlle. de Chantepe, 1857.

The ultimate question concerning any work of art is out of how deep a life does it come. But the question that must first be asked is whether it has a life of its own. And the life of art is in its form.

JOHN PEALE BISHOP, p. 183 in *Collected Essays*, edited by Edmund Wilson. Copyright 1948 by Charles Scribner's Sons. Reprint by permission of the publisher.

Fielding lifted life out of its setting, and arranged it for the delight of all who love symmetry.

GRAHAM GREENE, p. 288 in *From Anne to Victoria*, edited by Bonamy Dobrée. Copyright 1937 by Cassell, Ltd. Reprinted by permission of the publisher.

The Contrast

It must be every ambitious critic's aim to resolve the dichotomy between life and art; and every superficial critic does it constantly with negligent ease. EDGELL RICKWORD [1]

No question is of greater moment for the understanding of modern poetry than that of the relationship of art to life. The various schools and movements of the last hundred years have all been conditioned in one way or another by the disparity existing between the poet's private world and the public world in which he is situated as a social being and which, with the expansion of mechanical civilization, has increasingly separated itself from the private and personal values. In this way all later movements may be seen as offshoots of the Romantic Revival, which was the initial movement of the creative mind in its attempt deliberately to dissociate itself from the realm of collective values and to centre itself upon the personal life of the individual. After the romantics the movement known in France as Symbolism took the personalistic

[1] Review in *Scrutiny*, 1 (March 1933), 391.

revolution a stage further, purifying poetry of the social and moralistic elements within romanticism, and in doing this it helped to clarify the essential nature of poetry. D. S. SAVAGE [2]

And the greatest poetry seems to be that which has its roots deepest in human nature, deepest in passion, deepest in wonder and in worship, deepest among the infinite reverberations of the past. GILBERT MURRAY [3]

The artist is not distinguished either by the quality or the amount of his feeling, but by the intensity and comprehensiveness of his unifying perception. LEO STEIN [4]

The artist, as an artist, is not suffering life. He is looking at it, regarding it, contemplating it. That, I think, is part of what Mr. T. S. Eliot means when he says, in *The Sacred Wood*, that "Poetry is not a turning loose of emotion but an escape from emotion." In looking at life with the purely contemplative gaze of the Imagination, the poet is not enduring the emotions he looks upon; the thrill that he has is the thrill of the spectacle — of the recognition that that is what reality looks like when a searching gaze is turned upon it. This does not in the least mean that the poet has no emotions when he is making poetry, but only that they are not the same as the emotions which he is exhibiting; his may be the rapture of recognizing that his picture is a picture of life, and that he is making it well. His joy is the joy that arises from discerning the truth — a truth intuitively grasped, not logically stated. R. A. SCOTT-JAMES [5]

[2] *The Personal Principle*, p. 67. Copyright 1944 by George Routledge and Sons, Ltd. Reprinted by permission of the author and the publisher.
[3] *The Classical Tradition in Poetry*, p. 261. Copyright 1927 by Harvard University Press. Reprinted by permission of the publisher.
[4] *The A-B-C of Aesthetics*, p. 206. Copyright 1927 by Horace Liveright, Inc. Reprinted by permission of the publisher.
EDITOR'S NOTE. Rilke, I would add, was much mistaken when he said that "A work of art is good if it has sprung from necessity. In this nature of its origin lies its judgment: there is no other." Rainer Maria Rilke, *Letters to a Young Poet* (W. W. Norton and Co., Inc., 1934), p. 18.
[5] *The Making of Literature*, p. 343. Copyright 1930 by Martin Secker, Ltd. Reprinted by permission of the publisher.

The revolutionary task of literature today is to restore its great tradition, to break the bonds of subjectivism and narrow specialization, to bring the creative writer face to face with his only important task, that of winning the knowledge of truth, of reality. Art is one of the means by which man grapples with and assimilates reality. On the forge of his own inner consciousness the writer takes the white-hot metal of reality and hammers it out, refashions it to his own purpose, beats it out madly by the violences of thought, to steal a phrase from Naomi Mitchison. The whole procession of creation, the whole agony of the artist, is in this violent conflict with reality in the effort to fashion a truthful picture of the world.

. . .

Once this view was accepted the way was clear for the new "realism" which took the slice of life and described it minutely and objectively. But life, of course, proved too restive a creature to slice up artistically, so the novelist grew finicking about the choosing of his slice, demanding that it be cut off such a refined portion of life's anatomy that in the end he came to describe little more interesting than the suburban street, or the Mayfair party. RALPH FOX [6]

When novels with seemingly as little in common as *An American Tragedy* and *Remembrance of Things Past, My Antonia* and *Ulysses,* are all described as realistic, one obviously cannot set fixed boundaries to this literature. The meaning of "realism" has in fact never been very precise or generally agreed upon; as one looks at the word hard, one grows a little dizzy. All artists have at bottom the same subject matter, all deal somehow with life; and so far as they give the impression of actuality they are in a sense realistic. Who is to say that a "realist" like Dreiser gives a truer impression of life than a "romanticist" like Shakespeare?

Yet if all great artists arrive finally at the same goal, and the

[6] *The Novel and the People*, pp. 30–31, 67. Copyright 1945 by International Publishers, and 1937 and 1945 by Lawrence and Wishart, Ltd., and by Cobbett Press, Ltd. Reprinted by permission of the publishers.

distinctions among them resolve largely into differences of approach, these differences nevertheless lead to important consequences. The realist begins with the concrete and familiar in experience; his inspiration is less a cloudy imagining than observed fact. Although he does not and cannot exactly reproduce actual experience, although as an artist he inevitably recasts and imaginatively shapes, his primary effort is to represent without markedly idealizing, to remain close to actuality and impart its savor. Essentially, realism implies only so general a tendency or purpose — the purpose, as Professor W. L. Myers expresses it in *The Later Realism*, "of conveying to the reader, whatever else may be accomplished, a strong sense of things actual in experience and within the range of the average life." Its record may be drab or exciting, ugly or beautiful — "so long as it give the essential impression of actuality." HERBERT J. MULLER [7]

We have entered a universe that only answers to its own laws, supports itself, internally coheres, and has a new standard of truth. Information is true if it is accurate. A poem is true if it hangs together. Information points to something else. A poem points to nothing but itself. Information is relative. A poem is absolute. E. M. FORSTER [8]

Art as "A Criticism of Life"

It is important, therefore, to hold fast to this: that poetry is at bottom a criticism of life; that the greatness of a poet lies in his powerful and beautiful application of ideas to life — to the question: How to live. MATTHEW ARNOLD [9]

[7] *Modern Fiction*, p. 38. Copyright 1937 by Funk and Wagnalls Co. Reprinted by permission of the publisher.
[8] *Anonymity: An Enquiry*, p. 14. Copyright 1925 by Hogarth Press. Reprinted by permission of the publisher.
[9] Preface, p. 9 in *The Poems of Wordsworth*. Copyright 1879 by the Macmillan Co.

The spirit of the arts is dynamic. The arts are not passive, nor static, nor, in a sense, are they reflective, though reflection may assist at their birth.

Poetry is about as much a "criticism of life" as red-hot iron is a criticism of fire. EZRA POUND [10]

The seriousness with which he [Arnold] conceived the function and the importance he ascribed to poetry are more legitimately expressed in the phrase, the best-known tag from the essay, "criticism of life." That it is not altogether satisfactory the animadversion which it has been the object of must perhaps be taken to prove: at best we must admit that the intention it expresses hasn't, to a great many readers, made itself satisfactorily clear. Nevertheless Arnold leaves us with little excuse for supposing — as some of his most eminent critics have appeared to suppose — that he is demanding doctrine or moral commentary on life or explicit criticism. Nor should it be necessary to point out that all censure passed on him for having, in calling poetry "criticism of life," produced a bad definition is beside the mark. For it should be obvious to anyone who reads the phrase in its context that Arnold intends, not to define poetry, but, while insisting (a main concern of the essay) that there are different degrees of importance in poetry, to remind us of the nature of the criteria by which comparative judgments are made.

Why Arnold should have thought the insistence and the reminder worth while and should have hit on the given phrase as appropriate for his purpose is not difficult to understand if we think of that Pater with whom . . . he has been associated:

"Art for Art's sake" is the offspring of Arnold's culture; and we can hardly venture to say that it is even a perversion of Arnold's doctrine, considering how very vague and ambiguous that doctrine is.

At any rate, we can certainly not say that "Art for Art's sake" is the offspring of Arnold's "criticism of life." In fact, Arnold's

[10] *The Spirit of Romance*, p. 234. Copyright [1910] by J. M. Dent and Sons, Ltd., and by E. P. Dutton and Co., Inc. Reprinted by permission of the publishers.

phrase is sufficiently explained – and, I think, vindicated – as expressing an intention directly counter to the tendency that finds its consummation in "Art for Art's sake." F. R. LEAVIS [11]

We are reminded of Arnold again. All that he implied in his demand that poetry should be a "criticism of life" is present to a full degree in the poetry of Auden, Spender, and their contemporaries. We can read their verse for its interest even when we can no longer read it for its poetry. As their more youthful enthusiasms die and they grow in experience and wisdom, this quality should deepen – does deepen. But as Arnold said, "the criticism of life will be of power in proportion as the poetry conveying it is excellent rather than inferior, sound rather than unsound or half-sound, true rather than untrue or half-true." The problem of fusing thought and feeling into the formal unity of a work of art is the central problem of poetry. HERBERT READ [12]

However irritating the pontifical manner and occasionally unfortunate the vocabulary of Matthew Arnold, one must begin with his dictum: It is the business of art in some manner to offer a criticism of life. It must integrate, consolidate, interpret, and hence illumine our experience, give form and significance to facts that in their mere contiguity are meaningless. It is properly not an imitation of nature; in the words of Nietzsche, it is "a metaphysical supplement to the reality of nature." It has its own laws, its own logic, its own "truth." Its function is always in some measure to idealize – to select and filter, to exclude or minimize the trivial, irrelevant or grossly fortuitous, and in this way to detach meanings and values. This is not, of course, to demand of the novelist explicit instruction. He is not to be a Polonius, peddling precepts; his business is to state problems, not to solve them. But simply to make a vital statement, his work must have

[11] "Arnold as Critic," *Scrutiny*, 7 (December 1938), 323–24. This essay is reprinted in *The Importance of Scrutiny*, edited by Eric Bentley. Copyright 1949 by George W. Stewart, Inc. Reprinted by permission of the publisher.
[12] "The Present State of Poetry," *Kenyon Review*, 1 (Autumn 1939), 368.

an intellectual or spiritual center, must provide a point of view, must organize and not merely duplicate experience. HERBERT J. MULLER [13]

Criticism, I take it, is the formal discourse of an amateur. When there is enough love and enough knowledge represented in the discourse it is a self-sufficient but by no means an isolated art. It witnesses constantly in its own life its interdependence with the other arts. It lays out the terms and parallels of appreciation from the outside in order to convict itself of internal intimacy; it names and arranges what it knows and loves, and searches endlessly with every fresh impulse or impression for better names and more orderly arrangements. It is only in this sense that poetry (or some other art) is a criticism of life; poetry names and arranges, and thus arrests and transfixes its subject in a form which has a life of its own forever separate but springing from the life which confronts it. Poetry is life at the remove of form and meaning; not life lived but life framed and identified. So the criticism of poetry is bound to be occupied at once with the terms and modes by which the remove was made and with the relation between — in the ambiguous stock phrase — content and form; which is to say with the establishment and appreciation of human or moral value. R. P. BLACKMUR [14]

Art as the Mirror of Life

I suggest that it is time to get rid of the misleading current notion that art is not concerned with real life. I find that even Mr. E. M. Forster, in his *Aspects of the Novel*, lends countenance to this idea, and suggests that the reality of a character in a novel

[13] *Modern Fiction*, pp. 71-72. Copyright 1937 by Funk and Wagnalls Co. Reprinted by permission of the publisher.
[14] *The Double Agent*, p. 269. Copyright 1935 by Arrow Editions. Reprinted by permission of the author.

depends upon the laws of art, and not the laws of life. "The barrier of art," he says, divides us from Fielding's *Amelia* or Jane Austen's *Emma*. "They are real not because they are like ourselves . . . but because they are convincing."

But how will they ever be convincing unless they are like ourselves? The fact that the novelist knows more about his characters, as Mr. Forster tells us, than we can know about living individuals, is only another way of saying that the artist knows more about life than anyone can know without regarding life with the artist's eye. He gives us a semblance of reality which is more characteristic of life than anything which we discover in the duller glances of every day. The necessity of art for the spirit lies in just this, that it rescues us from the inattentiveness and obtuseness of so-called real life, from that diminished state of half-awareness in which daily impressions fly past us carelessly regarded, dulled by use-and-wont — a matter of sleeping and waking, knives and forks, bus fares and gossip — in which we lose the vividness of experience and miss the characteristics of the life that passes and passes. Art is concentration on those characteristics, those more deeply regarded aspects which might so easily pass unobserved. R. A. Scott-James [15]

"Right" for the spectator means aesthetically satisfying; for the artist at work it means the complete realisation of a conception, the perfect solution of a problem. The mistake that the vulgar make is to suppose that "right" means the solution of one particular problem. The vulgar are apt to suppose that the problem which all visual and literary artists set themselves is to make something lifelike. Now, all artistic problems — and their possible variety is infinite — must be the *foci* of one particular kind of emotion, that specific artistic emotion which I believe to be an emotion felt for reality, generally perceived through form: but the nature of the focus is immaterial. It is almost, though not quite, true to say that one problem is as good as another. Indeed

[15] *The Making of Literature*, pp. 343–44. Copyright 1930 by Martin Secker, Ltd. Reprinted by permission of the publisher.

all problems are in themselves equally good, though, owing to human infirmity, there are two which tend to turn out badly. One, as we have seen, is the pure aesthetic problem; the other is the problem of accurate representation.

The vulgar imagine that there is but one focus, that "right" means always the realisation of an accurate conception of life. They cannot understand that the immediate problem of the artist may be to express himself within a square or a circle or a cube, to balance certain harmonies, to reconcile certain dissonances, to achieve certain rhythms, or to conquer certain difficulties of medium, just as well as to catch a likeness. This error is at the root of the silly criticism that Mr. Shaw has made it fashionable to print. In the plays of Shakespeare there are details of psychology and portraiture so realistic as to astonish and enchant the multitude, but the conception, the thing that Shakespeare set himself to realise, was not a faithful presentation of life. The creation of Illusion was not the artistic problem that Shakespeare used as a channel for his artistic emotion and a focus for his energies. The world of Shakespeare's plays is by no means so lifelike as the world of Mr. Galsworthy's, and therefore those who imagine that the artistic problem must always be the achieving of a correspondence between printed words or painted forms and the world as they know it are right in judging the plays of Shakespeare inferior to those of Mr. Galsworthy. As a matter of fact, the achievement of verisimilitude, far from being the only possible problem, disputes with the achievement of beauty the honour of being the worst possible. It is so easy to be lifelike, that an attempt to be nothing more will never bring into play the highest emotional and intellectual powers of the artist. Just as the aesthetic problem is too vague, so the representative problem is too simple. CLIVE BELL [16]

There are three reasons why verisimilitude in imaginative literature is never conformity to the truth of actual life. In the first

place, actual life is too vast and various to be brought as a whole
within the compass of a novel, a narrative, or a dramatic representation. In the second place, the verisimilitude whereby any
piece of imaginative literature moves readers or auditors has to be
conformity to what is the truth about life for the readers or auditors, and, as is obvious, the nature of the truth about life differs
for different groups of these. In the third place, the imaginative
writer is as human as the rest of us: he thinks he is aware of the
truth about life, but what he takes to be this truth is no more than
one among a variety of conceptions or views of life. MONTGOMERY
BELGION [17]

The purpose of the novelist's ingenuity is always the same; it is
to give his subject the highest relief [not the closest verisimili-
tude] by which it is capable of profiting. PERCY LUBBOCK [18]

Plot, as the concrete epitome of such intricate interactions in
human life; conflict as the basic form of such contradictory interaction; parallelism and contrast as the manifestation of the direction in which human passions act for or against one another, and
so forth — all these fundamental principles of fact that the only
thing that is made into recreated reality is what existed in the
characters as a potentiality. . . .

But it is not only these forms. The general, typical phenomena
must at the same time be particular actions, the personal passions
of definite individuals. The artist invents situations and means of
expression with the aid of which he can demonstrate how these
individual passions grow beyond the confines of the merely individual world.

Herein lies the secret of elevating individuality to the typical
without depriving it of its individual contours, in fact by intensifying these individual contours. This concrete consciousness, like
fully developed, fully intensified passion, enables the individual to

[17] "The Testimony of Fiction," *Southern Review*, 4 (Summer 1938), 152.
[18] *The Craft of Fiction*, p. 173. Copyright 1947 by Peter Smith, Inc., and
1921 by Jonathan Cape, Ltd., and by Charles Scribner's Sons. Reprinted by
permission of the publishers.

unfold the abilities dormant within him, which in actual life he possesses only in a crippled form; only as a potentiality. Poetic truth in the reproduction of objective reality is based upon the fact that the only thing that is made into recreated reality is what existed in the characters as a potentiality. Poetic creativeness surpasses reality in that these dormant potentialities are allowed to develop fully.

And conversely. Created individualities' consciousness which is (at least partially) independent of these concrete potentialities of persons, which is not based upon such a rich and concrete interplay of human passions, and does not produce a new human quality solely through this intensification, as in Racine or Schiller, becomes abstract and anemic. The created character can be significant and typical only if the artist succeeds in disclosing the manifold connections between the individual traits of his heroes and the objective general problems of his time, if the character himself experiences the most abstract problems of his time as his own individual problems that are a matter of life and death for him.

It is obvious that the created character's ability to generalize intellectually is of extraordinary importance in this connection. Generalization sinks to the level of empty abstraction only when the bond between abstract thought and the personal experiences of the character disappear, when we do not experience this bond together with him. If the artist is able to recreate these bonds in all their vitality, the fact that the work of art abounds with ideas in no way impedes its artistic concreteness but, on the contrary, increases it. GEORGE LUKÁCS [19]

A "living" character is not necessarily "true to life." It is a person whom we can see and hear, whether he be true or false to human nature as we know it. What the creator of character needs is not so much knowledge of motives as keen sensibility; the

[19] "The Intellectual Physiognomy of Literary Characters," *International Literature*, 8 (August 1936), 58. (Translated from the German by Leonard E. Mins.)

dramatist need not understand people; but he must be exceptionally aware of them. T. S. ELIOT [20]

But this conclusion is reached without any direct examination of character as an illusion or as a symbol at all, for "character" is merely the term by which the reader alludes to the pseudo-objective image he composes of his responses to an author's verbal arrangements. Unfortunately, that image once composed, it can be criticized from many irrelevant angles — its moral, political, social or religious, significance considered, all as though it possessed actual objectivity, were a figure of the inferior realm of real life. And, because the annual cataract of serious fiction is as full of "life-like" little figures of such, and no more, significance as drinking water is of infusoria, it passes critical filters in undiminished volume and unrectified impunity while the meagre stream of genuine literature, being burdened with "the forms of things unknown," is anxiously traced to its hypothetical source — a veritable psychologico-biographical bog.

In this connexion, the main thing to be noted about the new "subjective" novelists is their increasing tendency to rely for their effect not on set pieces of character-drawing, but directly on the poetic properties of words. The idea of a character's consciousness is created in the reader by the exploitation of the emotive powers of language used to evoke concrete imagery and sensation. The idea so created has unusual reality; the idea of Dedalus, for instance, that is obtained from a compulsory experience of Dublin Beach as he would have experienced it is not unauthenticated by any suspicious connivance of Nature, as when the thunder rumbles conveniently over Egdon Heath.

. . .

. . . few great works are not ridiculous in synopsis. And for this reason — that the form of a novel only exists as a balance of response on the part of the reader. Hence schematic plot is a construction of the reader's that corresponds to an aspect of that re-

[20] *Selected Essays 1917–1932*, p. 188. Copyright 1932 by Harcourt, Brace and Co., and by Faber and Faber, Ltd. Reprinted by permission of the publishers.

sponse and stands in merely diagrammatic relationship in the source. Only as precipitates from the memory are plot or character tangible; yet only in solution have either any emotive valency. The composition of this metaphorical fluid is a technical matter. The technique of the novel is just as symphonic as the technique of the drama and as dependent, up to a point, on the dynamic devices of articulation and control of narrative tempo. But, though dependent, it is dependent as legs are on muscles, for the *how* but not the *why* of movement; and, interesting as functional technique may be to the mechanical minded and to workers in the same medium on the look-out for tips, the organic is the province of criticism. More important, then, than what may be called the tricks of the narrative is the status of the plot and its relation to the other elements of a novel, particularly its relation to character, in solution.

Modern opinion, commonly assuming that the novelist expresses himself primarily through character, tends to regard story as more or less incidental; either it is scorned as part of the "good old compromise . . . for the entertainment of the reader" or it is looked on as merely the expository structure—the Aintree, as it were, of character or, in less serious connexion, a modiste's parlour elegantly set for the mannequin parade.

Hence, though it is stipulated that plot be organic, it is required to be so in the sense that it may be said to arise out of, or be determined by, character. When a book is found satisfactory, this fundamental condition is said to be fulfilled, and "value" is attributed to it or quarried out of character. Only when an imaginative failure is perceived is the plot scrutinized and then only for the, as it were, temporal location of the lapse, whose occasion is still sought elsewhere.

This position is vulnerable from several points. In the first place, in any sense in which the terms used have a meaning at all, it is plain that character, that is, that idea of a human being that is carried away from a play or a novel, is a product of the narrative. Whereas it is impossible to attend to the barest recital of an event, or series of events without calling up for oneself an idea of the persons concerned, an equally bare description of character invokes no such animated notion. In fact, it is impossible to acquire from words any idea of a person unless that person is defined in time as well as in space. That is to say, action of some sort is indispensable. But though this be admitted, it may still be maintained that value, nevertheless, resides in the character thus created. C. H. RICKWORD [21]

We want a story that must be true only in the sense that it could have happened in the world of characters and events which the novelist has created. MORTIMER ADLER [22]

James carries Flaubert's conscious purpose a step farther. His details have the same solidity that Flaubert's have, but they are more *active*. Everything in a James novel *moves*. Even his houses, made up, like all matter, of quivering molecules, would not stand still long enough for Balzacian description.

The key to his method is to be found in his brilliant image of "The House of Fiction":

The House of Fiction has in short not one window, but a million, every one of which has been pierced or is still pierceable, in its vast front, by the need of the individual vision and by the pressure of the individual will. These apertures, of dissimilar shape and size . . . are but windows at the best, mere holes in a dead wall, disconnected, perched aloft; they are not hinged doors opening straight upon life. . . . at each of them stands a figure with a pair of eyes, or at least with a field glass, which forms, again and again, for observation, a unique instrument, insuring to the person making use of it an impression distinct from every other. . . .

The spreading field, the human scene, is "the choice of subject"; the pierced aperture, either broad or balconied or slit-like and low-browed, is "the literary form"; but they are, singly or together, as nothing without the posted presence of the watcher — without, in other words, the consciousness of the artist.

[21] "A Note on Fiction," pp. 31–32, 33–35 in *Towards Standards of Criticism*, edited by F. R. Leavis. Copyright 1933 by Lawrence and Wishart, Ltd. Reprinted by permission of the publisher.

[22] *How to Read a Book*, p. 306. Copyright 1940 by Simon and Schuster, Inc., and by Jarrolds, Ltd. Reprinted by permission of the publishers.

In Flaubert sensuous *perceptions* rest upon and sustain one another. James' *characters* exist, so to speak, *in terms of one another.* Everything in a James novel is seen through the eyes of one of the characters. This interaction gives the scenes a life-like quality — if we think of life as primarily movement or the capacity for movement — which no other writer has been able to achieve, for the very act of perceiving is made part of the drama. In *The Beast in the Jungle* John Marcher's thoughts, emotions and sensations are the actors, his consciousness the stage. But this circumscribing of the stage does not limit our view of "the spreading field." We see the world, too, as much of it, at least, as can be mirrored in the consciousness of one man, which is all that any of us can take in at one time. James has so maneuvered "the watcher at the window" that he contributes to the illusion of life, speeds up the action, rather than halts it. CAROLINE GORDON [23]

The Boundaries of Art

That it is a mistake to equate literature with life is a commonplace of criticism. Life creates its traditions, and literature creates its traditions; they are profoundly and subtly related, but they are not the same tradition. LASCELLES ABERCROMBIE [24]

Almost all works of art are more or less impure; that is to say, they allow or even excite in the contemplator echoes of the emotions which are aroused by actual life, such as pity, fear, desire, curiosity. So that our reaction to such works is (at all events for a time) compounded of certain emotional states which are con-

[23] "Notes on Faulkner and Flaubert," *Hudson Review*, 1 (Summer 1948), 225–26. Reprinted by permission of the author.
[24] *Year's Work in English Studies*, V (1924), p. 13. Copyright 1926 by Oxford University Press. Abercrombie is summing up E. E. Stoll's position in "Literature No 'Document'," *Modern Language Review*, April 1924.

nected with life, together with those purely detached emotions which are peculiar to esthetic apprehension.

. . . in proportion as he becomes more conscious of his purpose the artist tends towards purity — tends to concentrate his attention and his powers on the detached esthetic emotions. ROGER FRY [25]

The reason poetry and life can in no way be equivalent, and any assertion requiring that they should must be based on a misapprehension of the nature of aesthetic emotion, is, that the emotions which a poem offers to us are not the emotions of everyday life at all, but specifically poetic emotions. The fact has perhaps been most succinctly stated by Mr. Eliot, who, in a frequently quoted passage,* declares that "the business of the poet is not to find new emotions, but to use ordinary ones, and, in working them up into poetry, to express feelings which are not in actual emotions at all." That is to say, the emotion obtainable from a poem is to be found in the poem, and nowhere else. MONTGOMERY BELGION [26]

* "Tradition and the Individual Talent," *The Sacred Wood* (Methuen, 1928), p. 58.

Jonson's characters conform to the logic of the emotions of their world. It is a world like Lobatchevsky's; the worlds created by artists like Jonson are like systems of non-Euclidean geometry. They are not fancy, because they have a logic of their own; and this logic illuminates the actual world, because it gives us a new point of view from which to inspect it. T. S. ELIOT [27]

Art is autonomous, and to be pursued for its own sake, precisely because it comprehends the whole of human life; because it has reference to a more perfectly human morality than any other activity of man; because, in so far as it is truly art, it is indicative

[25] "Introduction," p. 295 in *Poems* by Stéphane Mallarmé, edited by Charles Mauron. Copyright 1938 by Chatto and Windus, Ltd., and by the Macmillan Co. of Canada. Reprinted by permission of the publishers.

[26] "What Is Criticism?" *Criterion*, 10 (October 1930), 126.

[27] *The Sacred Wood*, pp. 116–17. Copyright 1920 and 1928 by Methuen and Co., Ltd., and 1921 and 1930 by Alfred A. Knopf, Inc. This selection also appears in *Selected Essays 1917–1932*, pp. 135–36. Copyright 1932 by Harcourt,

of a more comprehensive and unchallengeable harmony in the spirit of man. It does not demand impossibilities, that man should be at one with the universe or in tune with the infinite; but it does envisage the highest of all attainable ideals, that man should be at one with himself, obedient to his own most musical law. JOHN MIDDLETON MURRY [28]

The champions of realism are suffering from a reaction against Pure Form, against Art for Art's Sake. It was quite right that a poet like W. H. Auden should reassert that a poem must be about something. It was right to go further and maintain that great poetry cannot be made out of subject matter which is essentially trivial. But it was a mistake to take subject matter, as some of the "realists" seemed to, as the sole, or even the chief, criterion of poetry. It was a mistake to fancy that criticism could ever devise a sliding scale which would assess the value of a poem by simple reference to the objective importance of its subject matter. The believers in Art for Art's Sake had gone too far in asserting that poetry can be judged without any reference to life. But the realists went too far in the other direction. A poem does not exist in a vacuum, but a poem at the same time *is* a unity, a creation. Criticism based on the assumption that a poem is a mere *translation* of facts outside itself is vicious criticism. The facts outside a poem, the facts which occasion a poem, are no longer the same facts when they have been fused into a poem. Or, looking at it in another way, one can say that the facts which occasion a poem are far too complex to be fully ascertainable by the critic. LOUIS MACNEICE [29]

Certainly tragedy is now often fairly unrecognizable if our notion of it is only as it was in its prime.

[28] *Aspects of Literature*, pp. 12–13. Copyright 1920 by Collins Sons and Co., Ltd. Reprinted by permission of the author and the publisher.
[29] *The Poetry of W. B. Yeats*, pp. 2–3. Copyright 1941 by Oxford University Press. Reprinted by permission of the publisher.

Is there a reason for this state of affairs? Mr. Krutch discovers it in our philosophy or in the life that we lead. It is because living is for us so mean and ignoble that our art is such. We bow or stumble under the load of our enlightenment. We have lost faith in God and even in man, and therefore it is impossible for us to make a hero of him on the stage. "We do not write about kings because we do not believe that any man is worthy to be one, and we do not write about courts because hovels seem to us to be dwellings more appropriate to the creatures who inhabit them. . . . We can no longer tell tales of the fall of noble men because we do not believe that noble men exist." The tragic conception has become for us "a fallacy."

There are, I think, several serious defects or shortcomings in the theory. The fundamental one is that the critic fails to remember the principle, which he incidentally, yet explicitly, acknowledges, of art as no mere imitation but a new creation. Since, as is admitted, art is no record, is no document, little or nothing can be proved by it; since art is a reflection of the taste of the time, it continually changes; and therefore the Spirit of Art is often, quite as Mr. Binyon finds it, "against the Spirit of the Age." ELMER EDGAR STOLL [30]

[30] *Shakespeare and Other Masters,* pp. 395–96. Copyright 1940 by Harvard University Press. Reprinted by permission of the publisher.

III

Form

To be beautiful, a living organism, or any other individual thing made up of parts, must possess not only an orderly arrangement of these parts, but also a proper magnitude; for beauty depends upon these two qualities, size and order. Hence an extremely minute creature cannot be beautiful to us; for we see the whole in an almost infinitesimal moment of time, and lose the pleasure that comes from a distinct perception of order in the parts. Nor could a creature of vast dimensions be beautiful to us — a beast, say, one thousand miles in length; for in that case the eye could not take all of the object in at once — we should see the parts, but not the unity of the whole.

ARISTOTLE

Form

But once his [Henry James'] imagination had been quite caught by an idea, he began working on it with all his powers of invention and manipulation. He turned it in every light; altered the sex and nationality of his characters; revised their marital status — single, married, lovers, widows; provided them with confidants, with foils, with fathers, with money; determined their occupation. He reversed the situation or in some way doubled it, trying for new "values" and points of reference, for some "turn of the screw" that would raise the situation to a higher pitch of intensity or rarity and squeeze out the last drop of "precious" meaning. He complicated the relations of his characters, gave them double and triple functions in reference to the theme and issue. He "squared" them, paired them off, set them in new and elaborate combinations. He arranged the material circumstances of his story so as to give freest play to his characters' penchant for spiritual intrigue. He always had something up his sleeve. He was as full of devices as a French exponent of the well-made play. His matter was as plastic to his hand as the matter of the cosmos to the Platonic demiurge.

And his matter was thus plastic because what he is primarily concerned with is not the gross substance so much as the ideal essence of life. In American scholarship there is a disposition to classify James as a realist . . . But if the realist is one who aims to tell the plain truth about human nature under ordinary or typical circumstances, then James will hardly qualify. For his aim is ever to tell the special truth about highly selected types under circumstances carefully arranged to give free play to their exceptionally refined sentimental reactions. The point is not that he does not tell the truth, and highly significant and illuminating truth, about human nature. But his stage is so set, his issues so drawn, his primary assumptions so determined, that the truth he tells is normative rather than descriptive and statistical. And that is surely not what is meant by realism when we are considering its main direction and intention. JOSEPH WARREN BEACH [1]

But as air, melody, is what strikes me most of all in music and design in painting, so design, pattern or what I am in the habit of calling "inscape" is what I above all aim at in poetry. Now it is the virtue of design, pattern, or inscape to be distinctive, and it is the vice of distinctiveness to be queer. This vice I cannot have escaped. GERARD MANLEY HOPKINS [2]

Of Hopkins's imagery, there is not much in general to be said, but that "not much" is all. He had that acute and sharp sensuous awareness essential to all great poets. He was physically aware of textures, surfaces, colours, patterns of every kind; aware acutely of the earth's diurnal course, of growth and decay, of animality in man and of vitality in all things. Everywhere there is passionate apprehension, passionate expression and equally that passion for form without which these other passions are spend-

[1] "The Witness of the Notebooks," pp. 51–52 in *Forms of Modern Fiction*, edited by William Van O'Connor. Copyright 1948 by the University of Minnesota Press. Reprinted by permission of the author.
[2] Letter LIII, p. 66 in *The Letters of Gerard Manley Hopkins to Robert Bridges*, edited by C. C. Abbott. Copyright 1935 by Oxford University Press. Reprinted by permission of the publisher.

thrift. But the form is inherent in the passion. For, as Emerson remarked with his occasional deep insight, "it is not metres, but a metre-making argument, that makes a poem — a thought so passionate and alive, that, like the spirit of a plant or an animal, it has an architecture of its own, and adorns nature with a new thing." HERBERT READ [3]

All sounds, all colours, all forms, either because of their preordained energies or because of long association, evoke indefinable and yet precise emotions, or, as I prefer to think, call down among us certain disembodied powers, whose footsteps over our hearts we call emotions; and when sound, and colour, and form are in a musical relation, a beautiful relation to one another, they become as it were one sound, one colour, one form, and evoke an emotion that is made out of their distinct evocations and yet is one emotion. The same relation exists between all portions of every work of art, whether it be an epic or a song, and the more perfect it is, and the more various and numerous the elements that have flowed into its perfection, the more powerful will be the emotion, the power, the god it calls among us. Because an emotion does not exist, or does not become perceptible and active among us, till it has found its expression, in colour or in sound or in form, or in all of these, and because no two modulations or arrangements of these evoke the same emotion, poets and painters and musicians, and in a less degree because their effects are momentary, day and night and cloud and shadow, are continually making and un-making mankind. WILLIAM BUTLER YEATS [4]

I conceived the form of the work of art to be its most essential quality, but I believed this form to be the direct outcome of an apprehension of some emotion of actual life by the artist, although, no doubt, that apprehension was of a special and peculiar

[3] *Form in Modern Poetry*, pp. 52–53. Copyright 1933 by Sheed and Ward, Inc. Reprinted by permission of the author and the publisher.
[4] *Essays*, pp. 192–93. Copyright 1912, 1918, and 1924 by the Macmillan Co. Reprinted by permission of Mrs. William Butler Yeats and the publisher.

kind and implied a certain detachment. I also conceived that the spectator in contemplating the form must inevitably travel in an opposite direction along the same road which the artist had taken, and himself feel the original emotion. I conceived the form and the emotion which it conveyed as being inextricably bound together in the aesthetic whole. ROGER FRY [5]

One word of warning is necessary. Let no one imagine that the expression of emotion is the outward and visible sign of a work of art. The characteristic of a work of art is its power of provoking aesthetic emotion; the expression of emotion is possibly what gives it that power. It is useless to go to a picture gallery in search of expression; you must go in search of significant form. When you have been moved by form, you may begin to consider what makes it moving. If my theory be correct, rightness of form is invariably a consequence of rightness of emotion. Right form, I suggest, is ordered and conditioned by a particular kind of emotion; but whether my theory be true or false, the form remains right. If the forms are satisfactory, the state of mind that ordained them must have been aesthetically right. If the forms are wrong, it does not follow that the state of mind was wrong; between the moment of inspiration and the finished work of art there is room for many a slip. Feeble or defective emotion is at best only one explanation of unsatisfactory form. Therefore, when the critic comes across satisfactory form he need not bother about the feelings of the artist; for him to feel the aesthetic significance of the artist's forms suffices. If the artist's state of mind be important, he may be sure that it was right because the forms are right. But when the critic attempts to account for the unsatisfactoriness of forms he may consider the state of mind of the artist. He cannot be sure that because the forms are wrong the state of mind was wrong; because right forms imply right feeling, wrong forms do not necessarily imply wrong feeling;

[5] *Vision and Design*, p. 294. Copyright 1920 by Chatto and Windus, Ltd. Reprinted by permission of the publisher.

but if he has got to explain the wrongness of form, here is a possibility he cannot overlook. He will have left the firm land of aesthetics to travel in an unstable element; in criticism one catches at any straw. There is no harm in that, provided the critic never forgets that, whatever ingenious theories he may put forward, they can be nothing more than attempts to explain the one central fact — that some forms move us aesthetically and others do not. CLIVE BELL [6]

To Mallarmé, no theme is *a priori* "poetic"; but this does not imply that all themes are of equal potential value for the purposes of poetry. He is determined to develop all the potentialities of the theme he has selected for treatment; he knows, however, that each theme has a different poetic charge. Thus he may consider a bicycle gliding down the road a wholly legitimate theme, yet he is far from asserting that the potentialities of this theme are equal to the potentialities of, say, the hair of a beautiful woman. In other words, even though he banishes no subject from the realm of poetry, he is convinced that there is a hierarchy of themes, governed not so much by the traditional notions of "loftiness" and "triviality" as by the richness of their poetic implications. Roger Fry, in the preface to his Mallarmé translation, comments very pertinently on this aspect of the poet's method. "The poetical poet," he writes, "makes use of words and material already consecrated by poetry, and with this he ornaments and embroiders his own theme. Mallarmé's method is the opposite of this. His poetry is the unfolding of something implicit in the theme. By the contemplation of the theme he discovers new and unsuspected relations. He is not concerned that the theme itself, or the objects it comprises, should already have poetical quality, nor does he seek to find relations with other things already charged with emotion." FRANCIS C. GOLFFING [7]

[6] *Art*, pp. 61–63. Copyright 1914 and 1947 by Chatto and Windus, Ltd. Reprinted by permission of the publisher.
[7] "Stéphane Mallarmé: A Reconsideration," *New Mexico Quarterly Review*, 16 (Spring 1946), 65.

[Dylan] Thomas has written some highly penetrating comments on his own poetry to his friend Henry Treece. In answer to the criticism that his poems are diffuse, the poet replies:

. . . a poem by myself needs a host of images, because its centre is a host of images. I make one image,— though "make" is not the word, I let, perhaps, an image be "made" emotionally in me and then apply to it what intellectual and critical forces I possess –, let it breed another, let that image contradict the first, make, of the third image bred out of the other two together, a fourth contradictory image, and let them all, within my imposed formal limits conflict. Each image holds within it the seed of its own destruction, and my dialectical method, as I understand it, is a constant building up and breaking down of the images that come out of the central seed, which is itself destructive and constructive at the same time.

What I want to try to explain — and it's necessarily vague to me — is that the life in any poem of mine cannot move concentrically round a central image; the life must come out of the centre; an image must be born and die in another; and any sequence of my images must be a sequence of creations, recreations, destructions, contradictions. . . . My object is, as you say, conventionally "to get things straight." Out of the inevitable conflict of images — inevitable, because of the creative, recreative, destructive and contradictory nature of the motivating centre, the womb of war — I try to make that momentary peace which is a poem. . . . A poem of mine is, or should be, a watertight section of a stream that is flowing all ways, all warring images within it reconciled for that small stop of time.

MARSHALL W. STEARNS [8]

What makes the aesthetic whole is the way the edges [of the perceived parts in the aesthetic object] grow together, as it were, the way one thing passes into another, the way the substance passes out of control of our measuring instruments, and in some indisputable way the local differences grow into one. LEO STEIN [9]

[8] "Unsex the Skeleton," *Sewanee Review*, 52 (Summer 1944), 434. Dylan Thomas's definition of his creative process is reprinted in C. Day Lewis, *The Poetic Image*, pp. 122ff. Copyright 1947 by Jonathan Cape, Ltd. Reprinted by permission of the publisher.
[9] *The A-B-C of Aesthetics*, p. 138. Copyright 1927 by Horace Liveright, Inc. Reprinted by permission of the publisher.

The descriptive meaning of artistic form as the total system of relations in the materials of the work of art is not to be confused with two other meanings. The first is pattern — the pattern of colors or lines in a painting, the pattern of shapes or masses in a statue or a building, the pattern of words or actions in a novel, poem, drama, or opera. Such patterns are true forms, but they are only fragments of artistic form in our sense. Artistic form is rather the system of such patterns found in any given creation. The second meaning defines artistic form as the total body of relations in a work of art. Artistic form includes not only the total system of relations of the materials but also the relation of this system to expression, function, and materials and the relation of these dimensions to each other and to the system of material relations. Artistic form is the interdimensional system of relations as well as a dimension of the public object. DILMAN WALTER GOTSHALK [10]

No survey, however brief, of the idea of form can omit reference to the distinction common in English criticism since Coleridge, between *organic* and *mechanic* (or abstract) form. "The form is mechanic," says Coleridge, "when on any given material we impress a pre-determined form, not necessarily arising out of the properties of the material; as when to a mass of wet clay we give whatever shape we wish it to retain when hardened. The organic form, on the other hand, is innate; it shapes, as it develops, itself from within, and the fullness of its development is one and the same with the perfection of its outward form. Such as the life is, such is the form." *(Lectures on Shakespeare,* i.) The intent of this passage is excellent, and the result of Coleridge's insistence upon this principle has been wholly good for criticism. But the terms of his statement involve a conflation of the distinction between form and matter with that between an expression and what it expresses, the ramifications of which it would take long to untangle. Fortunately the principle has been more accurately stated by T. S. Eliot in his recent Ker Memorial Lecture:

Some [structural] forms are more appropriate to some languages than to others, and all are more appropriate to some periods than to others. At one stage the stanza is a right and natural formalization of speech into a pattern. But the stanza — and the more elaborate it is, the more rules to be observed in its proper execution, the more surely this happens — tends to become fixed to the idiom of the moment of its perfection. It quickly loses contact with the changing colloquial speech, being possessed by the mental outlook of a past generation; it becomes discredited when employed solely by those writers who, having no impulse to form within them, have recourse to pouring their liquid sentiment into a ready-made mould in which they vainly hope that it will set. In a perfect sonnet, what you admire is not so much the author's skill in adapting himself to the pattern as the skill and power with which he makes the pattern comply with what he has to say. Without this fitness, which is contingent upon period as well as individual genius, the rest is at best virtuosity. . . . (*Partisan Review*, 9, 463f.)

Mr. Eliot does well to invoke the principle by name: *fitness*. It is not a question of the form's arising out of the properties of the "material," which is impossible; it is not a question of the "innate" except as genius for perceiving relations and establishing them is innate. The problem is that of such perfect fitting together of structural elements and meanings as will produce for a mind that contemplates the completed structure a sense of perfect harmony and consistency: that is, of perfect *order*. CRAIG LA DRIERE [11]

The difference in practice and criticism both is best explained by Mr. Charles Morgan's distinction between "suspense of plot" and "suspense of form." Suspense of plot, which has to do with the disclosure of a fact, like Epicene's sex or Tom Jones's pater-

[11] " 'Organic' Form," p. 253 in *Dictionary of World Literature*, edited by Joseph T. Shipley. Copyright 1943 by the Philosophical Library. Reprinted by permission of the publisher. The quotation from Eliot appears in *The Music of Poetry*, pp. 25-26. Copyright 1942 by Jackson, Son and Co., Ltd. Reprinted by permission of the publisher.

nity, or with that of motive or point of view, like Nora's and Helmer's in the *Doll's House,* has its indubitable value; but suspense of form, which has to do with the development and establishment of the emotional illusion, has a greater value, and in the best work of either Ibsen or Euripides the two sorts of suspense are conjoined. Suspense of form is the excited expectation not of the answer to a puzzle, or of the disclosure of a mystery, but — under the spell of illusion — of the rounding out of a harmony, like the rime to come at the end of a verse or the rest tone at the end of a song. It is the expectation of the way that Othello will receive the slander and afterwards the truth, or that Hamlet will baffle his enemies, have his revenge and meet his death.

Now with anticipation — this suspense of form — there is greater opportunity for irony; and in Shakespeare as in the ancients, not so continually but more variously, the contrast essential to drama, which holds it together, takes on this more accentuated and poignant aspect. ELMER EDGAR STOLL [12]

It is not, one will recall, until the fourth scene of the first act that Hamlet confronts the ghost of his father. As soon as the situation has been made clear, the audience has been, consciously or unconsciously, waiting for this ghost to appear, while in the fourth scene this moment has been definitely promised. For earlier in the play Hamlet had arranged to come to the platform at night with Horatio to meet the ghost, and it is now night, he is with Horatio and Marcellus, and they are standing on the platform. Hamlet asks Horatio the hour.

> HOR. I think it lacks of twelve.
> MAR. No, it is struck.
> HOR. Indeed? I heard it not: then it draws near the season
>   Wherein the spirit held his wont to walk.

Promptly hereafter there is a sound off-stage. "A flourish of trumpets, and ordnance shot off within." Hamlet's friends have es-

[12] *Shakespeare and Other Masters,* p. 13. Copyright 1940 by Harvard University Press. Reprinted by permission of the publisher.

tablished the hour as twelve. It is time for the ghost. Sounds off-stage, and of course it is not the ghost. It is, rather, the sound of the king's carousal, for the king "keeps wassail." A tricky, and effective detail. We have been waiting for a ghost, and get, start-lingly, a blare of trumpets. And again, once the trumpets are silent, we feel all the more just how desolate are these three men waiting for a ghost, on a bare "platform," feel it by this sudden juxtaposition of an imagined scene of lights and merriment. But the trumpets announcing a carousal have suggested a subject of conversation. In the darkness Hamlet discusses the excessive drinking of his countrymen. He points out that it tends to harm their reputation abroad, since, he argues, this one showy vice makes their virtues "in the general censure take corruption." And for this reason, although he himself is a native of this place, he does not approve of the custom. Indeed, there in the gloom he is talking very intelligently on these matters, and Horatio answers, "Look, my Lord, it comes." All this time we had been waiting for a ghost, and it comes at the one moment which was not pointing towards it. This ghost, so assiduously prepared for, is yet a surprise. And now that the ghost has come, we are wait-ing for something further. Programme: a speech from Hamlet. Hamlet must confront the ghost. Here again Shakespeare can feed well upon the use of contrast for his effects. Hamlet has just been talking in a sober, rather argumentative manner — but now the flood-gates are unloosed:

> Angels and ministers of grace defend us!
> Be thou a spirit of health or goblin damn'd,
> Bring with thee airs from heaven or blasts from hell . . .

and the transition from the matter-of-fact to the grandiose, the full-throated and full-vowelled, is a second burst of trumpets, perhaps even more effective than the first, since it is the rich fulfil-ment of a promise. Yet this satisfaction in turn becomes an allure-ment, an itch for further developments. At first desiring solely to see Hamlet confront the ghost, we now want Hamlet to learn from the ghost the details — which are, however, with shrewdness and husbandry, reserved for "Scene V. — Another Part of the Platform."

I have gone into this scene at some length, since it illustrates so perfectly the relationship between psychology and form, and so aptly indicates how the one is to be defined in terms of the other. That is, the psychology here is not the psychology of the *hero*, but the psychology of the *audience*. And by that distinction, form would be the psychology of the audience. Or, seen from another angle, form is the creation of an appetite in the mind of the auditor, and the adequate satisfying of that appetite. This satisfaction — so complicated is the human mechanism — at times involves a temporary set of frustrations, but in the end these frustrations prove to be simply a more involved kind of satisfaction, and furthermore serve to make the satisfaction of fulfilment more intense. If, in a work of art, the poet says something, let us say, about a meeting, writes in such a way that we desire to observe that meeting, and then, if he places that meeting before us — that is form. While obviously, that is also the psychology of the audience, since it involves desires and their appeasements. KENNETH BURKE [13]

In *Madame Bovary* is it not Flaubert's *anticipation* of Emma's collapse exactly what leads to it and makes it inevitable? There was nothing in the situation that might not have been changed by a single different step; but then the satisfaction of the anticipation would have been lost and the book would have fallen apart. Is it not perhaps the actuality of that anticipation that craves reality? Flaubert — his book — and, so, his character — had to look for, *to discover* the means and machinery of Emma's collapse; no recourse was too great, no resource too mean, for that purpose; Emma grows more lovely as her need grows more desperate; so, too, as her experience, and our experience of her, are based more and

[13] *Counter-Statement*, pp. 38–39. Copyright 1931 by Harcourt, Brace and Co. Reprinted by permission of the publisher. This essay is reprinted in *Critiques and Essays* in *Criticism*, edited by R. W. Stallman. Copyright 1949 by Ronald Press.

more upon the actual, the craving for the real becomes more intense: as she collapses she becomes a symbol satisfying Flaubert's anticipation and much more, articulating in her figure and in the configuration of the novel both the anticipation of the author and the actuality of her experience: she becomes, not a formula, but the unformulable whole of all that was meaningful in her: she becomes "Madame Bovary" — all we mean by the *title*. It is by these means that she becomes a symbol and takes on all the inexhaustible mode of being that goes with it. R. P. BLACKMUR [14]

Realization of such a synthesis, granted that the artist's experience is sufficiently rich and his attitude sufficiently comprehensive and profound, is essentially a problem of form, since form — in all the arts — is what Professor Greene calls "the artistically expressive organization . . . of the medium in which it has its being." The novelist, to borrow the words of the late Professor Rogers, "is attempting to convey a summation of the way life is grouped, at a particular moment or period, a summation, of course, which may give way to others in the future." To convey this summation he must, as Mr Tate has said that the poet must do, apprehend and concentrate our experience in the mysterious limitations of form. Mr. Ransom has defined poetry as "a structure with a texture." This definition, freely interpreted, may be applied to any type of imaginative literature. And both the structure and the texture have to do with the problem of form, since artistic form comes into being only when the two elements are successfully fused in the specific objectivity of the poem or the play or the novel.

All this implies no shallow "art for art's sake" doctrine or exclusively formalist esthetic, however, nor any belief in a priori patterns of composition, especially in the novel, which has always enjoyed more freedom than any other literary type. Gide would certainly subscribe to Percy Lubbock's assertion that "The best

[14] "Notes on Four Categories in Criticism," *Sewanee Review,* 54 (Autumn 1946), 589.

form is that which makes the most of its subject — there is no other definition of the meaning of form in fiction." Yet in France during the late nineteenth and early twentieth centuries there had developed a type of "well made" novel which, fortified by the academic prejudice that the French alone know how to "compose" and that such formal "composition" is essential to literature, tended to crystallize in a strict conventional mold into which the individual novelist was expected to stuff whatever material came to hand instead of actively shaping his experience into the unique form required by the subject. Against this kind of unintelligent, inartistic doctrine Gide rebels — Gide the master of style and composition himself and the exponent of the vital kind of "classicism" which he defines as the integration of the totality of the moral, intellectual, and emotional preoccupations of one's age in a synthesis allowing all the elements to assume their proper reciprocal relationships (*Oeuvres*, XI, 42–43). He is unwilling to accept any such ready-made frame for his own composition because he understands that the true novelist is a poet or "maker" whose task and privilege it is to shape his material into the specific form which *is* the novel just as surely as the form *is* the statue. As he insists in a preface written for a special edition of Baudelaire's *Fleurs du mal*: "La forme est le secret de l'oeuvre" (*Oeuvres*, VII, 500). CARLOS LYNES, JR.[15]

In an article in *The Third American Caravan*, entitled *The Extension and Re-Integration of the Human Spirit through the Poetry, chiefly French and American, since Poe and Baudelaire,* Mr. Yvor Winters discusses the several methods of constructing poems. There is, first, the "scattered" method, in which the several stanzas, or even the lines within a stanza, exhibit no progression, but are related to each other simply by their reference to a common theme. If I remember rightly, Nashe's *In Time of Pestilence*

---

[15] "André Gide and the Problem of Form in the Novel," pp. 178–79 in *Forms of Modern Fiction,* edited by William Van O'Connor. Copyright 1948 by the University of Minnesota Press. Reprinted by permission of the author.

is the example given. Most descriptions fall into this class. There is, next, the narrative method, which is too obvious to need comment. There is, third, the logical method in which the stanzas or lines of a poem follow logically from their predecessors. This method of development was characteristic of the seventeenth century Metaphysicals, and can be examined in such poems as Donne's *The Funeral*. Next, and specially characteristic of contemporary verse, there is the "psychological" method, in which there is from line to line, or from stanza to stanza, a progression not ordered by logic, but, in psychological terms, based on association of ideas. Mr. Winters, adopting a Freudian explanation, states that the method is a result of the lowering of the level of consciousness to a point where subconscious trains of thought become conscious. Mr. Read on the contrary would regard a non-logical progression in poetry as a result of thinking raised to a more than ordinary intensity. There is, doubtless, a difference between *uncontrolled* reverie and the purposive associations of poetry; and Mr. Winters' explanation, by suggesting the former rather than the latter, is misleading as a description of all but bad poetry using a psychological method. Lastly, there are poems which exhibit an alternation of method, or in which one method is applied to larger units, such as the stanza, and another method to smaller units, such as the line. Even though logical sequences, which are necessarily constituted by public or traditional connections, are ipso facto easier to apprehend than are psychological sequences, which at least so far have usually been private — that is to say, peculiar to the poet's mind — and have therefore exacted from readers not only a sustained intensity of attention, but often a considerable amount of bewildered fumbling, nevertheless poets are increasingly employing the psychological method. One reason may be given in the words of Mr. Crane . . .

. . . as a poet I may very possibly be more interested in the so-called illogical impingements of the connotations of words on the consciousness (and their combinations and interplay in metaphor on this basis) than I am interested in the preservation of their

logically rigid significations at the cost of limiting my subject matter and perceptions involved in the poem.

. . .

If the poet is to be held completely to the already evolved and
exploited sequences of imagery and logic — what field of added
consciousness and increased perceptions (the actual province of
poetry, if not lullabyes) can be expected when one has to relatively return to the alphabet every breath or so? In the minds
of people who have sensitively read, seen and experienced a great
deal, isn't there a terminology something like short-hand as compared to usual description and dialectics, which the artist ought to
be right in trusting as a reasonable connective agent toward fresh
concepts, more inclusive evaluations?

That is to say, logical sequences and traditional imagery are neither
flexible nor subtle enough to render accurately the nuances of
contemporary perception. F. CUDWORTH FLINT [16]

It should be unnecessary to devote this attention to these principles, principles which almost anyone will readily concede in
purely theoretical discussion. But that they need to be reiterated,
and that their opposites are smuggled into most attacks on modern
poetry, can be demonstrated. For instance, an able scholar and
distinguished critic will innocently rest his case against a contemporary poet in the following terms: "Is it beauty of sound? . . .
Is it a sequence of lovely images? That will be sought equally in
vain. Nor can the piece lay claim to intellectual interest: the
thought that appears to inform it is singularly commonplace."
Whether the poem in question is bad or good could never be
determined by this critical approach, for it leaves unanswered the
question of the relation of the parts of the poem to the total
intention. And another famous critic would ban the word *bloated*
from poetry because, as he affirms, it is "sacred to the memory
of dead fish." The word *bloated* may be the wrong word in any

[16] Metaphor in Contemporary Poetry," *Symposium*, I (July 1930),
319–21. The quotation from Crane (correspondence with Harriet Monroe
in *Poetry*, October 1926) appears in *Hart Crane*, by Brom Weber, pp. 417,
419. Copyright 1948 by the Bodley Press. Reprinted by permission of the
publisher.

given poem, but never for this reason. Indeed, most of the attacks on modern poetry involve this basic misconception as to the nature of poetry, a misconception which considers it a bundle of items intrinsically poetic in themselves and neglects the fundamental fact that the poetic effect is always dependent upon relationships. Indeed, most statements that any given poem is unintelligible are simply confessions to the failure to find the intrinsically poetic items existing in isolation.

But the general principle just laid down does not, or rather does not seem to, take into account the charge that is most often made against modern poetry — the charge of unintelligibility caused by an absence of logical links. The critic may hold that he is quite willing to accept the fact that a poem must be appreciated as a total organism but is unable to do so without benefit of logical connection. In almost all cases this critic will mean by logical connection the explicit statement — he does not mean that the connections between parts, or the general theme of the poem, are not susceptible to a logical statement. He merely refuses to attempt the leap himself. One critic, therefore, considers it a deadly attack on some modern poems to say that the parts of a poem "form a psychological, not a logical, unity." The answer to this sort of thing is simple: every successful poem creates a *psychological* unity, and not even the simplest metaphor fails to violate a *logical* unity. The distinction between the two kinds of unity is extremely important: Psychological unity is the aim of every poem; logical unity is a device to achieve this aim, and may or may not be used. CLEANTH BROOKS AND ROBERT PENN WARREN [17]

What is of more importance, however, is Ransom's tendency to praise — unless I misread him — Donne's logical rigor, not for its function in the development of the tone, but as an end in itself. The point is crucial, for it has everything to do with the essential function of metaphor. Does a poem find its unity in a rational or

[17] "The Reading of Modern Poetry," *American Review*, 8 (February 1937), 441–42.

logical unity? Or does it find its unity in a unity of tone? Or, to transpose the question: Does the poem find its "truth" in a scientific or philosophical truth? Or does it find its truth in a dramatic truth? Does the poem achieve coherence in a system of propositions logically related to each other? Or does it find its coherence in a complex of attitudes dramatically related to each other?

Donne's display of "logic" is frequently so brilliant that we may be tempted to say that it functions in the poems "logically." But an inspection of any one of his poems indicates what the "logic" is actually being used for. The logic of *The Canonization*, for example, will hardly satisfy the friend to whom it is addressed and who has (in the implied dramatic situation) been trying to persuade the lover to give up his love. The poem in which the logic is contained may well convince the friend that the lover is committed and determined, that he is not callow, that he is making his choice with open eyes. It will hardly convince him *logically* that the lover is a saint or that he is a phoenix or that he is winning a better world by giving up this world.

The real structure of *The Canonization* transcends the logical framework of its images. Moreover, it involves mixed metaphor and rapidly shifted figures. It achieves a unity, to be sure; but the unity which it achieves is an imaginative unity. It is not a logical unity unless we beg the whole question by adding "logic of its own nature." That, to be sure, it has; but so have most of the poems of Shakespeare. CLEANTH BROOKS [18]

Of course no work of literature is interesting or moving solely because of its intrinsic form. Art always relies at least partly on external associations. The main significance of form, however, is that in any portion of a work the rest is presumed and implied, just as in science, where a vast theoretical structure is implicit in any assertion. Sometimes more, of course, is presumed than merely the work of art: a knowledge of other works, for example, or of

[18] *The Well Wrought Urn*, p. 220. Copyright 1947 by Reynal and Hitchcock, and 1949 by Dennis Dobson, Ltd. Reprinted by permission of the publishers.

history. But to determine the nature of form in any literary work is to discover what each image or episode presupposes for its intelligibility and effect. The point is, again, the threefold equation of form and meaning on the one hand and emotion on the other. MARTIN LEBOWITZ [19]

Suppose the logical substance remained there all the time, and was in no way specially remarkable, while the particularity came in by accretion, so that the poem turned out partly universal, and partly particular, but with respect to different parts. I began to remark the dimensions of a poem, or other work of art. The poem was not a mere moment in time, nor a mere point in space. It was sizeable, like a house. Apparently it had a "plan" or a central frame of logic, but it had also a huge wealth of local detail, which sometimes fitted the plan functionally or served it, and sometimes only subsisted comfortably under it; in either case the house stood up. But it was the political way of thinking which gave me the first analogy which seemed valid. The poem was like a democratic state, in action, and observed both macroscopically and microscopically.

The house occurred also, and provided what seems to be a more negotiable trope under which to construe the poem. A poem is a *logical structure* having a *local texture*. These terms have been actually though not systematically employed in literary criticism. To my imagination they are architectural. The walls of my room are obviously structural; the beams and boards have a function; so does the plaster, which is the visible aspect of the final wall. The plaster might have remained naked, aspiring to no character, and purely functional. But actually it has been painted, receiving color; or it has been papered, receiving color and design, though these have no structural value; and perhaps it has been hung with tapestry, or with paintings for "decoration." The paint, the paper, the tapestry are texture. It is logically unrelated to structure. But

[19] "Thought and Sensibility," *Kenyon Review*, 5 (Spring 1943), 224–25. The quotation appears here as revised for this work by the author.

I indicate only a few of the textural possibilities in architecture. There are not fewer of them in poetry.

The intent of the good critic becomes therefore to examine and define the poem with respect to its structure and its texture. If he has nothing to say about its texture he has nothing to say about it specifically as a poem, but is treating it only insofar as it is prose. JOHN CROWE RANSOM [20]

[20] "Criticism as Pure Speculation," pp. 110–11 in *The Intent of the Critic*, edited by Donald A. Stauffer. Copyright 1941 by Princeton University Press. Reprinted by permission of the publisher.

IV

The
Problem of
Meaning

Horner (to Lady Fidget): "Alas, she has an innocent, literal under-standing."

WILLIAM WYCHERLEY, *The Country Wife* (IV, iii).

Stark naked thoughts and emotions are as weak as stark naked men. Therefore, they must be clothed.

How shameful to write without knowing the meaning of language, words, metaphors, changes of ideas and tone; without conceiving of the structure *of the work's duration, or the conditions of its end; hardly the why, and not at all the how!*

PAUL VALÉRY, "Literature," *Hudson Review*, 2 (Winter 1950), 538, 542.

The Nature of the Problem

A good poem, completely understood, must create in the reader
the feeling that he has not yet understood it at all.
The core of every poem is silence.
The poem is the better, the more indefiniteness it defines.
The poet always uses words as though he were the first one to
use them for the first time.

J. GRESHOFF [1]

Assuming that all art is symbol, you cannot on the stage present
the symbol, and leave aside the stuff of which it is made. Yet this
is precisely what M. Cocteau seems to be trying to do. Thus his
Orpheus and Eurydice remain symbols. . . . Thus in spite of its
great charm [i.e., the *Orphée*, acted at the Théâtre des Arts], its
high degree of theatrical skill, we have to apply our intellects to
apprehend the intuition, instead of ourselves apprehending intuitively through the aesthetic medium. We are left with no final
attitude, though we are made very alert. Perhaps it was the realiza-

[1] "Epigrams on Poetry," *Sewanee Review*, 54 (Winter 1946), 139, 143,
142, 141.

tion of this which led M. Cocteau into his greatest dramatic mistake, the direct statement; for on the stage, the meaning or the emotion should be implied. For Heurtebise the glazier to say that he was a guardian angel, for Eurydice to sum up by saying that it was ridiculous not to realise that our happiness lies in the everyday now, was wrong. We should be forced to guess these things: to have them told us destroys the validity of the symbol. Iago must not tell us he is the quintessence of evil; Tartuffe may not declare he is the incarnation of hypocrisy: then they would merely be statements of what their creators intended them to be. BONAMY DOBRÉE [2]

Thus explained, *The Echoing Green* [by Blake] is as nearly perfect an example of poetical obliquity as can be found. The main sense is stated in no particular whatever, but is diffused through every part of the poem and can be apprehended as a whole only through the synthesis of all those parts. The abstract idea, far from being stated, has been translated into completely concrete form; it has disappeared into apparently alien facts. Through its major obliquity *The Echoing Green* is in a different category from Goldsmith's lines [in *The Deserted Village*] and must be judged by different standards.

Even if this interpretation of *The Echoing Green* were wrong (and such bold guesses at obliquity are likely to please oneself better than others), the *principle* illustrated is not thereby invalidated. Those who reject this instance may find a better and agree that directness and obliquity must vary widely from poem to poem and that to judge an oblique poem as if it were direct, and the other way round, can only lead to disaster.

. . .

In a general sense, then, plot signifies order and control: it is the chief means of giving the impression of what we loosely call *greatness*. But besides this it can have other less general meanings. First and most important, it is the commonest and most effective

[2] Review in *New Criterion*, 4 (October 1926), 767.

means of putting the great commonplaces obliquely. Out of the mere bringing together of the different sorrows of Priam and Achilles Homer extracts his commonplace that the things that unite mankind count for more than those that divide them. Such a juxtaposition would be useless, even ridiculous, without the qualities of human insight, closeness to actual life, rhythmic skill and so on that Homer commands; but co-existing with them it expresses most of all. Moreover it is totally oblique, giving its meaning without any trace of statement whatever.

Secondly, plot expresses most effectively the adaptable comprehensiveness of a fine mind. Plot is the largest but the least obtrusive manifestation of wit (in the seventeenth century sense). One of the reasons why Marvell's *To His Coy Mistress* satisfies us so thoroughly is that the minor manifestations of wit gracefully subordinate themselves to the plot of the poem, to the major contrasts between the poem's three paragraphs. E. M. W. TILLYARD [3]

But let me here say at once that although the poet may be conscious of this aspect of his vision [that his poem, or part of it, has symbolic value], it is exactly what he wants to avoid stating, or even being too concerned with. His job is to recreate his vision, and let it speak its moral for itself. The poet must distinguish clearly in his own mind between that which most definitely must be said and that which must not be said. The unsaid inner meaning is revealed in the music and the tonality of the poem, and the poet is conscious of it in his knowledge that a certain tone of voice, a certain rhythm, are necessary. STEPHEN SPENDER [4]

And what are we to say about the text which we never think of paraphrasing, and nobody asks us to paraphrase? It is in the same position as the text which we have paraphrased already, and

---

[3] *Poetry Direct and Oblique* (1945), pp. 15, 76. Copyright 1934, 1945, and 1948 by Chatto and Windus, Ltd., and 1948 by the Macmillan Co. Reprinted by permission of the publishers.

[4] "The Making of a Poem," *Partisan Review*, 13 (Summer 1946), 298-99. This essay is reprinted in *Critiques and Essays in Criticism*, edited by R. W. Stallman. Copyright 1949 by Ronald Press.

therefore think we have disposed of. The text which does not invite paraphrase is one whose logic we obtain intuitively and at once; it is logically transparent. And what do we find to say about it? I will suggest an easy paradox, whose two terms do not exclude each other but fit together with perfect nicety: Analysis of the difficult text is easy, and analysis of the easy text is difficult. Mr. T. S. Eliot remarked sagely that the argument of a poem is sometimes like the biscuit which the burglar takes along for the dog. Mr. Eliot does not approve of psychological speculation about poetry, and that is a strategic position which is respectable though in the present juncture of affairs I do not share it. But it is significant that he should liken the poet to a burglar, placating the public censor with a logical argument as the burglar placates the dog with the biscuit, and then, we must suppose, going on with business which is also like the burglar's; business done better in the dark, and not for the public eye. On the occasion we are considering now, however, the faithful watchdog is confident that the burglar carries no equipment besides the biscuit, and the public censor basks in the belief that the poet does not intend anything but his argument. JOHN CROWE RANSOM [5]

Most human utterances can be regarded from four points of view, viz: *Sense, Feeling, Tone,* and *Intention.* (1) *Sense.* We use words to direct our hearers' attention upon some state of affairs, to present to them some items for consideration and to excite some thoughts about these items.

(2) *Feeling.* But we also, as a rule, have some feelings about these items, about the state of affairs we are referring to. We have some special bias of interest towards it, some personal coloring of feeling, and we use language to express these feelings, this nuance of interest.

(3) *Tone.* The speaker has ordinarily an attitude to his listener. He chooses or arranges his words differently as his audiences vary, in automatic or deliberate consequence of his relation to them.

[5] "Poetry, the Formal Analysis," *Kenyon Review,* 9 (Summer 1947), 443.

The tone of his utterance reflects this relation, his sense of how he stands towards those he is addressing.

(4) *Intention.* Apart from what he says (Sense), his attitude to what he is talking about (Feeling), and his attitude to his listener (Tone) there is the speaker's intention, his aim, conscious or unconscious, the effect he is endeavoring to promote. Ordinarily he speaks for a purpose; this modifies his speech. The understanding of it is part of the whole business of apprehending his meaning. Unless we know what he is trying to do, we can hardly estimate the measure of his success. He may purpose no more than to state his thoughts, or to express his feelings about what he is thinking of, *e.g.*, Hurrah! Damn!, or to express his attitude to his listener as in the case of endearments and abuse.

Frequently intention operates through a combination of other functions, but it has effects that are peculiarly its own. . . . It controls the "plot" in the largest sense of the word, and is at work whenever the author is "hiding his hand." I. A. RICHARDS [6]

All the critical parings scattered about by the new thought yield in point of practical importance to Richards' "four kinds of meanings," which have through various text books become quite common property, and which pretty well include many of the other subjects of the new investigations. . . . In the second and third, and to some extent in the fourth of these meanings, Richards is dealing directly with the infra-intellectual components of words. The four meanings or functions, as their discoverer sometimes designates them, are important because they include the total meaning of discourse (sensory or concrete and intellectual meanings taken together), grouping the concrete handily around two referents and giving a special place to the speaker's intention or ultimate purpose. Having placed under "sense" the function of words in communicating abstract meaning, Richards

[6] *Practical Criticism*, pp. 181-83. Copyright 1929 by Harcourt, Brace and Co., and by George Routledge and Sons, Ltd. Reprinted by permission of the publishers. This essay appears in revised form in *Dictionary of World Literature*, edited by Joseph Shipley. Copyright 1943 by the Philosophical Library.

considers in Functions 2 and 3 the direct or non-abstractive communications of language, grouping under "feeling" the "whole conative-affective aspect of life — emotions, emotional attitudes, the will, desire, pleasure — unpleasure and the rest" as these things are conveyed when they are not the subject of the abstract meaning of the discourse. Similarly, under "tone" he considers the speaker's or writer's "sense of how he stands towards those he is addressing." In either tone or feeling, abstract meaning may play an indirect part as a component in the whole context which effects the communication, but in considering tone or feeling we hold in our direct view the discourse as a whole — as affording not only words from which conventially established abstractions may be made, but a complex texture or "total meaning" from which, together with these conventional abstractions, other abstractions as well as various sense knowledges may be had.

Taken in themselves, feeling and tone, under one name or another, form a part of the field of almost any criticism. Richards' functions are new only in presenting themselves not as satellites of a system of abstractions projected from the mind, but as integral parts of a system of communication of which one aspect is abstract knowledge. Because he recognizes abstract meaning itself as imbedded in the matter of discourse and especially of nonscientific discourse, he provides for the understanding of poetic organization which makes the new criticism. W. J. Ong [7]

Poetry moves on many levels simultaneously. Dante in his *Convivio* holds that writings may be understood in four senses — the *literal*, the *allegorical*, the *moral*, and the *anagogic*, which might be called the spiritual or mystical sense. As an illustration of the "anagogic, that is, above or beyond sense," he cites "that hymn of the prophet [114th Psalm] which says that when the people of Israel went out of Egypt, Judaea became holy and free. Now, although this is obviously true according to the letter, the spiritual

[7] "The Meaning of the 'New Criticism'," pp. 359–60 in *Twentieth Century English*, edited by W. S. Knickerbocker. Copyright 1946 by the Philosophical Library. Reprinted by permission of the publisher.

meaning is nevertheless true also: that when the soul makes its exodus from sin it becomes holy and free in its own nature." DONALD A. STAUFFER [8]

What the Poem Means

It is never what a poem *says* which matters, but what it *is*. I. A. RICHARDS [9]

On the other hand, while it is thus useful to remember that poetry is an art of "saying" we must beware of a misunderstanding. What the poet "says" must not be identified with the apparent (i.e. the grammatical) propositions in his poem. This is the error which Dr. I. A. Richards has so long and usefully combated — the error under which the late Professor Babbitt, though wise, wrote much of his *Rousseau and Romanticism*. The poet is not "saying" that his soul is an enchanted boat. Poetry is an exploitation of language to convey the concrete; one of the means by which it does this is a free use of propositions which have logically only the remotest connexion with its real utterance. What it "says" is the total, concrete experience it gives to the right reader — the πεπαιδευμένος. The means are art; the thing conveyed, said, or uttered is not. It is everybody's business. C. S. LEWIS [10]

As for the meaning of the Cantos, that never worries me, and I do not believe that I care. I know that Pound has a scheme and a

---

[8] *The Nature of Poetry*, pp. 155–56. Copyright 1946 by W. W. Norton and Co., Inc. Reprinted by permission of the publisher.

EDITOR'S NOTE. As Mr. Stauffer points out, "All four of Dante's divisions would fall under the first of Mr. Richards' categories, its *sense*."

[9] *Science and Poetry*, pp. 34–35. Copyright 1926 by W. W. Norton and Co., Inc., and by the Orthological Institute. Reprinted by permission of the publishers.

[10] *The Personal Heresy*, pp. 113–14. Copyright 1939 by Oxford University Press. Reprinted by permission of the publisher.

kind of philosophy behind it; it is quite enough for me that he thinks he knows what he is doing; I am glad that the philosophy is there, but I am not interested in it.

This brings us to the second problem about Pound. I confess that I am seldom interested in what he is saying, but only in the way he says it. That does not mean that he is saying nothing; for ways of saying nothing are not interesting. Swinburne's form is uninteresting, because he is literally saying next to nothing, and unless you mean something with your words they will do nothing for you. T. S. ELIOT [11]

D. H. Lawrence . . . wrote in a letter:

The essence of poetry in this age of stark and unlovely actualities is a stark directness, without a shadow of a lie, or a shadow of a deflection anywhere. Everything can go, but this stark, bare, rocky directness of statement, this alone makes poetry today.

Eliot commented on this passage: *

This speaks to me of that at which I have long aimed, in writing poetry; to write poetry which should be essentially poetry, with nothing poetic about it, poetry standing naked in its bare bones, or poetry so transparent that we should not see the poetry, but that which we are meant to see through the poetry, poetry so transparent that in reading it we are intent on what the poem *points at,* and not on the poetry, this seems to me the thing to try for. To get *beyond poetry* as Beethoven in his later works, strove to get *beyond music.*

ELIZABETH DREW [12]

* In an unpublished lecture, quoted in *The Achievement of T. S. Eliot* by F. O. Matthiessen.

The Language of Poetry

Language in a healthy state presents the object, is so close to the object that the two are identified.

[11] "Isolated Superiority," *Dial*, 84 (January 1928), 6.
[12] In collaboration with John L. Sweeney, *Directions in Modern Poetry*, p. 186. Copyright 1940 by W. W. Norton and Co., Inc. Reprinted by permission of the publisher.

They are identified in the verse of Swinburne solely because the object has ceased to exist, because the meaning is merely the hallucination of meaning, because language, uprooted, has adapted itself to an independent life of atmospheric nourishment. In Swinburne, for example, we see the word "weary" flourishing in this way independent of the particular and actual weariness of flesh or spirit. The bad poet dwells partly in a world of objects and partly in a world of words, and he never can get them to fit. Only a man of genius could dwell so exclusively and consistently among words as Swinburne. His language is not, like the language of bad poetry, dead. It is very much alive, with this singular life of its own. But the language which is more important to us is that which is struggling to digest and express new objects, new groups of objects, new feelings, new aspects, as, for instance, the prose of Mr. James Joyce or the earlier Conrad. T. S. ELIOT [13]

The difficulties that most of us have felt at one time or another with Racine can probably be reduced to vocabulary and diction. Words like *feux, flamme, courroux, haine,* and *âme* recur with such frequency that they sometimes strike one as a poetic jargon which is not unlike the jargon of the weaker eighteenth-century poets in England. These words have of course been debased by later French poets and their impact has to some extent lost the freshness that it had for a seventeenth-century audience. It must be remembered, however, that society was such that these words did, as in Racine's poetry they still do, signify completely realized and often incomparably presented emotional states. This correspondence between words and things they signify (Eliot's "intellect at the tip of the senses") is always the sign of a very high degree of civilization; and it is a remarkable fact that as soon as civilization begins to decline language tends to lose its power of translating sensation into precise terms. The formal diction, which has seemed to some readers frigid and mechanical, is perfectly adequate to Racine's experience and is in fact the vehicle of feel-

[13] *Selected Essays 1917–1932*, p. 285. Copyright 1932 by Harcourt, Brace and Co., and by Faber and Faber, Ltd. Reprinted by permission of the publishers.

ings whose incredible ferocity appalled Racine's own age as it fascinates ours. MARTIN TURNELL [14]

The conventional vocabulary has sometimes appeared to English readers to be colourless and inexpressive; but Racine's style is not only perfectly adequate to his experience, it is an instrument of extraordinary delicacy in revealing emotional states. His method is entirely different from that of English poets. English poetry is remarkable for the richness and variety of its imagery and for its accumulation of sense-perceptions. In Racine's poetry there are comparatively few images and no accumulation; there is often simply bare *statement*. He owes nearly everything to the *precision* with which his language renders the obscurest sensations and to his exquisite sensibility. The simple, conventional words seem somehow to penetrate into the furthest layers of the mind, to catch and fix emotion at the moment of its formation. MARTIN TURNELL [15]

The meaning of a poem is the meaning of its words, but that meaning does not lie in the words or on the paper in any neatly determinable sense; rather it lies outside the words, in their whole history and the contexts in which they have been used. . . .

Professor Olson has touched on another facet of the same question in his analysis of Yeats's *Sailing to Byzantium*. He tells us that the words of a poem do not have "their dictionary meaning"; rather, "they take their significance from their context, through juxtaposition to other terms with which they are equated, contrasted, correlated, or combined." The "words of a poem have meanings which the poet may arbitrarily determine." But is not this to make the words lift themselves by their bootstraps — or subsist by taking in one another's washing? How can the words as context give one another meaning unless they have some meaning, dictionary

---

[14] "Racine," *Scrutiny*, 6 (March 1938), 453–54.

[15] *The Classical Moment*, pp. 202–3. Copyright 1947 by Hamish Hamilton, Ltd., and 1948 by New Directions Books. Reprinted by permission of the publishers.

meaning, to start with? The situation would seem to be more like this: in interpreting a poem, one has to take into account the meaning of the words, the whole meaning; if some of the meaning is highly complex or multiple, then the total design of the poem may help one to eliminate or neglect what would be irrelevant — unless the irrelevant is too strong or conspicuous in its dictionary right, in which case it will be a blemish. There is nothing "arbitrary" in the meaning which the skilful poet manages to convey in the total of words which is the poem. He deals with material which continually clamors in its own right to mean what he does not want it to mean; when he succeeds it is because by selection and combination he crowds out the dissonance, the static. Professor Olson has come to the verge of a very serious fallacy, that of making the intention of the author equal to the intent or total design of the poem itself. . . .

Professor Olson carries his argument into its most dangerous extreme when he says that "the co-ordination of elements in a poem cannot involve reference to anything outside the poem." Here again is the poem sustaining itself, the words in a vacuum, instead of rooted in life. The "Essays in Practical Criticism" are here at last on truly controversial ground — in that no critic, from Plato to Allen Tate, seems able to persuade the others what the relation of poetry to the rest of life is. W. K. WIMSATT, JR.[16]

The "Sound" and the "Sense"

In nearly all poetry the sound and feel of the words, what is often called the *form* of the poem in opposition to its *content*, get to work first, and the sense in which the words are taken is subtly influenced by this fact. Most words are ambiguous as regards their plain sense, especially in poetry. We can take them as we please in a variety of senses. The sense we are pleased to choose is the one

[16] "Comment on 'Two Essays in Practical Criticism'," *University Review*, 9 (Winter 1942), 141, 142. "Essays in Practical Criticism" appeared in *University Review*, 8 (Spring 1942), 198–219. Professor Olson's essay is reprinted as an appendix to "An Outline of Poetic Theory," pp. 284–88 in *Critiques and Essays in Criticism*, edited by R. W. Stallman. Copyright 1949 by Ronald Press.

which most suits the impulses already stirred through the form of the verse. I. A. RICHARDS [17]

Now, in Swinburne the meaning and the sound are one thing. He is concerned with the meaning of the word in a peculiar way: he employs, or rather "works," the word's meaning. And this is connected with an interesting fact about his vocabulary: he uses the most general word, because his emotion is never particular, never in direct line of vision, never focused; it is emotion reinforced, not by intensification, but by expansion. . . . Swinburne defines the place by the most general word, which has for him its own value. "Gold," "ruin," "dolorous": it is not merely the sound that he wants, but the vague associations of idea that the words give him. He has not his eye on a particular place. . . . It is, in fact, the word that gives him the thrill, not the object. When you take to pieces any verse of Swinburne, you find always that the object was not there — only the word. T. S. ELIOT [18]

The meaning of poetry — I do not say its source — has never been distinguishable from its sound. Most of the traditional devices of the poet have been connected with pointing up the sound, and almost all the difficulties of reading poetry can be associated with the difficulty of finding out how the lines sound. Words build into their poetic meaning by building into sound. Flaccidity of meaning almost always goes with flaccidity of sound. By sound I mean, of course, sound in composition: music. Music is most likely not the most important or the primary element of great poetry — which is what we are after — but it is the crowning grace without which we could not know that it was great. R. P. BLACK-MUR [19]

[17] *Science and Poetry*, p. 32. Copyright 1926 by W. W. Norton and Co., Inc., and by the Orthological Institute. Reprinted by permission of the publishers.

[18] *Selected Essays 1917–1932*, pp. 283–84. Copyright 1932 by Harcourt, Brace and Co., and by Faber and Faber, Ltd. Reprinted by permission of the publishers.

[19] "Twelve Poets," *Southern Review*, 7 (Summer 1941), 209.

In nearly every chapter Miss Atkins [Elizabeth Atkins, *Edna St. Vincent Millay and Her Times*] would show us that the Millay sound-patterns are peculiarly descriptive of their logical contents. There is a fallacy here which is common, and must be of rather hoary lineage. We may say that Miss Millay's arrangement of vowels and consonants, runs and rests, suits the particular sense she would convey, if we mean simply that it is not unsuitable. Very little more can be said for any poet. If Miss Atkins seems to me to make absurd claims for Miss Millay's ability to suggest the thing by the sounds, and apart from the logical associations of the words, my criticism is of Miss Atkins, not of Miss Millay, who does everything that is possible, but hardly that. Miss Millay is said at one place to have

the fluent pentameter line that had seemed to belong to Shakespeare alone, a line in which the syllables are like leaves springing from a twig, so subtly are their vowels and consonants varied and repeated. Such a line as the dying Hamlet's

Absent thee from felicity awhile,

with its panting *f's*, its languid *l's*, and its darker vowels around the three short *i's* together in one climactic word, so that "felicity" seems lifted into a glimmer of sunlight in a gloom, such a line seems to have as much living oneness as a green branch has.

But it is far from clear whether, and how, she is the sole inheritor of Shakespeare's pentameter line; and it hardly defines that line to liken it to a green branch. The variation of the vowels and consonants may be very intricate, but so is that in a weather report, and it is a question if it is subtle, or deliberate, for it would probably obtain anyway. The quoted line from Shakespeare is a famous one, but why? We use *f's* too freely (as *philosophy, fluffy, ruffles, fortify, falsify*) to identify them with panting, and *l's* too freely (as in *syllable, golly, laughable, Lilliput*) to identify them with languidness. *Felicity* is climactic, but the climax has little to do with the short *i's*, for *lubricity* or *acidity* would not work at all. It is easy to imagine an occasion on which the line might stand intact and yet have no poetic effect, least of all the effect of sunlight in gloom. For example, if a graduate English student were urging a friend to stay and discuss meters with him awhile, and not rush off to the beer party. Then

> Absent thee from felicity awhile

becomes a euphuism, a piece of university diction, faintly facetious. And so it may have been for Shakespeare's Hamlet, who was an incorrigible alumnus of Wittenberg, as some of Shakespeare's colleagues were of Oxford and Cambridge, and who in his dying speech said to his best friend,

> If thou didst ever hold me in thy heart,
> Absent thee from felicity awhile.
> And in this harsh world draw thy breath in pain,
> To tell my story.

The line in question is the odd thing about the speech, but this is due to logical and not phonetic causes; *felicity* is its oddest word, because the least emphatic, but *absent thee* is nearly as odd, because nearly as weak. Lines 1, 3, and 4 are in strong monosyllabic Saxon diction, but line 2, our line, is Latinistic, foppish, and amazing. That may be why it is memorable, and in that case it has accidentally, and not in its own right, become the eternal expression of a thought which might be paraphrased

> Seek not thy Heav'n's bliss quickly, stay awhile.

Poor as this version is, it suits an earnest sentiment better than the other; it would serve Moody and Sankey better, if they needed a line. The phonetic quality is trifling in any case. JOHN CROWE RANSOM [20]

A poet does not compose *in order to* make of language delightful and exciting music; he composes a delightful and exciting music in language *in order to* make what he has to say peculiarly efficacious in our minds. The audible half of his art is the portion which is most easily explained, and of which an intelligent appreciation can be most easily acquired. But we can never be sure, from the

[20] *The World's Body*, pp. 92–94. Copyright 1938 by Charles Scribner's Sons. Reprinted by permission of the publisher.

music alone, that we are in the real presence of poetry. What does convince us of that is something in the *meaning* of the words. LASCELLES ABERCROMBIE [21]

How the Meaning Is Said
(Poetic Techniques)

Whether or not there is anything resembling dramatic technique, there is always a situation. A poem makes statements, but not at random: there is exclusion, concentration, with a resulting intensity of apprehension. A situation, a context, grows, is established. Here is a world quite to itself, isolated, with its own regulating principles and laws. Feelings and perceptions are made articulate by being given a pattern within which to develop and organize. As readers we are not required to project ourselves into the poet's mind in an effort to explain in psychological terms what is taking place there as he creates this situation. For us the situation *is* the poem. It is there in the form and language of the poem, and our full response to this form and language is acknowledgment that we too have found our way into the unique situation. RICARDO QUINTANA [22]

In a note to *Art and Scholasticism* (116b, pp. 191–3 of the English translation), M. Jacques Maritain quotes a contemporary French poet, Paul Reverdy:

The image [writes Reverdy] is a pure creation of the mind. It cannot emerge from a comparison but only from the bringing together of two more or less distant realities. . . . An image is not striking because it is *brutal* or *fantastic* — but because the association of ideas is remote and exact. . . . No image is produced by comparing (always inadequately) two disproportionate realities.

[21] *Poetry: Its Music and Meaning*, p. 43. Copyright 1932 by Oxford University Press. Reprinted by permission of the publisher.
[22] *Two Hundred Poems*, p. xxv. Copyright 1947 by Longmans, Green and Co. Reprinted by permission of the publisher.

A striking image, on the contrary, one new to the mind, is produced by bringing into relation without comparison two distant realities whose relations *the mind alone* has seized.

That is the whole secret of the so-called obscurity of modern poetry, and M. Maritain's comment on Reverdy's distinction is charged with sympathetic light and understanding:

The besetting sin of such a writer as Hugo is staking all upon the material dynamism of the word-*thing*. I think on the contrary that it is the province of the poet, who uses words as the material of his work, to react against this tendency of the symbol to transform itself into a thing, and so to maintain or recover by force, in the sensitive flesh of the word, the spirituality of language. Hence an invention, a creation of fresh images, which may appear obscure but is nevertheless imposed by absolute precision. Modern poetry, with a courage which is sometimes ridiculous, has undertaken to scour language. In spite of contradictory appearances and stray phenomena, like Dadaism some years ago and "free" words, it is making rather towards objectivity, trying to find a form of expression which will not convey a lie, but in which the mind will force the word with its whole weight of matter to be faithfully significant in the cloistered world of the poem.

HERBERT READ [23]

It is no accident that the method of art involves symbolism. For the artist must work with single instances; he can tell only one story at a time, paint only one picture or sing one song. The story, the picture or the song, would mean nothing artistically unless it dragged in its wake a wide penumbra of meaning. Behind every concrete object of art is reflected the shadows of countless absent particulars which it affectively symbolizes. The hold upon us of a character in fiction, for instance, is its ability to remind us of all those actual people who are therein described. It is not the particularity of such a figure but rather its valuational generality which carries the appeal. We have never met Polonius nor shall

[23] "The Form of Modern Poetry," *Symposium*, I (July 1930), 308–9.

The English translation, by J. F. Scanlan, of Maritain's *Art and Scholasticism*, is copyright 1935 and 1943 by Charles Scribner's Sons, and by Geoffrey Bles, Ltd. The excerpts are reprinted by permission of the publishers.

we ever meet him: there is no such person. Yet we meet him every day and he lives for us because we have met so many dull, busy-body, meddling bores in high places. Needless to emphasize, the abstract qualities which are embodied in a fictional character do not of themselves constitute the artistic property, and indeed they are incapable by themselves of carrying it. They require embodiment, embodiment in a particular symbolism; and it is just this step which the artist is obliged to furnish. JAMES FEIBLEMAN [24]

Have we, in these four terms, a single referent? Semantically, the terms overlap; they clearly point to the same area of interest. Perhaps our sequence — image, metaphor, symbol, and myth — may be said to represent the convergence of two lines, both important for the theory of poetry. One is sensuous particularity, or the sensuous and aesthetic continuum, which connects poetry with music and painting and disconnects it from philosophy and science; the other is "figuration" or "tropology" — the "oblique" discourse which speaks in metonyms and metaphors, partially comparing worlds, precising its themes by giving them impractical translations into other idioms. These are both characteristics, *differentiae*, of literature, in contrast to scientific discourse. Instead of aiming at a system of abstractions consistently expressed by a system of monosigns, poetry organizes a unique, unrepeatable pattern of words, each an object as well as a sign and used in a fashion unpredictable by any system outside of the poem.

Like "image," "symbol" has given its name to a specific literary movement. Like "image," again, it continues to appear in widely different contexts and very different purposes. It appears as a term in logic, in mathematics, in semantics and semiotics and epistemology; it has also had a long history in the worlds of theology ("symbol" is one synonym for "creed"), of liturgy, of the fine arts, and of poetry. The shared element in all these current uses is probably that of something standing for, representing, something

---

[24] *Aesthetics*, p. 405. Copyright 1949 by Duell, Sloan and Pearce, Inc. Reprinted by permission of the publisher.

else. But the Greek verb, which means to throw together, to compare, suggests that the idea of analogy between sign and signified was originally present. It still survives in some of the modern uses of the term. Algebraic and logical "symbols" are conventional, agreed-upon signs; but religious symbols are based on some intrinsic relation between "sign" and thing "signified," metonymic or metaphoric: the Cross, the Lamb, the Good Shepherd. In literary theory, it seems desirable that the word should be used in this sense: as an object which refers to another object but which demands attention also in its own right, as a presentation.

There is a kind of mind which speaks of "mere symbolism," either reducing religion and poetry to sensuous images ritualistically arranged or evacuating the presented "signs" or "images" in behalf of the transcendental realities, moral or philosophical, which lie beyond them. Another kind of mind thinks of a symbolism as something calculated and willed, a deliberate mental translation of concepts into illustrative, pedagogic, sensuous terms. But, says Coleridge, while allegory is merely "a translation of abstract notions into a picture language, which is itself nothing but an abstraction from objects of the senses . . ." a symbol "is characterized by a translucence of the special [the species] in the individual, or of the general [genus] in the special. . . . above all, by the translucence of the eternal through and in the temporal." *

Is there any important sense in which "symbol" differs from "image" and "metaphor"? Primarily, we think, in the recurrence and persistence of the "symbol." An "image" may be invoked once as a metaphor, but if it persistently recurs, both as presentation and representation, it becomes a symbol, may even become part of a symbolic (or mythic) system. Of Blake's early lyrics, the *Songs of Innocence* and *Of Experience*, J. H. Wicksteed writes: "There is comparatively little *actual symbolism*, but there is constant and abundant use of *symbolic metaphor*." Yeats has an early essay on the "Ruling Symbols" in Shelley's poetry. "One finds in his poetry, besides innumerable images that have not the definiteness [fixity?] of symbols, many images that are certainly symbols, and as the years went by he began to use these with more and more deliberately symbolic purpose – such images as caves and towers. †

What happens with impressive frequency is the turning of what, in a writer's early work, is "property" into the "symbol" of his later work. Thus in his early novels, Henry James painstakingly visualizes persons and places, while, in the later novels, all the images have become metaphoric or symbolic. AUSTIN WARREN AND RENÉ WELLEK [25]

* S. T. Coleridge, *The Statesmen's Manual: Complete Works* (ed. Shedd, New York, 1853), Vol. I, pp. 437–8. This distinction between symbol and allegory was first clearly drawn by Goethe.

† J. H. Wicksteed, *Blake's Innocence and Experience* . . . , London, 1928, p. 23; W. B. Yeats, *Essays*, London, 1924, p. 95ff., on Shelley's "Ruling Symbols."

Of the two kinds of sensibility that we can identify in examining works of poetry the first would seem to be incapable of receiving impressions except through the prism of an already acquired set of language symbols. It is as if poets with this type of sensibility are uncontrollably *determined* in the kind of response they can make to reality. And because they are so determined in their initial response they are determined also in their manner of expression. The original language-symbols, acquired through culture, training, or unconscious immersion in some tradition, are infinitely perpetuated in their writing. At its worst such writing is anemic and invertebrate, like the minor verse of any period or like the earlier work of many excellent poets. In such verse the language gives the effect of having occasioned the feeling more often than the feeling the language. At its most sophisticated, however, this verse is capable of achieving a certain superficial quality of distinction all its own. It is a quality of distinction undoubtedly made possible by the reduced effort to discover precise images to convey very definite and particular sensations or emotions. It may consist in the pure musicalization

[25] *Theory of Literature*, pp. 190, 193–94. Copyright 1949 by Harcourt, Brace and Co. Reprinted by permission of the publisher.

of language through the draining of all specific content from the imagery that we find in Mallarmé or (on a lower plane) in Swinburne. Or it may consist in that plastic manipulation of surfaces which is another department of the interesting verse of any period. The effect in either case is the same, that of a resuscitation rather than a re-creation of language.

The other type of sensibility, of course, is in the habit of receiving direct impressions, of forming images which possess the freshness, uniqueness, and body of the original object. It has the faculty of creating new language-symbols to convey what it has perceived or, as sometimes happens, of re-creating traditional symbols with enough force to make them serve again. (For used symbols are capable of being recharged, so to speak, under the pressure of the new emotion they are called upon to convey.) Only when the original perception is solid and clear is it able to crystallize into images capable of transmitting emotion; and only when the emotion is adequate are these images capable of creating or re-creating language. The difference is between language which is made its own object and language which is made to realize emotion by evoking particular objects of concrete experience. It is the difference between writing which secures a certain effectiveness through being recognizable in a particular tradition and writing which is an exact verbal equivalent for a precise emotion or set of emotions. WILLIAM TROY [26]

"Life is not a series of gig lamps symmetrically arranged," declares Virginia Woolf; "life is a luminous halo." Her whole effort is accordingly to render the "myriad impressions" that we daily receive, the "semi-transparent envelope" veiling all our activities. She is, in short, an impressionist; and as such she joins the large company, including Conrad, Proust, and Lawrence, who have extended into literature the method of the French painters: a projection of the artist's immediate sense impression as opposed to a

[26] "Virginia Woolf: The Novel of Sensibility," pp. 353–54 in *Literary Opinion in America*. Copyright 1937 by Harper and Brothers. Reprinted by permission of the author.

literal reproduction of surfaces or an intellectual analysis of what underlies them. The impressionists substitute the subtle evocation of atmosphere for inventory, the direct rendering of sensation for analysis; they strive to achieve a greater intimacy with the experiencing self rather than with objective reality, to impart a full *realization* instead of a mere comprehension of experience. All greatly extend the limits of realistic investigation — Lawrence so far that he approaches the mystical. Yet even when they deliberately distort appearances for the sake of essences, the aim of these writers remains fundamentally realistic. They have simply developed finer instruments than the earlier realists and penetrated farther below the surface of the familiar. They are simply striving to convey in purer form the impression life makes upon us.

More difficult of classification, however, are other more extreme developments in recent fiction. Kaleidoscopic pictures like Evelyn Scott's *The Wave* and all the later novels of John Dos Passos give only momentary trouble; these novelists are merely assembling their bits of reality in unusual combinations. Similarly when Aldous Huxley in *Point Counterpoint* and André Gide in *The Counterfeiters* toy with the principles of musical composition, and when Proust actually writes a Time Symphony, they are nevertheless presenting a realistic picture of a cross-section of their society. But beyond these experimenters is a more advanced group whom in *The Twentieth Century Novel* Professor Beach aptly describes as "expressionists." In certain chapters of *Ulysses* James Joyce definitely departs from the world of appearances and employs the principles of abstract composition illustrated in the paintings of Picasso: the creation of a "generalized atmosphere," the presentation in some abstract form of the underlying meaning of a scene. HERBERT J. MULLER [27]

Religious symbols, such as myths, legends, and the acts and stage properties of ritual, are like aesthetic symbols in that they do not merely indicate objects and instigate operations, as do the

[27] *Modern Fiction*, pp. 40–41. Copyright 1937 by Funk and Wagnalls Co. Reprinted by permission of the publisher.

symbols of science, but depict or enact or evoke what they signify; and at least part of what they signify consists of certain
value qualities, which convey immediacy and particularity of the
object as experienced. The two types of symbols agree further in
that they, or some of them, may organize a considerable area of
experience by their systematic ambiguity or multiple reference,
whereas the symbols of science are chosen for their univocal signi-
fication. Thus the crimson carpet in the *Agamemnon* organizes
the play by bringing into focus at least three elements: the blood-
soaked atmosphere of the play in general, and more specifically
the bloody deeds of Agamemnon and Clytemnestra; Agamemnon's hybris — Oriental despots walk into their palaces on crimson
carpets, which in Greece are spread only for the statues of gods
entering their temples; and the blood feud whose struggle with
civic justice is the main theme of the trilogy. In the Joseph story
a like role is played by such symbols as the bridal veil, the Nile,
the dying god, the strife of brothers over the blessing.

In their aesthetic functioning, such symbols are intransitive; they
organize only the little world of the poem or the novel, and
they organize it for perceptual or contemplative enjoyment. Their
meanings may be derived from the great world of practical and
cognitive experience, and are potentially extensible into it; but in
so far as we adopt the aesthetic attitude — and perhaps we can
never do so completely — such reference to the great world is excluded, suspended.

Symbols functioning aesthetically are not assertions; they do
not give us transitive knowledge. Poetry of course contains sen-
tences in the indicative mood: we are told that Macbeth killed
Duncan. But this is a pseudo-assertion, or an assertion about the
imaginary world of the play, not about the great world in space-
time.

Such considerations are behind the denial of empiricists that art
when it is functioning aesthetically gives us knowledge in the full
sense. They may grant that it gives us "knowledge" by "acquaintance" of value qualities, as *Macbeth* can show us what it feels like

to commit a murder. But value qualities are predicates, or propositional functions, and not propositions. In the aesthetic experience the subject of which they are predicated is the aesthetic object itself; the symbols function reflexively, within a microcosm. Even when we say that *Macbeth* shows us what it feels like to commit a murder, we are overstating the case. Responded to aesthetically, the play merely shows us what an imaginary character was imagined to feel like upon committing an imaginary murder. When we generalize from this we are not necessarily saying something false, but we are going beyond the evidence supplied by the aesthetic experience itself, and we must verify the statement by scrutinizing the reactions of real murderers, or at least by inference from our own experiences of transgression.

So far, all this is in accord not only with empiricist logic but with everyday observation. Any one who has fed on imaginative literature in adolescence must undergo a series of shocks in order to learn that his fund of vicarious experience derived from literature cannot be carried over directly to life without much painstaking and painful "verification."

Presentational symbols when functioning aesthetically, then, do not give us warranted knowledge; but such symbols when functioning in other ways may contribute to both knowledge and practice. Rather than to establish moral and cosmological truth forthwith, the transitive use of aesthetic experience is to help us discriminate immediate qualities, to stamp in attitudes, and to supply us with "hypotheses" which subsequent experience can confirm or disconfirm. When we exploit aesthetic symbols for these purposes, we may be doing something legitimate, but we are no longer using them aesthetically. PHILIP BLAIR RICE [28]

[28] "Thomas Mann and the Religious Revival," *Kenyon Review*, 7 (Summer 1945), 374–76.

Poetic Meaning and Reader's Response
(the Paraphrase)

Poetry is not the thing said but a way of saying it. Can it then be isolated and studied by itself? for the combination of language with its intellectual content, its meaning, is as close a union as can well be imagined. Is there such a thing as pure unmingled poetry, poetry independent of meaning?

Even when poetry has a meaning, as it usually has, it may be inadvisable to draw it out. "Poetry gives most pleasure" said Coleridge "when only generally and not perfectly understood"; and perfect understanding will sometimes almost extinguish pleasure. The Haunted Palace is one of Poe's best poems so long as we are content to swim in the sensations it evokes and only vaguely to apprehend the allegory. We are roused to discomfort, at least I am, when we begin to perceive how exact in detail the allegory is; when it dawns upon us that the fair palace door is Roderick Usher's mouth, the pearl and ruby his teeth and lips, the yellow banners his hair, the ramparts plumed and pallid his forehead, and when we are reduced to hoping, for it is no more than a hope, that the wingèd odours have no connexion with hair-oil.

Meaning is of the intellect, poetry is not. If it were, the eighteenth century would have been able to write it better. A. E. Housman [29]

This is what Mr. Frost said: "Poetry is implication. Let implication be implication. Don't try to turn implication into explication. If I had wanted to say anything definite I would have put it into the poem."

I said: "Would you say the meaning could be expressed as —" He held up his hand. "Stop. Don't say anything. Don't put anything in words."

[29] *The Name and Nature of Poetry*, pp. 35–37. Copyright 1933 by the Macmillan Co., and by Cambridge University Press. Reprinted by permission of the publishers.

Later, in discussing poetry in general, he said: "Poetry is not communication in the sense of giving a message. The object is to strike the reader in a vital spot." CECILIA HENNEL HENDRICKS [30]

Because aesthetic analysis is so nearly impossible, so nearly meaningless, aesthetic education can only take the form of practice. One can only be taught how one ought to look, what positions to take with reference to that which is to be seen aesthetically, and where the attention should be directed in order that what is looked at should be seen.

. . .

It is remarkable how often a painter "is discovered," after hundreds of people have seen his work again and again, after they have written about it, apparently without having *seen* it, and how they all see it as soon as it has been discovered. LEO STEIN [31]

Qua work of art, the work of art cannot be interpreted; there is nothing to interpret; we can only criticise it according to standards, in comparison to other works of art; and for "interpretation" the chief task is the presentation of relevant historical facts which the reader is not assumed to know. T. S. ELIOT [32]

If *The Ancient Mariner* has a meaning, what is that meaning?

It is true that a poem may mean a number of different things. By this I do not intend to say that a poem means different things to different readers. That is, of course, true in one sense, but true, first, only in so far as the poet fails, as fail he must in some degree, in the exercise of his creative control, and second, in so far as each reader must, as a result of his own history and nature, bring to the poem a different mass of experience, strength of intellect, and intensity of feeling. In this second sense we may

[30] Writing about Frost's *Neither Out Far Nor In Deep*, in the *Explicator*, 1 (May 1943).
[31] *The A-B-C of Aesthetics*, pp. 153, 222. Copyright 1927 by Horace Liveright, Inc. Reprinted by permission of the publisher.
[32] *Selected Essays 1917–1932*, p. 122. Copyright 1932 by Harcourt, Brace and Co., and by Faber and Faber, Ltd. Reprinted by permission of the publishers.

say that the reader does not interpret the poem but the poem interprets the reader. We may say that the poem is the light and not the thing seen by the light. The poem is the light by which the reader may view and review all the area of experience with which he is acquainted. ROBERT PENN WARREN [33]

. . . in fact there is hardly a poem of his [Hart Crane's] which has not something in it, and a very definite something, worth saving.

The nature of that saving quality, for it saves him no less than ourselves, Crane has himself most clearly expressed in a stanza from the poem called "Wine Menagerie."

> New thresholds, new anatomies! Wine talons
> Build freedom up about me and distill
> This competence — to travel in a tear
> Sparkling alone, within another's will.

I hope to show that this stanza illustrates almost inexhaustibly, to minds at all aware, both the substance and the aspiration of Crane's poetry, the character and value of his perceptions, and his method of handling words to control them. If we accept the stanza as a sort of declaration of policy and apply it as our own provisional policy to the sum of his work, although we limit its scope we shall deepen and articulate our appreciation, — a process, that of appreciation, which amounts not to wringing a few figs from thistles but to expressing the wine itself.

Paraphrase does not greatly help. We can, for the meat of it, no more be concerned with the prose sense of the words than Crane evidently was. Crane habitually re-created his words from within, developing meaning to the point of idiom; and that habit is the constant and indubitable sign of talent. The meanings themselves are the idioms and have a twist and life of their own. It is only by ourselves meditating on and *using* these idioms, — it is only by emulation, — that we can master them and accede to their life.

[33] Essay, pp. 69–70 in *The Rime of the Ancient Mariner.* Copyright 1946 by Reynal and Hitchcock. Reprinted by permission of Harcourt, Brace and Co.

Analysis, however, does help, and in two directions. It will by itself increase our intimacy with the words as they appear; and it will as the nexus among comparisons disclose that standard of achievement, inherent in this special use of poetic language, by which alone the value of the work may be judged. (Analysis, in these uses, does not cut deep, it does not cut at all: it merely distinguishes particulars; and the particulars must be re-seen in their proper focus before the labour benefits.)

Moving in the first direction, towards intimacy, we can say that Crane employed an extreme mode of free association; that operation among words where it is the product rather than the addition that counts. There was, for example, no logical or emotional connection between thresholds and anatomies until Crane verbally juxtaposed them and tied them together with the cohesive of his metre. Yet, so associated, they modify and act upon each other mutually and produce a fresh meaning of which the parts cannot be segregated. Some latent, unsuspected part of the cumulus of meaning in each word has excited, so to speak, and affected a corresponding part in the others. It is the juxtaposition which is the agent of selection, and it is a combination of metre and the carried-over influence of the rest of the poem, plus the as yet undetermined expectations aroused, which is the agent of emphasis and identification. It should be noted that, so far as the poem is concerned, the words themselves contain and do not merely indicate the feelings which compose the meaning; the poet's job was to put the words together like bricks in a wall. In lesser poetry of the same order, and in poetry of different orders, words may only indicate or refer to or substitute for the feelings; then we have the poetry of vicarious statement, which takes the place of, often to the highest purpose, the actual complete presentation, such as we have here. Here there is nothing for the words to take the place of; they are their own life, and have an organic continuity, not with the poet's mind nor with the experience they represent, but with themselves. We see that thresholds open upon anatomies: upon things to be explored and understood and felt freshly as an adventure; and we see that the anatomies, what is to be explored, are known from a new vantage, and that the vantage is part of the anatomy. The separate meanings of the words fairly rush at each other; the right ones join and those irrelevant to the juncture are for the moment — the whole time of the poem — lost in limbo. Thus the association "New Thresholds, new anatomies!" which at first inspection might seem specious or arbitrary (were we not used to reading poetry) not only does not produce a distortion but, the stress and strain being equal, turns out wholly natural and independently alive.

In the next phrase the association of the word "talons" with the context seems less significantly performed. So far as it refers back and expresses a seizing together, a clutching by a bird of prey, it is an excellent word well-chosen and spliced in. The further notion, suggested by the word "wine," of release, would also seem relevant. There is, too, an unidentifiable possibility — for Crane used words in very special senses indeed — of "talons" in the sense of cards left after the deal; and there is even, to push matters to the limit, a bare chance that some element of the etymon — ankle, heel — has been pressed into service. But the possibilities have among them none specially discriminated, and whichever you choose for use, the dead weight of the others must be provisionally carried along, which is what makes the phrase slightly fuzzy. And however you construe "wine talons" you cannot, without distorting what you have and allowing for the gap or lacuna of what you have not, make your construction fit either or both of the verbs which it governs. Talons neither build nor distill even when salvation by rhyme is in question. If Crane meant —as indeed he may have — that wines are distilled and become brandies or spirits, then he showed a poverty of technique in using the transitive instead of the intransitive form. Objection can be carried too far, when it renders itself nugatory. These remarks are meant as a kind of exploration; and if we now make the allowance for the unidentified distortion and supply with good will the lacuna in the very heart of the middle phrases, the rest of the stanza becomes as plain and vivid as poetry of this order need ever be. To complete the whole association, the reader need only remember that Crane probably had in mind, and made new use of Blake's lines:

> For a Tear is an Intellectual Thing,
> And a Sigh is the Sword of an Angel King.

It is interesting to observe that Blake was talking against war and that his primary meaning was much the same as that expressed negatively in "Auguries of Innocence" by the following couplet:

> He who shall train the Horse to War
> Shall never pass the Polar Bar.

Crane ignored the primary meaning, and extracted and emphasized what was in Blake's image a latent or secondary meaning. Or possibly he combined — made a free association of — the intellectual tear with

> Every Tear from Every Eye
> Becomes a Babe in Eternity;

only substituting the more dramatic notion of will for intellect. What is important to note is that, whatever its origin, the meaning as Crane presents it is completely transformed and subjugated to the control of the "new thresholds, new anatomies!"

The stanza we have been considering is only arbitrarily separated from the whole poem — just as the poem itself ought to be read in the context of the whole "White Buildings" section. The point is, that for appreciation — and for denigration — all of Crane should be read thoroughly, at least once, with similar attention to detail. That is the way in which Crane worked. Later readings may be more liberated and more irresponsible — as some people read the Bible for what they call poetry or a case-history for its thrill; but they never get either the poetry or the thrill without a preliminary fundamental intimacy with the rational technique involved. Here is a question of achieving some notion of a special poetic process. The principle of association which controls this stanza resembles the notion of wine as escape, release, father of insight and seed of metamorphosis, which controls the poem; and, in its turn, the notion of extra-logical, intoxicated metamorphosis of the senses controls and innervates Crane's whole sensibility. R. P. BLACKMUR [34]

Poetry is the art of patterned language. No amount of prose interpretation or elucidation or appreciation or analysis of its various parts by the reader can be the same thing as the poem, though they may be an essential preliminary to the complete enjoyment of the poem. But the poem is the full and unique expression in language of the impact between a certain piece of experience and the poet's consciousness. What the reader can do, is to make the results of this impact as fully conscious to himself as possible, by opening his own faculties as widely as he can to the inflow of all that the poet has communicated by his use of words. "Attention of perusal . . . is what I at every point . . . absolutely invoke or take for granted," says Henry James, and this is what the reader can give. He can *live into* the poetry, can re-create it in himself, can feel its vibrations in his own senses, as completely as his capacities and equipment allow. And to do this he must yield himself and be borrowed by the wind that flows through the poem. ELIZABETH DREW [35]

We can very properly use paraphrases as pointers and as shorthand references provided that we know what we are doing. But it is highly important that we know what we are doing and that we see plainly that the paraphrase is not the real core of meaning which constitutes the essence of the poem. CLEANTH BROOKS [36]

[34] *The Double Agent*, pp. 130–35. Copyright 1935 by Arrow Editions. Reprinted by permission of the author.
[35] In collaboration with John L. Sweeney, *Directions in Modern Poetry*, p. 179. Copyright 1940 by W. W. Norton and Co., Inc. Reprinted by permission of the publisher.
[36] *The Well Wrought Urn*, p. 180. Copyright 1947 by Reynal and Hitchcock, and 1949 by Dennis Dobson, Ltd. Reprinted by permission of the publishers.

The truth of the matter is that all such formulations lead away from the center of the poem — not toward it; that the "prose-sense" of the poem is not a rack on which the stuff of the poem is hung; that it does not represent the "inner" structure or the "essential" structure or the "real" structure of the poem. We may use — and in many connections must use — such formulations as more or less convenient ways of referring to parts of the poem. But such formulations are scaffoldings which we may properly for certain purposes throw about the building: we must not mistake them for the internal and essential structure of the building itself.

. . .

Mr. Winters' position will furnish perhaps the most respectable example of the paraphrastic heresy. He assigns primacy to the "rational meaning" of the poem. "The relationship, in the poem, between rational statement and feeling," he remarks in his latest book, "is thus seen to be that of motive to emotion." He goes on to illustrate his point by a brief and excellent analysis of the following lines from Browning:

> So wore night; the East was gray,
> White the broad-faced hemlock flowers. . . .

"The verb *wore*," he continues, "means literally that the night passed, but it carries with it connotations of exhaustion and attrition which belong to the condition of the protagonist; and grayness is a color which we associate with such a condition. If we change the phrase to read: 'Thus night passed,' we shall have the same rational meaning, and a meter quite as respectable, but no trace of the power of the line: the connotation of *wore* will be lost, and the connotation of *gray* will remain in a state of ineffective potentiality."

But the word *wore* does not mean *literally* "that the night passed," it means literally "that the night *wore*" — whatever *wore* may mean, and as Winters' own admirable analysis indicates, *wore* "means," whether *rationally* or *irrationally*, a great deal. Furthermore, "So wore night" and "Thus night passed" can be said to have "the same rational meaning" only if we equate "rational meaning" with the meaning of a loose paraphrase. And can a loose paraphrase be said to be the "motive to emotion"? Can it be said to "generate" the feelings in question? (Or, would Mr. Winters not have us equate "rational statement" and "rational meaning"?)

Much more is at stake here than any quibble. In view of the store which Winters sets by rationality and of his penchant for poems which make their evaluations overtly, and in view of his frequent blindness to those poems which do not — in view of these considerations, it is important to see that what "So wore night" and "Thus night passed" have in common as their "rational meaning" is not the "rational meaning" of each but the lowest common denominator of both. To refer the structure of the poem to what is finally a paraphrase of the poem is to refer it to something outside the poem. CLEANTH BROOKS [37]

In authentic poetry the total statement is identical with the poem itself. As it can find expression only through the component statements that constitute the poem, it cannot be summarized without essential loss. The "scenario content" of the poem can be summarized, as in Lamb's *Tales* and in many a college syllabus, but the poetic statement is destroyed in translation. . . . My answer is that while no poetic statement can ever be translated or summarized into literal language adequately, there are cases in which a literal restatement can approximate the poetic original more nearly than in other cases, and that light can be thrown upon the nature of the poetic statement by comparing such approximations. PHILIP WHEELWRIGHT [38]

The trouble is that the word *missed* here falsifies the relationship between the reader and the poem. It implies a matter of yes-

[37] *The Well Wrought Urn*, pp. 182, 183–84. Copyright 1947 by Reynal and Hitchcock, and 1949 by Dennis Dobson, Ltd. Reprinted by permission of the publishers.
[38] "On the Semantics of Poetry," *Kenyon Review*, 2 (Summer 1940), 279.

and-no. Actually, the relationship is not one of yes-and-no, but of degree, of gradual exploration of deeper and deeper levels of application within the symbol. And this process of exploration of deeper and deeper levels of the poem may be immediate and intuitive. The reader may be profoundly affected — his sense of the world may be greatly altered — even though he has not tried to frame in words the nature of the change wrought upon him, or having tried to do so, has failed (as all critics must fail in some degree, for the simple reason that the analysis cannot render the poem, the discursive activity cannot render the symbolical). As for *The Ancient Mariner* itself, the great central fact of the poem, the fact which no reader could miss — the broken tabu, the torments of guilt and punishment, the joy of reconciliation — is enough to account for the first impact of the poem upon a reader. But beyond that, the vividness of the presentation and the symbolic coherence may do their work — as blessing sprang to the Mariner's lips — "unawares." For the good poem may work something of its spell even upon readers who are critically inarticulate.

If this is true — if ideally appreciation is immediate and intuitive — why should critical analysis ever be interposed between the reader and the poem? The answer is simple: in order that the intuition may be fuller, that detail may be more richly and the central symbols more deeply realized. But in this case what becomes of immediacy of appreciation? Nothing becomes of it, if "immediacy" is read properly — if it is read as signifying "without mediation" of critical analysis and not as signifying "upon the first instant of contact." Let me put it this way: A poem works immediately upon us when we are ready for it. And it may require the mediation of a great deal of critical activity by ourselves and by others before we are ready. And for the greater works we are never fully ready. That is why criticism is a never-ending process. ROBERT PENN WARREN [39]

[39] Essay, pp. 116–17 in *The Rime of the Ancient Mariner*. Copyright 1946 by Reynal and Hitchcock. Reprinted by permission of Harcourt, Brace and Co.

It is the reading of the poem that is the poem. Without the reading, this succession of curiously assembled words is an inexplicable fabrication. PAUL VALÉRY. [40]

[40] "A Course in Poetics: First Lesson," *Southern Review*, 5 (Winter 1940), 409.

V

The
Concept of the
"Objective
Correlative"

So, too, is the external world to the mind; which needs, also, as the condition of its manifestation, its objective correlative. Hence the pressure of some outward object, predetermined to correspond to the preexisting idea in its living power, is essential to the evolution of its proper end, — the pleasurable emotion.

WASHINGTON ALLSTON, *Lectures on Art*, edited by R. H. Dana, p. 16. Copyright 1850 by Baker and Scribner.

The unique, unduplicated character of experienced events and situations impregnates the emotion that is evoked. . . . In reality . . . poet and novelist have an immense advantage over even an expert psychologist in dealing with an emotion. For the former build up a concrete situation and permit it to evoke emotional response. Instead of a description of an emotion in intellectual and symbolic terms, the artist "does the deed that breeds" the emotion.

JOHN DEWEY, *Art as Experience*, p. 67. Copyright 1934 by Minton, Balch. Reprinted by permission of G. P. Putnam's Sons.

Parallelisms and Echoes of the Concept

The poet's art is to a great extent the art of intensifying emotions by assembling the scattered objects that naturally arouse
them. He sees the affinities of things by seeing their common
affinities with passion. As the guiding principle of practical thinking is some interest, so that only what is pertinent to that interest
is selected by the attention; as the guiding principle of scientific
thinking is some connection of things in time or space, or some
identity of law; so in poetic thinking the guiding principle is
often a mood or a quality of sentiment. By this union of disparate
things having a common overtone of feeling, the feeling is itself
evoked in all its strength; nay, it is often created for the first time,
much as by a new mixture of old pigments Perugino could produce the unprecedented limpidity of his colour, or Titian the
unprecedented glow of his. Poets can thus arouse sentiments finer
than any which they have known, and in the act of composition
become discoverers of new realms of delightfulness and grief.
Expression is a misleading term which suggests that something
previously known is rendered or imitated; whereas the expression

is itself an original fact, the values of which are then referred to the thing expressed. . . .

. . .

The thrilling adventures which he [the poet] craves demand an appropriate theatre; the glorious emotions with which he bubbles over must at all hazards find or feign their correlative objects. GEORGE SANTAYANA [1]

. . . it is because *there are no images of feeling.* . . . The only effective way of arousing any particular feeling that is more than mere bodily feeling is to call up the images that are naturally connected with that feeling. ARTHUR H. R. FAIRCHILD [2]

When the artist passes from pure sensations to emotions aroused by means of sensations, he uses natural forms which, in themselves, are calculated to move our emotions, and he presents these in such a manner that the forms themselves generate in us emotional states, based upon the fundamental necessities of our physical and physiological nature. The artist's attitude to natural form is, therefore, infinitely various according to the emotions he wishes to arouse. He may require for his purpose the most complete representation of a figure, he may be intensely realistic, provided that his presentment, in spite of its closeness to natural appearance, disengages clearly for us the appropriate emotional elements. Or he may give us the merest suggestion of natural forms, and rely almost entirely upon the force and intensity of the emotional elements involved in his presentment. ROGER FRY [3]

For a tragedy, and no one will disagree with Aristotle in this, should contain only what is necessary to it, and nothing else. For if a work of art succeeds through the measure in which it arouses

[1] *Interpretations in Poetry and Religion,* pp. 263–64, 277. Copyright 1918 by Charles Scribner's Sons, and by Constable and Sons, Ltd. Reprinted by permission of the publishers.

[2] *The Making of Poetry,* pp. 24, 25. Copyright 1912 by G. P. Putnam's Sons. Reprinted by permission of the author and the publisher.

[3] *Vision and Design,* pp. 37–38. Copyright 1920 by Chatto and Windus, Ltd. Reprinted by permission of the publisher.

appetencies in us, and satisfies them, the appetency and the satisfaction must not be in excess of each other; nor must each kind of art involve more impulses than it requires for its resultant emotion. In the last analysis, the structure of a play is made up of the relation between themselves of the emotions we are made to feel. BONAMY DOBRÉE [4]

The only way of expressing emotion in the form of art is by finding an "objective correlative"; in other words, a set of objects, a situation, a chain of events which shall be the formula of that *particular* emotion; such that when the external facts, which must terminate in sensory experience, are given, the emotion is immediately evoked. . . . The artistic "inevitability" lies in this complete adequacy of the external to the emotion; and this is precisely what is deficient in *Hamlet*. Hamlet (the man) is dominated by an emotion which is inexpressible, because it is in *excess* of the facts as they appear. T. S. ELIOT [5]

Here [in A. E. Housman's *Epitaph*], a particular situation has produced a tragic emotion; whatever is lacking we can supply, so that the event behind the lines is adequate to the emotion. But this is not always so in Housman. . . . And yet, in Housman's poetry as a whole, something is lacking. Despite an apparent clarity such that almost any poem seems ready to deliver its meaning at once, there is always something that is not clear, something not brought into the open, something that is left in doubt.

. . .

Of the suffering we have no doubt, but something, it seems, has been suppressed that it is essential to know of the particular situation of the human sufferer. There is an emotion here that is unaccounted for. It is apparently united to the secret cause.

. . .

[4] *Restoration Tragedy*, p. 71. Copyright 1929 by Clarendon Press. Reprinted by permission of the publisher.
[5] "Hamlet and His Problems," pp. 124–25 in *Selected Essays 1917–1932*. Copyright 1932 by Harcourt, Brace and Co., and by Faber and Faber, Ltd. Reprinted by permission of the publishers.

Perfect understanding of his poems depends upon knowledge of his personal plight, for until that is known, the emotion must seem in excess of its object. JOHN PEALE BISHOP [6]

The Threefold Aspects of the Concept

[Three aspects of the work of art are predicated in the concept of the "objective correlative": the poem in relation to the poet (the creative process); the poem as a thing in itself (the work of art as an objectified autonomous creation); and the poem in relation to the critic or reader (poetic appreciation).]

The Poem in Relation to the Poet (the Creative Process)

At the very heart of the thinking of any scholar or artist deeply absorbed in his work, seemingly quite cut off from the outside world, and face to face with what is most himself and most impersonal, there lies I do not know what presentiment of the external reactions which the work in progress will provoke. It is hard for a man to be alone.

The influence of this presence may always be supposed, without fear of error; but it is compounded so subtly with the other factors of the work, is sometimes disguised so well, that it is almost impossible to isolate it.

Nevertheless we know that the true meaning of a certain choice or a certain effort of a creator is often outside the demands of the thing created, and results from a more or less conscious concern with the effect which will be produced and with its consequences for the producer. Thus, during its activity, the mind goes and comes continually from Self to Other, and modifies what its most intimate being produces, by this particular consciousness of the

[6] *Collected Essays of John Peale Bishop*, edited by Edmund Wilson, pp. 141, 142. Copyright 1948 by Charles Scribner's Sons. Reprinted by permission of the publisher.

judgment of a third. Therefore, in our reflections upon a work of art we may take one or the other of these two mutually exclusive attitudes. If we intend to proceed as rigorously as such a matter deserves, we must take great pains to separate our study of the production of a work of art from our study of the production of its value, that is to say, of the effects which it may produce here or there, in such and such a head, at such and such a time.

To demonstrate this, it is sufficient to remark that what we can really know or think we know in any field is nothing else than what we can either *observe* or *make* ourselves, and that it is impossible to gather into one condition and into one effort of attention the observation of the mind which produces the work and the observation of the mind which produces some value of this work. There is no grasp capable of spanning these two functions at once; producer and consumer are two essentially separate orders. The work of art is for one the terminus, for the other the origin of developments which may be as foreign as you please one from the other.

We must conclude then that any judgment which declares a threefold relationship between the producer, the work of art, and the consumer — and judgments of this kind are not rare in criticism — is an illusion which can have no meaning and which the slightest reflection will dissipate. We may consider only the relationship of the work to its producer, or again the relationship of the work, once finished, to the one whom it affects. The action of the first and the reaction of the second must never be confused. One's conception of the work is incompatible with the other's. PAUL VALÉRY [7]

It is not in his personal emotions, the emotions provoked by particular events in his life, that the poet is in any way remarkable or interesting. His particular emotions may be simple, or crude, or flat. The emotion in his poetry will be a very complex thing, but not with the complexity of the emotions of people who have very complex or unusual emotions in life. One error, in fact,

[7] "A First Course in Poetics," *Southern Review*, 6 (Winter 1940), 405-6.

of eccentricity in poetry is to seek for new human emotions to express; and in this search for novelty in the wrong place it discovers the perverse. The business of the poet is not to find new emotions but to use the ordinary ones and, in working them up into poetry, to express feelings which are not in actual emotions at all. And emotions which he has never experienced will serve his turn as well as those familiar to him. Consequently, we must believe that "emotion recollected in tranquility" is an inexact formula. For it is neither emotion, nor recollection, nor, without distortion of meaning, tranquility. It is a concentration, and a new thing resulting from the concentration, of a very great number of experiences which to the practical and active person would not seem to be experiences at all; it is a concentration which does not happen consciously or of deliberation. These experiences are not "recollected" and they finally unite in an atmosphere which is "tranquil" only in that it is a passive attending upon the event. Of course this is not quite the whole story. There is a great deal, in the writing of poetry, which must be conscious and deliberate. In fact, the bad poet is usually unconscious where he ought to be conscious, and conscious where he ought to be unconscious. T. S. ELIOT [8]

. . . we should not lend too docile ears to similar errors of artists when they talk of their artistic aims and methods, or describe their inspired experience and the usual physical symptoms which precede, accompany, and follow it. Such accounts are not very weighty and do not deserve to be taken as philosophically or scientifically sound. Many years ago a man with one of the most purely poetic talents that I have ever intimately known — a poet of the Neapolitan dialect named Salvatore di Giacomo — told me that poetry always came to him in the shape of an overmastering stomach-ache; and, while he made the confession, his face exhibited every mark of agony and nausea. And lately, in a lecture given by an English poet this year at Cambridge [*The Name and Nature of Poetry*, by A. E. Housman, 1933], I met with a mention of the same part of his anatomy. For there I read that poetry is a "secretion," like the resin which exudes from a pine-tree, or the pearl formed in a diseased oyster, and that its birth-place is in "the pit of the stomach." And this reminded me that Goethe too, in a like context, talked about his stomach: but his experience, on the contrary, was that if he were to conceive and bring forth good poetry this digestive organ must be in sound condition, and he concluded that, to judge from his extraordinary powers of creation, nobody had ever so fine a stomach as William Shakespeare. But whatever action poetic travail may have upon the stomach . . . we are, none the less, entitled to reject the conclusion drawn in the Cambridge lecture quoted above, that poetry "is rather physical than intellectual," or only to accept it, in the sense perhaps intended, as a curiosity or whimsical paradox. BENEDETTO CROCE [9]

What made Housman write a poem instead of shedding tears or killing himself or dreaming bad dreams or telling his troubles to a friend — was the fact that for a time something else replaced pain as the center of his experience. Through some yet unexplained change, a change involving the whole meaning of *poet*, other things took on new light to his imagination, and a feeling of synthesis replaced in some degree that pain; everything seemed to be one: end of work, end of life, death of the year, all conceivable endings in fact, or even *ending* as an abstract idea. All that is different and yet not different, like a fugue in words, is united into identity. The experience then becomes a satisfying one, yet without destroying altogether the quality of pain in it.

This is essentially the same experience as the Aristotelian catharsis in tragedy, through pity and terror. Is it not possible that from among the painful human emotions these two occurred to

---

[9] *The Defence of Poetry*, pp. 24–25. Copyright 1933 by the Clarendon Press. Reprinted by permission of the publisher.

Aristotle, not because they in fact are the primary feelings aroused by every tragedy, but rather because they are the two emotions utterly irreconcilable in real life? We cannot actually, I think, in our own life experience pity and terror at the same time: one drives the other out. But we can and do experience these or their analogues together — along with other emotions — in witnessing a tragedy. Precisely because of their irreconcilability in life we receive the greatest pleasure from their union in art. And so the pleasurable aesthetic feeling that results from the synthesis predominates easily over the painful character of the content without obliterating altogether the pain. It is through form, as we have tried to show very roughly in the case of Housman's poem, that this shift of value takes place: the painful becomes partially transformed through imaginative gratification of man's deep desire, the desire for unity of all things. ELISABETH SCHNEIDER [10]

All art originates in an act of intuition, or *vision*. But such *intuition* or vision must be identified with *knowledge*, being fully present only when consciously objectified. This act of vision or intuition is, physically, a state of concentration or tension in the mind. The *process* of poetry consists firstly in maintaining this vision in its integrity, and secondly in expressing this vision in words. Words are generally (that is to say, in prose) the *analysis* of a mental state. But in the process of poetic composition words rise into the conscious mind as isolated objective "things" with a definite equivalence in the poet's state of mental intensity. They are arranged or composed in a sequence or rhythm which is sustained until the mental state of tension in the poet is exhausted or released by this objective equivalence. HERBERT READ [11]

[10] *Aesthetic Motive*, pp. 103–4. Copyright 1939 by the Macmillan Co. Reprinted by permission of the publisher.
[11] *Form in Modern Poetry*, pp. 39–40. Copyright 1933 by Sheed and Ward, Inc. This essay is reprinted in *Collected Essays*, p. 44. Copyright 1938 by Faber and Faber, Ltd. Reprinted by permission of the publishers.
"This 'objective equivalence' is the poem, and the 'fumbling' by which the artist gets it out of himself is very largely a matter of hard work, of pure critical intelligence. We have to go to the poets themselves (always the best

This quality of pure being, which characterizes the Greek soul, was for Keats the required immediate prelude to creation. Since "poetry should be tranquil and sumptuous," the moment of creation should be one of tranquility. The sole aim of poetry (for Keats) was the submission of mind to things in their eternal aspect, to the real. The creative spirit attained this vision only in moments of wise passiveness (the "passive contemplativeness" of the Classical being), in self-detachment and self-annihilation, in states of "negative capability." The mind in aesthetic experience submits to sensations of the instant: all intellect is suspended, and the soul (as Yeats likewise reports) passes into a slight trance. Creation, particularly in its initial phases, did not mean for Keats — or again for Housman — an activity of the intellect. The experience of the poet (for Keats) is located in the point-present now, the point-present now being identical with static-unconsciousness. The submission of the conscious to the unconscious (according to John Middleton Murry) is Keats' declared philosophy, and by means of it he achieved his greatest works. He not only celebrates tranquility as theme (the tranquility of emotions harmonized in aesthetic experience) but creates tranquility in immediacy. What the poetry reflects, on its great occasions, is this extra-temporal quality of being.

Where the temporal relation of things is conceived as of a present mode, the present transposes into sensuous immediacy. Thought in Keats is conceived as a time-free present and felt consequently "as immediately as the odour of a rose." In D. H. Lawrence's preface to *New Poems* (1920) poetry is defined as the instantaneous expression of image in "the insurgent naked throb of the instant moment." Keats is the most sensuous of all our poets. He creates that "spot of time" which Wordsworth translates into past or future; Wordsworth embraces the past and Shelley the future, as Keats embraces the present. Shelley's thematic perspective, perspectives of life not yet brought to pass, are fu-

authorities on poetry) to see that this is so." Elizabeth Drew, in collaboration with John L. Sweeney, *Directions in Modern Poetry* (W. W. Norton and Co., Inc., 1940), p. 192.

turistic. To operate through the future is to repudiate the sensuous particulars of present reality. Shelley's poetic experience possesses the Faustian tendency, from particular to infinite. Wordsworth dictates what his senses are going to perceive or what his senses have perceived, transposing his sense-impressions into memories, overriding thus the sense-present. In Wordsworth's famous preface to *Lyrical Ballads* (I quote John Crowe Ransom's reading), Wordsworth "is repeatedly on the verge of laying down the principle that poetry looks necessarily to the past. For example, he says poetry is essentially an emotion *recollected*, it is not itself the original emotion. . . ." His *Intimations of Immortality* is a perspective of the past, and of the future as viewed from the past. Conversely, Shelley's *Music When Soft Voices Die* anticipates retrospection. Here the futuristic Shelley, as Kenneth Burke phrases it, "is looking forward to looking back. The form of thought is naturalistic and temporalistic in terms of *past* and *future*. But the form of thought in Keats is mystical, in terms of an *eternal present*. The Ode [*On a Grecian Urn*] is striving to move beyond the region of becoming into the realm of *being*." The static quality of the *Ode on a Grecian Urn* mirrors Keats' imagination, static in that instant of a sensation of things *as they are*, the perception of which is felt and not reflected upon. So it is with the entire poems or with their minute particulars. "Or with a finger stayed Ixion's wheel" is the objective correlative of Keats' static imagination. R. W. STALLMAN [12]

The poetic process is twofold: The one part, the discovery of the symbol, the establishment of an equivalence, is what we may call poetic method. It is concerned with the transposition and communication of emotion, no matter what the emotion may be; for the poetic method the emotional material is, strictly, indifferent. The other part is an aesthetic apprehension of significance, the recognition of the all in the one. This is specifically poetic act, or rather the supreme poetic act. Yet it may be absent from

[12] "Keats the Apollinian," *University of Toronto Quarterly*, 16 (January 1947), 147-49.

poetry. There is no necessary connection between poetic apprehension and poetic method, which frequently exists without
poetic apprehension; and no reason to suppose that the reverse is
also true, for the recognition of greatness in poetry is probably
not the peculiar privilege of great poets. We have here, at least, a
principle of division between major and minor poetry. JOHN
MIDDLETON MURRY [13]

Objective Correlatives

Clear visual images [and] a concise and luminous language:
these are the two qualities of Dante Eliot has in mind. The former
is the "objective correlative" of the emotions they intend to suggest, the latter appeals to the auditory imagination: there is an
element of extreme precision and an element of vagueness in both;
for the mind of the reader is stirred by the symbolical import of
the precise images, whereas — in contrast with the apparent terse-
ness of the vocabulary — "the feeling for syllable and rhythm
penetrates far below the conscious levels of thought and feeling,
invigorates every word; sinks to the most primitive and forgotten,
returns to the origin and brings something back, seeks the beginning and the end" (essay on Arnold). MARIO PRAZ [14]

Pound's idea of poetry [in *The Spirit of Romance*, 1910, p. 5]
as of "a sort of inspired mathematics, which gives us equations,
not for abstract figures, triangles, spheres, and the like, but equations for the human emotions," may be said to be the starting
point of Eliot's theory of the "objective correlative" ("Hamlet
and His Problems"). . . . Pound's statements are not so clear-cut
as Eliot's, but I think that, by reading the following passages, in
the light of the definition of poetry quoted above, we have the
chief elements of Eliot's theory of the "objective correlative," as
well as of his interpretation of Dante's vision:

The cult of Provençe had been a cult of the emotions; and with
it there had been some, hardly conscious, study of emotional psy-

[13] *Aspects of Literature*, p. 135. Copyright 1920 by Collins Sons and Co.,
Ltd. Reprinted by permission of the author and the publisher.
[14] "T. S. Eliot and Dante," *Southern Review*, 2 (Winter 1937), 539.

chology. In Tuscany the cult is a cult of the harmonies of the mind. If one is in sympathy with this form of *objective imagination* [*italics mine*] and this quality of vision, there is no poetry which has such enduring, such, if I may say so, indestructible charm (p. 103).

Apropos of Guinizelli's sonnet *Vedut'ho la lucente stella diana*, Pound writes (p. 92):

Here the preciseness of the description denotes, I think, a clarity of imaginative vision. In more sophisticated poetry an epithet would suffice, the picture would be suggested. The dawn would be "rosy-fingered" or "in russet clad." The Tuscan poetry is, however, of a time when the seeing of visions was considered respectable, and the poet takes delight in definite portrayal of his vision. The use of epithet is an advance on this method only when it suggests a vision not less clear, and its danger is obvious. In Milton or Swinburne, for example, it is too often merely a high-sounding word, and not a swift symbol of vanished beauty.

In general, on Tuscan poetry (p. 104):

Faults this poetry may have. . . . this virtue it ever has, it is not rhetorical, it aims to be what it is, and never pretends to be something which it is not.

And on the *Vita Nuova* in particular (p. 114):

Anyone who has in any degree the faculty of vision will know that the so-called personifications are real and not artificial. Dante's precision both in the *Vita Nuova* and in the *Commedia* comes from the attempt to reproduce exactly the thing which has been clearly seen. The "Lord of terrible aspect" is no abstraction, no figure of speech. There are some who can not or will not understand these things.

This passage must be read in connection with what Pound says of allegory (p. 85):

With the Romaunt of the Rose we come to a third thing. . . . we get the allegory, a sort of extension of the fable. . . . In the romances he [the medieval author] has told of actions and speech and has generalized about the emotions. In the allegory he learns to separate himself, not yet from complete moods, but from simple qualities and passions, and to visualize them.

128

These are, then, the points made by Pound in *The Spirit of Romance*: allegory is a means for the poet to separate himself from the emotions, to visualize them; this kind of vision is not a pretence; there is nothing rhetorical about it; in the Middle Ages the seeing of visions was considered respectable; the attempt of the poet to reproduce exactly the thing he has *actually* seen makes for clarity.

If now we read what Eliot says on the same subject in his *Dante* we will easily perceive the affinities:

The simplicity of Dante has another detailed reason . . . What is important for my purpose is the fact that the allegorical method was a definite method not confined to Italy; and the fact, apparently paradoxical, that the allegorical method makes for simplicity and intelligibility. We incline to think of allegory as a tiresome cross-word puzzle. We incline to associate it with dull poems (at best, *The Romance of the Rose*), and in a great poem to ignore it as irrelevant. What we ignore is, in a case like Dante's, its particular effect towards lucidity of style. . . . We have to consider the type of mind which by nature and *practice* tended to express itself in allegory; and for a competent poet, allegory means *clear visual images*. . . . Allegory is only one poetic method, but it is a method which has very great advantages. Dante's is a *visual* imagination. . . . it is visual in the sense that he lived in an age in which men still saw visions. . . . We have nothing but dreams, and we have forgotten that seeing visions . . . was once a more significant, interesting, and disciplined kind of dreaming. . . . All I ask of the reader, at this point, is to clear his mind, if he can, of every prejudice against allegory, and to admit at least that it was not a device to enable the uninspired to write verses, but really a mental habit, which when raised to the point of genius can make a great poet as well as a great mystic or saint. And it is the allegory which makes it possible for the reader who is not even a good Italian scholar to enjoy Dante. Speech varies, but our eyes are all the same. . . . Dante's attempt is to make us see what he saw.

This passage (*Dante*, pp. 22–23) is closer to *The Spirit of Romance* than the passage on allegory in the short essay in *The Sacred Wood*, but the conclusion is the same. In the short essay

Eliot justifies the usefulness of allegory in a poem of so vast an
ambit as the *Commedia,* but he calls it an artificial and mechanical
framework, whose intelligence is not necessary: "The emotional
structure within the scaffold is what must be understood, the structure made possible by the scaffold. This structure is an ordered
scale of human emotions. . . . Dante's is the most comprehensive, and the most *ordered* presentation of emotions that has
ever been made." Of Dante's use of elaborate imagery such as
that of the figure of the Eagle composed by the spirits of the just
in the Paradise (XVIII and following cantos), Eliot says (p. 54):
"Such figures are not merely antiquated rhetorical devices, but
serious and practical means of making the spiritual visible."

Another passage of Pound (p. 117) illustrates for the *Commedia* the point of view which is in everything but in name Eliot's
theory of the "objective correlative":

There is little doubt that Dante conceived the real Hell, Purga-
tory, and Paradise as states, and not places. Richard St. Victor
had, somewhile before, voiced this belief, and it is, moreover, a part
of the esoteric and mystic dogma. *For the purposes of art* and
popular religion it is more convenient to deal with such matters
objectively; this also was most natural in an age wherein it was
the poetic convention to personify abstractions, thoughts, and the
spirits of the eyes and senses, and indeed nearly everything that
could be regarded as an object, an essence or a quality. It is therefore expedient in reading the *Commedia* to regard Dante's descriptions of the actions and conditions of the shades as descriptions
of men's mental states in life, in which they are, after death, compelled to continue: that is to say, *men's inner selves stand visibly
before the eyes of Dante's intellect* [*italics mine*].

We shall see how Eliot as a poet has tried to revive this practice chiefly in *Ash-Wednesday*: to find clear images, or rather
symbols, appealing to the senses, apt to evoke the emotions of
which they are the "objective correlative."

It may be noted incidentally that Pound's definition of the nature of an image in such a way as to stress the union of sense and
thought, the presence of the idea *in* the image ("An 'Image' is that

which presents an intellectual and emotional complex in an instant of time") — a definition intimately connected with Pound's knowledge of Dante's practice — was capable of establishing at once a link between the poetry of Dante and his circle and that of the English metaphysical poets of the Seventeenth Century of whom Eliot was to write that they felt "their thought as immediately as the odor of a rose. A thought to Donne was an experience, it modified his sensibility." MARIO PRAZ [15]

Pound, after de Gourmont, had described this transference of vision more precisely: "Poetry is a sort of inspired mathematics which gives us equations not for abstract figures, triangles, spheres, and the like, but equations for the human emotions. If we have a mind which inclines to magic rather than to science, we will prefer to speak of these equations as spells or incantations; it sounds more arcane, mysterious, recondite." Eliot records a detachment somewhat more complete and a literary structure more complex. Following Pound, but with different intentions, he looks for the definition of his classicism in the writings of the Greeks and the Middle Ages. The vision which he aims at seems to him to be contained in the *Divine Comedy*. Pound has studied Dante's poem, but not categorically. Both poets consider it a masterpiece in which the emotions are perfectly projected in objects raised into relief. RENÉ TAUPIN [16]

M. René Taupin, * following Ramón Gómez de la Serna, finds it difficult to distinguish Apollinaire from his symbolist predecessors, whose influence he was instrumental in reviving. Indeed Apollinaire could write well in the symbolist manner; such poems as *La Chanson du Mal-Aimé, Le Brasier* and *L'Ermite* might have been written by any inspired disciple of Mallarmé. He profited, furthermore, from the symbolists' orchestration of sound, their discoveries in prosody and their widened range of imagery. Although he often used regular verse-forms, he resumed their ex-

---

[15] "T. S. Eliot and Dante," *Southern Review*, 2 (Winter 1937), 528–31.
[16] "The Classicism of T. S. Eliot," *Symposium*, 3 (January 1932), 64–65.

periments with free verse, which he made into a suppler and more precise instrument. Finally, and perhaps most important of all, he too sought concrete objective equivalents for every emotion and every abstract idea.

But a fundamental divergence from them may be found in Apollinaire's use of these "objective correlatives." The symbol can be considered as a truncated metaphor, one term of which may be "suggested" but is not stated. At its logical extreme, then, the symbolist poem tends to become a pattern of symbol-images, with the things symbolised projected darkly on to a plane behind the poem. The reference of the symbol is often ambiguous; hence much of the obscurity of this sort of poetry. With Apollinaire, however, all is crystal-clear; he leaves no room for misinterpretation, because he usually gives both terms of the metaphor — the thing symbolised together with the symbol. His method is statement rather than evocation. PHILIP BLAIR RICE [17]

* *L'Influence du Symbolisme français sur la Poésie américaine*, p. 221.

Symbolism in one form or another has been used by nearly every great European poet and Baudelaire's definition * could without violence be applied to their practice. The use of symbols is simply one aspect of language; the mistake lies in trying to invest them with some sort of transcendental significance instead of regarding them as a technical device of the same order as simile or metaphor. A symbol is nothing more than a vehicle for imaginative experience. What is essential is that it should correspond to the emotion evoked, and a great deal of Mallarmé's obscurity is due to the fact that he tried to use symbols to convey experiences which had not been transmuted into poetry. Baudelaire himself cannot be altogether exonerated from the charge of adding to the confusion and it is unfortunate that his *Correspondances* have been used by critics as a text instead of being treated as a piece of muddled psychology.

This does not mean that Baudelaire and his followers did not

[17] "A Modern Poet's Technique: Guillaume Apollinaire," *Symposium*, 2 (October 1931), 476–77.

extend and develop the use of symbols. They undoubtedly did. Now the term has a variety of meanings. It includes the expanded image in *l'Albatros*, the use of the "sea" as a symbol of liberation in the work of both Baudelaire and Mallarmé and Mallarmé's way of "working" words in the *Swan*. These are straightforward examples. What is more interesting is Baudelaire's use of the *néant* and the *gouffre* to symbolise the void behind the façade of contemporary civilization. MARTIN TURNELL [18]

* Baudelaire writes in his diary: "Dans certains états de l'âme presque surnaturels, la profondeur de la vie se révèle tout entière dans le spectacle, si ordinaire qu'il soit, qu'on a sous les yeux. Il en devient le Symbole."

They are without idea [Gautier's poems], and almost without emotions; or rather, their emotions are always implicit in *things*, in visible objects which are sometimes employed as symbols; more often Gautier describes them for their own sake. MALCOLM COWLEY [19]

When we look at *Heraclitus* we see that the directly emotional and personal insistence distinguishing it is associated with an absence of core or substance: the poem seems to be all emotional comment, the alleged justifying situation, the subject of comment, being represented by loosely evocative generalities, about which the poet feels vaguely if "intensely" (the "intensity" of this kind of thing is conditioned by vagueness). Again, the emotion seems to be out there on the page, whereas in reading *Proud Maisie* we never seem to be offered emotions as such; the emotion develops and defines itself as we grasp the dramatic elements the poem does offer — the data it presents (that is the effect) with emotional "disinterestedness." For "disinterestedness" we can substitute "impersonality," with which term we introduce a critical topic of the first importance. F. R. LEAVIS [20]

[18] "The Heirs of Baudelaire," *Scrutiny*, 11 (Summer 1943), 295–96.
[19] "The Art of Visible Things," *Dial*, 82 (March 1927), 247.
[20] " 'Thought' and Emotional Quality," *Scrutiny*, 13 (Spring 1945), 53.
The poem "Heraclitus," by Callimachus, is found on p. 584 of *The Oxford Book of Greek Verse in Translation*, edited by T. F. Higham and C. M. Bowra. Copyright 1938 by the Clarendon Press.

But we should linger over this scene [in *Madame Bovary*, II, XIII] if only to try our hands at what I shall now, for the first time, call sub-criticism, or the animal tact which permits us occasionally to see connections and correspondences which our rational powers, unaided, cannot detect. What capital feature of the scene seems (if it does) to render the actuality more than any other? The great fact, I think, is the actuality, and your sense of it is all that is necessary. Yet I like to linger over the whirring lathe of old Binet, a lay figure or "flat character" who has done little in the novel and will never do much, and whose lathe we merely noted from the beginning as a common feature of a small town like Yonville. I should like to know when Flaubert gave him the lathe, whether just to tag him for us; whether, writing the present scene, he went back and gave it to him as a "plant" for use here later; or whether, having given him the lathe, he decided it would be useful in this scene.

What is its use? James said that the work of fiction must be "a direct impression of life," a very general requirement; but in the perspective of nearly ninety years since the publication of *Madame Bovary* and the rise of the Impressionist novel through Henry James, James Joyce, and Virginia Woolf, the phrase takes on a more specific sense. Mind you the phrase is not "direct representation," which only the stage can give us. But here, using this mechanic's tool [the whirring lathe of Binet] Flaubert gives us a direct *impression* of Emma's sensation at a particular moment (which not even the drama could accomplish), and thus by rendering audible to us what Emma alone could hear he charged the entire scene with actuality. As Emma goes to the window she merely notes that Binet's lathe is turning — "*C'était Binet qui tournait.*" Then she looks down at the street which seems to rise towards her — "*Allons! Allons!*" she whispers, because she cannot find the will to jump. We have had rendered to us visually the shock of violent suicide. Now comes the subtle fusion of the reaction and of the pull towards self-destruction, which is the humming in her head: how can Flaubert *render* it for us? Shall we not have to take his word for it? Shall we not have to imagine for him? No: "*l'air circulait dans sa tête creuse*," he says; and then: "*le ronflement du tour ne discontinuait pas, comme une voix furieuse qui l'appelait*" — "the whirring of the lathe never stopped, like a voice of fury calling her." The humming vertigo that draws the street towards her is rendered audible to us by the correlative sound of the lathe. ALLEN TATE [21]

. . . I have chosen as my final instance of tension — the instance itself relieves me of the responsibility of the term — not a great and difficult passage, but only a slight and perfect one. It is from a scene that has always been the delight of the amateur reader of Dante; we can know more about it with less knowledge than about any other, perhaps, in the poem. The damned of the Second Circle are equivocally damned: Paolo and Francesca were illicit lovers but their crime was incontinence; neither adultery nor pandering, the two crimes of sex for which Dante seems to find any real theological reprobation; for they are committed with the intent of injury.

You will remember that when Dante first sees the lovers they are whirling in a high wind, the symbol here of lust. When Francesca's conversation with the poet begins, the wind dies down, and she tells him where she was born, in these lines:

> Siede la terra dove nata fui
> Sulla marina dove il Po discende
> Per aver pace co' seguaci sui.

Mr. Courtney Landon renders the tercet:

> The town where I was born sits on the shore,
> Whither the Po descends to be at peace
> Together with the streams that follow him.

But it misses a good deal; it misses the force of *seguaci* by rendering it as a verb. Professor Grandgent translates the third line:

[21] *On the Limits of Poetry: Selected Essays 1928–1948*, pp. 144–45. Copyright 1941 and 1948 by Allen Tate. Reprinted by permission of the Swallow Press and William Morrow and Co., Inc.

"To have peace with its pursuers," and comments: "The tributaries are conceived as chasing the Po down to the sea." Precisely; for if the *seguaci* are merely followers, and not pursuers also, the wonderfully ordered density of this simple passage is sacrificed. For although Francesca has told Dante where she lives, in the most directly descriptive language possible, she has told him more than that. Without the least imposition of strain upon the firmly denoted natural setting, she fuses herself with the river Po near which she was born. By a subtle shift of focus we see the pursued river as Francesca in Hell: the pursuing tributaries are a new visual image for the pursuing winds of lust. A further glance yields even more: as the winds, so the tributaries at once pursue and become one with the pursued: that is to say, Francesca has completely absorbed the substance of her sin — she is the sin; as, I believe it is said, the damned of the *Inferno* are plenary incarnations of the sin that has put them there. The tributaries of the Po are not only the winds of lust by analogy of visual images; they become identified by means of sound:

> *. . . discende*
> *Per aver pace co' seguaci sui*

The sibilants dominate the line; they are the hissing of the wind. But in the last line of the preceding tercet Francesca has been grateful that the wind has subsided so that she can be heard —

> *Mentre che il ventro, come fa, si tace.*

After the wind has abated, then, we hear in the silence, for the first time, its hiss, in the susurration of the descending Po. The river is thus both a visual and an auditory image, and since Francesca is her sin and her sin is embodied in this image, we are entitled to say that it is a sin that we can both hear and see. ALLEN TATE [22]

[22] *On the Limits of Poetry: Selected Essays 1928–1948*, pp. 88–90. Copyright 1941 and 1948 by Allen Tate. Reprinted by permission of the Swallow Press and William Morrow and Co., Inc.

The Recognition-Test (the Affective Fallacy)

Set beside that stanza of Daniel's these lines from Bruce's or Logan's
Cuckoo:

> Sweet bird, thy bower is ever green,
> Thy sky is ever clear;
> Thou hast no sorrow in thy song,
> No winter in thy year.

There is a new element has stolen in, a tinge of emotion. And I
think that to transfuse emotion — not to transmit thought but to set
up in the reader's sense a vibration corresponding to what was
felt by the writer — is the peculiar function of poetry. Even where
the verse is not thus beautiful and engaging in its external form, as
in Johnson's lines,

> His virtues walked their narrow round,
> Nor made a pause, nor left a void;
> And sure the Eternal Master found
> The single talent well employed,

it may yet possess the same virtue and elicit a like response.

Further than this I will not now ascend the stair of poetry. I
have chosen these two examples because they may almost be
called humble, and contain hardly more than the promise of what
poetry attains to be. Here it is not lofty or magnificent or intense; it does not transport with rapture nor overwhelm with awe;
it does not stab the heart nor shake the soul nor take the breath
away. But it is poetry, though not in the highest, yet in the highest definable sense.

> Duncan is in his grave;
> After life's fitful fever he sleeps well.

Even for that poetry there is no other name. A. E. HOUSMAN [23]

[Poetic inspiration, for Housman, had its source in the "pit of
the stomach"; and the pit of the stomach is also the inspirational

[23] *The Name and Nature of Poetry*, pp. 8–9. Copyright 1933 by the Macmillan Co., and by Cambridge University Press. Reprinted by permission of
the publishers.

source, according to Housman, for poetic judgment. To a request that he define poetry:] I replied that I could no more define poetry than a terrier can define a rat, but that I thought we both recognised the object by the symptoms which it provokes in us. One of these symptoms was described in connexion with another object by Eliphaz the Temanite: "A Spirit passed before my face: the hair of my flesh stood up." Experience has taught me, when I am shaving of a morning, to keep watch over my thoughts, because, if a line of poetry strays into my memory, my skin bristles so that the razor ceases to act. This particular symptom is accompanied by a shiver down the spine; there is another which consists in a constriction of the throat and a precipitation of water to the eyes; and there is a third which I can only describe by borrowing a phrase from one of Keats's last letters, where he says, speaking of Fanny Brawne, "everything that reminds me of her goes through me like a spear." The seat of this sensation is the pit of the stomach. A. E. HOUSMAN [24]

I cannot find my thrill in Schiller, nor even in Kleist. Even in Goethe the pleasure is intermittent; it is only a few of his lyrics that yield their essence or, to make the metaphor more exact, that

[24] *The Name and Nature of Poetry*, p. 46. Copyright 1933 by the Macmillan Co., and by Cambridge University Press. Reprinted by permission of the publishers.

EDITOR'S NOTE. Compare Housman's Recognition Test with Emily Dickinson's: "If I read a book and it makes my whole body so cold no fire can ever warm me, I know it is poetry. If I feel physically as if the top of my head were taken off, I know this is poetry."

Or compare Housman's test with C. Day Lewis' testimony that his sensations are "one of suffocation, followed by a sense of physical lightening and relief. . . . There can be little doubt that this emotional disturbance in the reader is a reproduction of the disturbance which was the poetical impulse of the writer; and this reproduction is the first aim and effect of poetry." C. Day Lewis, *Collected Poems: 1929–1933* (Random House, 1935), pp. 250–51.

Other critics, following Housman's example, apply to his own poetry his Lump-in-the-Throat Criterion, the Stab-in-the-Heart Test. But even T. S. Eliot gets shudders from certain poems: "Tennyson's *In Memoriam* gives me the shudder that I fail to get from anything in Maud." T. S. Eliot, *Essays Ancient and Modern* (Faber and Faber, Ltd., and Harcourt, Brace and Co., 1936), p. 195. See also pp. 491–94 of my "Annotated Bibliography of A. E. Housman: A Critical Study," *P.M.L.A.*, 55 (June 1945), 463–502.

give me the necessary shock. In these lyrics . . . I experience the poetry as a direct *impact*; a sensation of sound, and of sound allied to expressive epithet and metaphor. But in the case of George and Rilke the sensation is almost one of sight. Light seems to be involved: a visual perception. . . .

Actually I believe the sensation has to do with the immediate obscurity of the verse, and is strictly parallel to the pleasure I derive from obscurity in English poetry. Rilke in one of his poems cries:

> *Singe die Gärten, mein Herz, die du nicht kennst;*
> *Wie in Glas eingegossene Gärten, klar, unerreichbar.*

And that is the perfect analysis of the sensation: the vision of an unknown garden, embedded in glass, clear but unattainable. Vision without meaning, concrete, synthetic, but held in suspense, contemplated without question. HERBERT READ [25]

Art as the Expression of Emotion

. . . to transfuse emotion — not to transmit thought but to set up in the reader's sense a vibration corresponding to what was felt by the writer — is the peculiar function of poetry. A. E. HOUSMAN [26]

Tolstoy's famous definition of the process of art is expressed in these words:

To evoke in oneself a feeling one has experienced, and having evoked it in oneself, then by means of movement, lines, colours, sounds, or forms expressed in words so to transmit that feeling that others experience the same feeling — this is the activity of art.

Art is a human activity consisting in this, that one man con-

---

[25] *Collected Essays,* pp. 90–91. Copyright 1938 by Faber and Faber, Ltd. Reprinted by permission of the publisher.

[26] *The Name and Nature of Poetry,* p. 8. Copyright 1933 by the Macmillan Co., and by Cambridge University Press. Reprinted by permission of the publishers.

sciously, by means of certain external signs, hands on to others feelings he has lived through, and that others are infected by these feelings and also experience them.

. . .

The amendment I want to make in Tolstoy's definition . . . is simple. I would say that the function of art is not to transmit *feeling* so that others may experience the same *feeling*. That is only the function of the crudest forms of art — "programme music," melodrama, sentimental fiction and the like. The real function of art is to express *feeling* and transmit *understanding*. That is what the Greeks so perfectly realized and that is what, I think, Aristotle meant when he said that the purpose of drama was to purge our emotions. We come to the work of art already charged with emotional complexes; we find in the genuine work of art, not an excitation of these emotions, but peace, repose, equanimity. HERBERT READ [27]

. . . any emotion (pity; horror; amusement; love) can be evoked by countless formulae. If by emphasizing "particular" [emotion] Eliot means the complex of feelings summoned by the unique set of external facts, he is remarking merely that in art as in life each individual set of circumstances is attended by concordant feelings. It is no novelty to state that the artist must create the combination that will produce the effect he desires — though Eliot confuses expression of an emotion in the work with its arousal in the receptor. JOSEPH T. SHIPLEY [28]

It should now be clear that Eliot hesitates between the following two propositions — or perhaps it were better to say that he has not considered the important differences that exist between them: I) Poetry arouses emotion in the reader; II) The poem ex-

[27] *The Meaning of Art*, pp. 218–19, 222. Copyright 1931 by Faber and Faber, Ltd. Reprinted by permission of the publisher.
[28] "Objective Correlative," p. 410 in *Dictionary of World Literature*. Copyright 1943 by the Philosophical Library. Reprinted by permission of the publisher.

presses emotion. The first proposition needs qualification, but does not require an explanation; the second, however, does. We must therefore take up these propositions and see in what sense each can be held.

I) There is no question that poetry can and often indeed does make us sad, or compassionate, or angry, or fires us with patriotic fervor. It may even evoke or arouse specific but very complex emotions that language is too crude to denote adequately. But in the light of the facts uncovered by psychological investigations in the last fifty years about the diversity of aesthetic responses I doubt whether we can maintain that art always arouses emotion in every spectator. It depends on the art and on the spectator, and on his attention. Not all spectators are dionysian or want to be.* But even if poetry always did arouse emotion, we would still have to ask whether poetry *should* seek to arouse emotion — for we cannot confuse the merely descriptive with the normative question. And it would also be a question, whether, if we did hold that poetry *should* arouse emotion, we would not make it entirely impossible to draw the distinction between art and something else — between the aesthetic transaction and some other mode of experience. For the aesthetic would now be defined functionally by the presence of emotion, but the emotion aroused could be only ordinary emotion, since psychology does not recognize *sui generis* aesthetic emotions. Should we hold that poetry ought to arouse emotion, we also run up against a statement of Eliot's in an essay entitled "The Perfect Critic" † in which he tells us that "the end of the enjoyment of poetry is a pure contemplation from which all the accidents of personal emotion are removed." And yet, that the arousal of the emotion in the reader seems to be the way in which at least at times Eliot conceives the expression of emotion is to be gathered from his definition of the "objective correlative," ‡ and which Matthiessen considers a *locus classicus* of contemporary criticism; § for in this passage we are told that when the objective correlative is presented "the emotion is immediately evoked." Eliot may answer that there is no contradiction between these two statements. For what he is opposed to is the indulgence of *personal* emotion, which is precisely what a correlative that is truly objective controls. But if there is one fact for which we have ample evidence in aesthetics today it is the fact that no artist, however skillful, can possibly control the subjective affective responses of his readers, and this is all the truer to the extent to which the culture to which either poet or reader belongs (or both of course) is complex and in a state of flux, and where therefore to accidental personal idiosyncracies must be added the differences caused by heterogeneity of social determinants.

II) Poetry may legitimately be said to "express" emotion in two senses, but the first of these is trivial.

a) In a dramatic scene, you know that the actor is feeling a certain emotion. And you are able to say, "What an intense scene!" Whether or not the actor really does feel the emotion he is expressing through representation is a question we need not ask here. It would seem that some actors need to feel what they are acting, while others act poorly when they are the victims of the emotion they must represent. In any case, all that an actor needs to do to be faithful to the exigencies of the drama is to simulate the emotion. Consider, let us say, Giotto's *Pieta*. The figures represented clearly express by their gesture the intense emotions that they are supposed to be feeling. This sense neither furthers nor delays critical analysis of art.

b) Poetry may also express emotion in another way. The poem may be about a situation or an object which socially is connected or invariably associated — whether naturally or conventionally — with an emotion. This is perhaps the only legitimate and unambiguous meaning that we can give the term "objective correlative." But in this case all the term means is that poetry refers denotatively to emotions, not by means of direct verbal reference, but through the whole poem itself — and how this takes place is precisely what calls for explanation and what the term "objective correlative" perhaps labels but otherwise leaves us in the dark about. Somehow, because of a complex connection which is not yet understood, the poem presents itself as a composite symbol, but not as a neutral, semantic, one; rather, as one which refers reflexibility to a fully qualitied, self-consistent whole, more heavily loaded with value than things of ordinary life usually are. These values, not without some reason, *may be called* emotions, though they are objective characters of the value-freighted reality present for the experiencer, since they seem to be the factors in the object that account for the rapturous quality of the experience. But to suppose that they alone function in this manner seems to me utterly erroneous, since the poem and its parts function as wholes whose form and content cannot be separated from each other. . . . In any case poetry may legitimately be said to express emotion for any member of a group for whom a connection exists — conventionally or naturally — between the situation or object used by the poet and an emotion; and it expresses it whether it arouses it or not.

. . .

Be that as it may, a poem expresses all that which the poet presents objectively in it for apprehension; true, among the elements making up the object there are some that we find easier to denote when we wish to refer to them verbally, through the terms which we use to denote emotions. But I see no reason to assume that all else in the poem is put there merely to arouse an emotion in us or to bring about its objective denotation. Surface, formal, and ideational elements are all in their own right of intrinsic interest. And while the emotion expressed is also of interest, it is not, and it should not be, of chief or exclusive interest to the reader.

It is too much to expect that a theory so popular as the expression theory shall be abandoned on account of its ultimate unintelligibility. But because it will continue to be used, it is of the uttermost importance for criticism to realize that the emotion expressed through the objective correlative is not that which the poet felt before the poem was written. The emotion as well as the correlative, are *found* through the process of *creation*. But if the term "creation" is taken seriously, the consequences for Eliot's critical approach are devastating. For it means that once finished no one can go behind the poem, not even the artist himself. Otherwise put, the emotion itself, naked and unexpressed, cannot be had for comparison with its expression through its objective correlative. And the assumption therefore that we can criticize the play *Hamlet* by comparing the emotion expressed in the play with Shakespeare's emotions, or that through the play we can discover the emotions that went into it, is a confusing illusion. The vocabulary of the emotions is thus confusing, if not indeed irrevelant, to literary criticism; and if it were dropped, and the critic confined himself only to the objects and situations and values communicated by the poem, there would ensue an enormous clarification in the practice of criticism. ELISEO VIVAS [29]

* The evidence is to be found conveniently summarized in A. R. Chandler, *Beauty and Human Nature*, Chapters 6 and 12, pp. 230–36. See also Vernon Lee, *Music and its Lovers*, Chapters I and II.
† *The Sacred Wood*, pp. 14–15.
‡ *The Sacred Wood*, p. 100.
§ F. O. Matthiessen: *The Achievement of T. S. Eliot* (1935), p. 57.

It [the creative process of objectification of the self] is an active "enjoyment," not a passive "suffering," of his experiences. Instead, therefore, of restraint of emotion, it would be better to speak of a strengthening of self-consciousness in proportion to the strength of the experience. Without this, lyrical poetry would never be possible; the lyrical poet must "enjoy" his sorrows as well as his joys. In other words, behind all the emotional sensitiveness of the poet is the creative imagination operating on the "material" of emotion. And for our present purpose, what we emphasize is not the strength or vividness of his emotional reactions, but the ordering activity of the imagination which gives significance to emotion. Mere emotion in itself is something and nothing; what is necessary for poetry is the imaginative command of this emo-

[29] "The Objective Correlative of T. S. Eliot," pp. 392–95, 400, in *Critiques and Essays in Criticism*, edited by R. W. Stallman. Copyright 1949 by Ronald Press. Reprinted by permission of the author.

tion. The life of art is in this sense a strenuous effort after release from emotion in the very act of experiencing it. There must go on a certain depersonalization, a quietness in the midst of the speed of passion. It is from the "balance of those opposites" that poetry is born. Hence in lyrical poetry what is conveyed is not mere emotion, but the imaginative prehension of emotional states, which is a different thing. It is true that the object of imaginative prehension in this case is the poet himself; but it does not follow that language as it is used in lyrical poetry is any more "emotive" than in other kinds of poetry. Shelley's *Lines Written in Dejection* is as "objective" as *King Lear* or *Othello*. It is subjective only in the sense that it happens to be concerned with an emotional state which actually occurred in the life of the writer. Aesthetically, however, this fact is irrelevant.

. . .

Poetry is never concerned primarily to awake "emotion" and "attitude"; its concern is to convey imaginative ideas of, among other things, emotions. Successful conveyance of such imaginative prehension will certainly be accompanied by excitement — but excitement of a unique kind, which is not itself part of the content of the poem, for it is that which accompanies contemplation of the object. This contemplative excitement is impersonal, as impersonal as that which may accompany intellectual comprehension. Poetry can be as impersonal as science — and in relation to matters in which impersonality is enormously difficult. This is not, of course, to say that Shelley does not effect a self-expression in his poetry. Of course he does; as also does Shakespeare for that matter in his plays. D. G. JAMES [30]

A great art does not require us to undergo the same experience from which it has arisen; its only requirement is that we heed the form given to that experience. WALLACE FOWLIE [31]

[30] *Scepticism and Poetry*, pp. 114–15, 119–20. Copyright 1937 by Allen and Unwin, Ltd. Reprinted by permission of the publisher.
[31] *Clowns and Angels*, p. 126. Copyright 1943 by Sheed and Ward, Inc. Reprinted by permission of the publisher.

The experience which the poet offers to his auditor, or reader, is not the original experience which has provided him with a subject for his poem. There may even not have been, strictly speaking, any original experience. And also, what he feels in composing the poem is not what the auditor, or reader, can feel from hearing, or reading, it. MONTGOMERY BELGION [32]

Beauty's the form loves gives to things. JOSEPH T. SHIPLEY [33]

One definition of the beautiful which has been popular for a number of years among exponents of the principles of aesthetics continues at the moment to be that perhaps most generally accepted. It is that beauty is the expression of emotion. I have to confess an inability to understand what these words mean.

A first possibility is that the condition of the artist on the occasions when he succeeds in producing a beautiful work is held to be akin to the condition of the man who sings at his job. The vocal performance of such a man may not be of a very high order; but it implies an absorption by his task and a certain exaltation. I cannot discern, however, the existence of any ascertainable relation between the mood in which an artist works and the presence or absence of beauty in what he produces; and I suspect that, on the contrary, as it is the errand boy whistling merrily on his round who is as likely as not to leave his parcels at the wrong addresses, so it is the artist too readily transported by the promise of his subject who will be the more prone to fail in the control of both his material and his inspiration.

Another possibility is that the artist, when achieving the beautiful, is thought to succeed in conveying or communicating emotion. But against this being so there are what seem to me fatal objections.

Any acceptable description of beauty must undoubted apply to natural beauty as well as to that which happens to be embodied

[32] "What Is Criticism?" *Criterion*, 10 (October 1930), 128.
[33] *The Quest for Literature*, p. 220. Copyright 1931 by Richard R. Smith, Inc.

in much of the handiwork of man. But as soon as we consider natural beauty we see that the definition, "The expression of emotion," does not account for it. Where emotion exists, and *a fortiori* where it is expressed, it must be the emotion of some being. There is no such thing as emotion in the abstract. In the case of natural beauty, then, we are at once led to ask whose would be the emotion it expressed. Another modern view in aesthetics is that the essential pleasure afforded in the presence of a work of art consists in the spectator's admiration of the artist's skill; and a reputable philosopher, satisfied that the beautiful is the expression of emotion, very pertinently condemns this other view on the ground that when we find a piece of natural scenery enjoyable we can hardly be admiring the brushwork of the Creator. Yet, since this philosopher can raise that objection, it is curious he should be content with the doctrine he himself defends. For you would think it was equally undeniable that when we find beauty in natural scenery what we are finding is not the expression of Divine emotion. Assuredly, at any rate, we have no right to suppose in the piece of scenery the presence of anything of the kind.

If we confine our attention to works of human art, the obscurity of the definition is by no means dissipated. Unquestionably it is at least an element in the nature of beauty to arouse a particular emotion in the spectator; but when this beauty is the beauty of a work of human art the emotion felt by the spectator as he takes stock of the work can hardly be the emotion which the artist might be said to have put into it. Yet how believe that the definition does not imply some identity of this sort? That emotion has gone to the making of the work we must not deny, but, on the contrary, insist upon. Yet, on the one hand, there can have been emotion in the making without the achievement of beauty; and, on the other hand, where there is beauty in the work the emotion which the maker felt as he made it is not an emotion of the same kind as is aroused in the spectator who, upon beholding the work, is affected by its beauty. . . .

. . .

Now Cézanne, being himself a painter, was able to observe and enumerate the elements of beauty in this picture [*The Wedding of Cana*] with great precision. A less expert spectator would, if sufficiently receptive and observant, have been affected by the same features, but more vaguely and indistinctly. Cézanne, that is to say, missed nothing of what the picture offers. Yet it seems to me unmistakable that Cézanne, although himself a painter, was not feeling in the presence of the picture the emotion which we must suppose Paolo Veronese to have had when he painted it. I say, "which we must suppose," because Veronese has not told us — he may not have been conscious of — what he was feeling; and yet nobody, I fancy, will refuse to grant that the conditions in which art is produced are invariably the same, whatever the quality of the art, provided we ignore — as we may — the consequences of the wide variation of capacity in different artists. There is no need to claim a privileged psychological insight regarding what Veronese was feeling at every one of the successive stages in the composition of this particular picture. It will be enough if we consider quite generally the artist's emotion in regard to those specific effects which, since their quality moved Cézanne so greatly more than three hundred years after they had been wrought, can be said to constitute a typical specimen of pictorial beauty. The emotion of Veronese was, then, the emotion, first of trying to conceive these effects, next of having conceived them — the artist's delight that he could now set to work — thirdly of trying to execute them, and finally of executing and of having executed them. Among these, the last — the emotion of having successfully executed the effects which he wished to produce — has alone any kinship with the emotion which we have found Cézanne to display as spectator. Even so, it was entirely other. For Veronese, while painting, must have been undergoing the emotion that fills a man when conscious of causing effects; Cézanne, while beholding, the emotion of a man being subjected to effects. Nor does the second emotion become a replica of the first because Cézanne was able, as he was moved, to detect the devices in the disposition of pigment and application of the brush whereby the effects were obtained.

Between this consciousness of causing and this undergoing of effects there is no mere distinction without a difference. The artist is moved by his activity, the spectator in what is relatively his passivity. . . . The point is, that no painter, when beholding or imagining the subject of a prospective work, thinks, "This moves me mightily; I shall move other people as I am being moved by transmitting to them with the help of brush, pigment, and canvas, the beauty in what I now see"; for then, on beholding *The Wedding of Cana*, Cézanne would have wanted, above all, to copy it; and some one else have wanted to copy his copy; and so on *ad infinitum*. The painter need not, *a priori*, see anything emotional in a subject. MONTGOMERY BELGION [34]

It may be that in the complete apprehension of a work of art there occurs more than one kind of feeling. There is generally a basis of purely physiological pleasure, as in seeing pure colours or hearing pure sounds; then there is the specifically aesthetic emotion by means of which the necessity of relations is apprehended, and which corresponds in science to the purely logical process; and finally there is the unity-emotion, which may not improbably be of an identical kind in both art and science.

In the art of painting we may distinguish between the unity of texture and the unity of design. I know quite well that these are not really completely separable, and that they are to some extent mutually dependent; but they may be regarded as separate for the purpose of focussing our attention. Certainly we can think of pictures in which the general architecture of the design is in no way striking or remarkable which yet please us by the perfection of the texture, that is to say, the ease with which we apprehend the necessary relationship of one shape, tone or colour with its immediately surrounding shapes, tones or colours; our aesthetic sense is continually aroused and satisfied by the succession of in-

[34] "The Expression of Emotion," *Southern Review*, 3 (Spring 1938), 783-84, 785-86.

evitable relationships. On the other hand, we know of works of art in which the unity and complexity of the texture strike us far less than the inevitable and significant relationship of the main divisions of the design — pictures in which we should say that the composition was the most striking beauty. It is when the composition of a picture adequately supported as it must be by significance of texture, reveals to us the most surprising and yet inevitable relationships that we get most strongly the final unity-emotion of a work of art. ROGER FRY [35]

[Concerning T. S. Eliot's theory of poetry as expressed in "Tradition and the Individual Talent," *Selected Essays*, p. 8:]

One of the contributions of this argument to theory is the aesthetic truth that the emotion we have for the artistic object cannot be the same as the emotion we might have had for the natural or original object; we have often received that truth, through the doctrine of "psychic distance," or of artistic "detachment," or even of art as "imitation." But in what lies the difference in the emotions? And what is a "transmuted" emotion? I think it is impossible to talk clearly about these matters until we drop the vocabulary of emotions and talk about the respective cognitive objects, or the cognitive situations, which identify them. . . . Perhaps we might call it [the original emotion] a practical emotion; and then we should distinguish the emotion which attaches to the mere image of the object, when called up for retrospect or put together by inventive imagination, as at best an experimental or tentative emotion, or a self-conscious, philosophical, or speculative emotion: whatever would constitute an *aesthetic* emotion. But probably the most important thing in Eliot's statement is his recognition of *big* emotions as set off against *little* feelings; and I should say the big emotion refers to our reception of the main situation, or situation as a whole, and the little feelings refer to our reception of the heterogeneous detail of the situation. Or, the emotion attaches to the main *struc-*

[35] *Vision and Design*, pp. 83–84. Copyright 1920 by Chatto and Windus, Ltd. Reprinted by permission of the publisher.

ture, the feelings attach to the local *texture*. These are the terms which seem to me most practical in critical analysis. JOHN CROWE RANSOM [36]

Art as the Union of "Thought" and "Feeling"

I doubt whether the *sound* of two poems can be very similar, when the *sense* is entirely different. At any rate, I have found that the more I studied the meaning of Crashaw's verse, and his peculiar use of image and conceit, the less resemblance the music of it seemed to have to Shelley's. . . . Crashaw's images, even when entirely preposterous — for there is no warrant for bringing a pillow (and what a pillow!) for the *head* of a *tear* — give a kind of intellectual pleasure — it is a deliberate conscious perversity of language, a perversity like that of the amazing and amazingly impressive interior of St. Peter's. There is brain work in it. But in *The Skylark* there is no brain work. For the first time perhaps in verse of such eminence, sound exists without sense. Crashaw would never have written so shabby a line as "That from heaven or near it" merely to provide an imperfect rhyme for *spirit*.

> Keen as are the arrows
>   Of that silver sphere
> Whose intense lamp narrows
>   In the white dawn clear,
> Until we hardly see, we feel that it is there.

I should be grateful for any explanation of this stanza; until now I am still ignorant of what Sphere Shelley refers to, or why it should have silver arrows, or what the devil he means by any intense lamp narrowing in the white dawn; though I can understand that we could hardly see the lamp of a *silver* sphere narrowing in *white* dawn (why dawn? as he has just referred to the pale purple even). There may be some clue for persons more learned than I;

---

[36] *The New Criticism*, pp. 155–56. Copyright 1941 by New Directions. Reprinted by permission of the publisher.

but Shelley should have provided notes. Crashaw does not need *such* notes.

And when Shelley has some definite statement to make, he simply says it; keeps his images on one side and his meanings on the other: T. S. ELIOT [37]

We say, in a vague way, that Shakespeare, or Dante, or Lucretius, is a poet who thinks, and that Swinburne is a poet who does not think, even that Tennyson is a poet who does not think. But what we really mean is not a difference in quality of thought, but a difference in quality of emotion. The poet who "thinks" is merely the poet who can express the emotional equivalent of thought. But he is not necessarily interested in the thought itself. We talk as if thought was precise and emotion was vague. In reality there is precise emotion and there is vague emotion. To express precise emotion requires as great intellectual power as to express precise thought. T. S. ELIOT [38]

Poetry cannot prove that anything is *true*; it can only create a variety of wholes composed of intellectual and emotional constitu-

[37] "The Poems of Richard Crashaw," *Dial*, 84 (March 1928), 248-49.

EDITOR'S NOTE. Eliot's request for an explanation of this stanza of "To a Skylark" was answered by A. E. Housman in the *Times Literary Supplement*, 1403 (December 20, 1928), 1011. Here is his explanation:

"Although this ode is not one of Shelley's best poems and enjoys more fame than it deserves, it is good enough to be worth interpreting. Quintilian says that you will never understand the poets unless you learn astronomy; and as this subject is not now much studied in girls' schools it was only to be expected that Mr. Moore's *Egeria* should darken with misinformation the ignorance of Mr. Eliot. In the stanza . . . the silver sphere is the Morning Star, the planet Venus; and Shelley is giving a true description of her disappearance and using an apt comparison. The moon, when her intense lamp narrows in the white dawn clear, is not a sphere but a sickle: when she is a sphere at sunrise she is near the western horizon, visible in broad daylight and disappearing only when she sets; so that nothing could be less like the vanishing of the skylark. A.E.H." Quoted in Grant Richards, *Housman 1897–1936* (Oxford University Press, 1941), p. 246. Reprinted by permission of Jonathan Cape, Ltd., and by the British Society of Authors. See also T. Sturge Moore, *Armour for Aphrodite* (Grant Richards and Humphrey Toulin, Cayne Press, Ltd., 1929), pp. 180, 206-7.

[38] *Selected Essays 1917–1932*, p. 115. Copyright 1932 by Harcourt, Brace and Co., and by Faber and Faber, Ltd. Reprinted by permission of the publishers.

ents, justifying the emotion by the thought and the thought by the emotion; it proves successively, or fails to prove, that certain worlds of thought and feeling are *possible*. It provides intellectual sanction for feeling, and esthetic sanction for thought. T. S. ELIOT [39]

And the relation between "thought" and "feeling" is illustrated by Tennyson's poem — a note of Yeats' on his own work comes to mind here: "I tried after the publication of *The Wanderings of Oisin* to write of nothing but emotion, and in the simplest language, and now I have had to go through it all, cutting out or altering passages that are sentimental for lack of thought." This has an obvious bearing on *The Lake Isle of Innisfree. Tears, idle tears* . . . may fairly be classed with *Innisfree.* Whether we are to call it "sentimental" or not, it certainly bears to *Break, break, break* a relation that gives force to the suggestion made in regard to this last poem. The poet who wrote the one wrote the other: they are both highly characteristic; and it is plain that habitual indulgence of the kind represented by *Tears, idle tears* — indulgence not accompanied and virtually disowned by a critical placing — would be, on grounds of emotional and spiritual hygiene, something to deplore. There is nothing gross about the poem; it exhibits its author's highly personal distinction; but it unquestionably offers emotion directly, emotion for its own sake without a justifying situation, and, in the comparison, its inferiority to Lawrence's poem [*Piano*] compels a largely disparaging commentary.

. . .

There is, then, an obvious sense in which Shelley's poetry offers feeling divorced from thought — offers it as something opposed to thought. Along with this characteristic goes Shelley's notable inability to *grasp* anything — to present any situation, any observed or imagined actuality, or any experience, as an object existing independently in its own nature and in its own right.

[39] "Poetry and Propaganda," *Bookman*, 70 (February 1930), 602.

Correlatively there is the direct offer of emotion — emotion insistently explicit — in itself, for itself, for its own sake: we find our description merging into criticism. F. R. Leavis [40]

Poetry is an expressive art, we say, and perhaps presently we are explaining that what it expresses is its poet; a dangerous locution, because the public value of the poem would seem to lie theoretically in the competence with which it expresses its object. There is no reason why it should not offer an absolute knowledge of this object, so far as the adjective is ever applicable to a human knowledge, including a scientific knowledge, and a knowledge however "objective." Nevertheless one knowledge will differ from another knowledge in glory, that is, in the purity of intention, and sometimes it is scarcely a knowledge at all; it is rather a self-expression. There is probably a poetry of the feelings just as much as there is a poetry of knowledge; for we may hardly deny to a word its common usage, and poetry is an experience so various as to be entertained by everybody. But the poetry of the feelings is not the one that the critic is compelled to prefer, especially if he can say that it taints us with subjectivism, sentimentality, and self-indulgence. This is the poetry, I think, which we sometimes dispose of a little distastefully as "romantic." It does not pursue its object with much zeal, and it is so common that it involves in a general disrepute all poets, the innocent as well as the guilty, by comparison with those importunate pursuers, the scientists — who may not exactly be expected to fail to make the most of the comparison.

This sort of poetry, I am afraid, is as natural to Shakespeare as language is, and he is a great master in it. John Crowe Ransom [41]

So I infer that Swinburne found an adequate outlet for the creative impulse in his poetry; and none of it was forced back and out through his critical prose. . . . The disturbance in Mr.

[40] "'Thought' and Emotional Quality," *Scrutiny*, 13 (Spring 1945), 59, 60.
[41] *The World's Body*, pp. 278-79. Copyright 1938 by Charles Scribner's Sons. Reprinted by permission of the publisher.

[Arthur] Symons is almost, but not quite, to the point of creating; the reading sometimes fecundates his emotions to produce something new which is not criticism, but is not the expulsion, the ejection, the birth of creativeness.

The type is not uncommon, although Mr. Symons is far superior to most of the type. Some writers are essentially of the type that reacts in excess of the stimulus, making something new out of the impressions, but suffer from a defect of vitality or an obscure obstruction which prevents nature from taking its course. Their sensibility alters the object, but never transforms it. Their reaction is that of the ordinary emotional person developed to an exceptional degree. For this ordinary emotional person, experiencing a work of art, has a mixed critical and creative reaction. It is made up of comment and opinion, and also new emotions which are vaguely applied to his own life. The sentimental person, in whom a work of art arouses all sorts of emotions which have nothing to do with that work of art whatever, but are accidents of personal association, is an incomplete artist. For in an artist these suggestions made by a work of art, which are purely personal, become fused with a multitude of other suggestions from multitudinous experience, and result in the production of a new object which is no longer purely personal, because it is a work of art itself. T. S. ELIOT [42]

In every effective symbolism there are certain aesthetic features shared in common. The meaning acquires emotion and feeling directly excited by the symbol. This is the whole basis of the art of literature, namely that emotions and feelings directly excited by the words should fitly intensify our emotions and feelings arising from contemplation of the meaning. ALFRED NORTH WHITE-HEAD [43]

[42] *The Sacred Wood*, pp. 6-7. Copyright 1920 and 1928 by Methuen and Co., Ltd., and 1921 and 1930 by Alfred A. Knopf, Inc. Reprinted by permission of the author and the publishers.

[43] *Symbolism: Its Meaning and Effect*, pp. 83–84. Copyright 1927 by the Macmillan Co., and by Cambridge University Press. Reprinted by permission of the publishers.

In conclusion it is suggestive to think of metaphysical poetry as lying between romantic and classical poetry, as the product of an angle of vision in which the subjective and objective meet, in which dialectical subtlety and impassioned majesty unite, in which the most inward experience may join the wide horizon of the sky. The result is a metaphysic of imaginative form which renders a complex introspective emotion by an objective equivalent that is both sensuous and intellectual. It is an effort to support imagination by reason when the conventions and beliefs which verify that imagination are disintegrating and can no longer connect the emotions. To create new imaginative connections for emotion the metaphysical poet introduces new psychological and realistic elements, sometimes neglecting the common emotional connectives which govern communication. This metaphysic might be called an effort to impose intellectual form upon intuitions which would normally be expressed by a free sequence of images.

In romantic poetry the sequence of images is free in the sense that it is directed by "emotion recollected in tranquillity." This carries with it the associative form of creative emotion. Donne's "conceptual" form, on the other hand, gives his emotion the exciting concision of an intellectual skeleton. At other times his imaginative form derives from the logic of the image – from the simplest form of expanded conceit to the subtle figure of *Air and Angels* or the extensive but powerful image of the *First Anniversary*. This imaginative form may be regarded as a form between the emotionally organized form of the Romantic and the rationally organized form of the Classic: the Metaphysical seizes emotionally the idea or symbol which imposes its own logic upon the emotion. This metaphorical logic helps to explain the intimate union of dialectical subtlety and impassioned majesty which De Quincey detected in Donne and which T. S. Eliot finds disintegrated in Milton and Dryden. It is just in this "dissociation of sensibility" that one finds the imaginative form of the Classic and Romantic inferior to that of the Metaphysical. And it is the desire to make the whole mind operative on the poetic level that has led contemporary poets back to the study of Donne and the Elizabethans. GEORGE WILLIAMSON [44]

It seems to me that the power to give the illusion of "thought" by written words is a power of *dramatizing*; it is the power possessed by the later Elizabethan dramatists who split up, as Mr. Eliot says, "the primitive rhetoric, developing out of it subtler poetry and subtler tones of conversation, eventually mingling, as no other school of dramatists has done, the oratorical, the conversational, the elaborate and the simple, the direct and the indirect." The power is dramatic in that it gives us the illusion of "thought" *in action*, of "thought" growing, hesitating, changing, violently reversing; and all through the medium of words.

Eliot and Donne resemble each other in this particular above all, that they both, though not dramatic poets, possess this "dramatic" power. The metaphysical relationship seems to me of less significance. To bring out more clearly what I mean, I should like to glance a little more closely at Donne. In an interesting pamphlet, *Donne the Craftsman*, Mr. Pierre Legouis takes up the question of "dramatic power," which, he says, it "has generally been acknowledged" Donne possessed. "Still," he complains, "that general agreement upon the epithet 'dramatic' tends to confusion [rather] than enlightenment because no two critics seem to understand it in the same sense, and it may well be applied to Donne's poetry in more than one" (p. 48). Mr. Legouis then distinguishes three senses. One is the pictorial conception of the "dramatic": "what stirs the emotions through the sight, especially,

[44] "Donne and the Poetry of Today," pp. 175–76 in *A Garland for John Donne*, edited by Theodore Spencer. Copyright 1931 by Harvard University Press. Reprinted by permission of the publisher.

EDITOR'S NOTE. See Herbert J. C. Grierson's "Introduction" to *Metaphysical Lyrics and Poems* (Oxford University Press, 1921), pp. xv–xvi. The peculiar quality of the metaphysical poetry of Donne and his followers includes, among other ingredients, "the more intellectual, less verbal, character, of their wit . . . the finer psychology of which their conceits are often the expression; their learned imagery; the argumentative, subtle evolution of their lyrics; above all the peculiar blend of passion and thought, feeling and ratiocination which is the greatest achievement."

of attitudes and gestures." A second is the psychological conception: Mr. Legouis does not develop this in any detail, but it appears to correspond to the illusion of "thought" in action. A third,
which Mr. Legouis favors, is the implying, in addition to the
character who is speaking, of a second character, a mute listener,
whose actions and feelings are hinted at. The first and third of
these conceptions of the "dramatic" seem to me to be subordinate
or auxiliary to the second: first of all, the language itself must
give, by rhythm, syntax and vocabulary, the illusion of "thought"
in action. The "dramatic" power of Donne, in the second sense,
comes out clearly:

> I wonder by my troth, what thou, and I
> Did, till we lov'd? were we not wean'd till then?
> But suck'd on countrey pleasures, childishly?
> Or snorted we in the seven sleepers den?
> T'was so; But this, all pleasures fancies bee.
> If ever any beauty I did see,
> Which I desir'd, and got, t'was but a dreame of thee.

The rhythm, the syntax, the vocabulary are all conversational.
Even a listener is implied, but that seems to me of secondary importance. Whoever the "I" is — and I do not see any reason one
should assume that it is Donne himself — he is apparently speaking
to some one; but I also do not see any reason the some one should
not be an *imaginary* listener, present only in the mind of the "I."
But what is of primary importance is that the "thought" seems
to issue forth spontaneously as it forms in the mind. FRANKLIN
GARY [45]

[45] Review in *Symposium*, 3 (October 1932), 528–29.

VI

The
Problem of the
Personal
Element

———————————————

In Matthew Arnold the pose of impersonality is carried with such art that it would be absurd to withhold our admiration. If he passes judgement, it is not he that does it, but the orbis terrarum, *the whole congregation of saints. For him criticism knows nothing of persons; nor poetry either — the poet has neither father nor mother, nor any place in the history of literature; or if he has, it is a kind of impertinence, and is not going to help him in the day of judgement.*

H. W. GARROD, *Poetry and the Criticism of Life*, p. 158. Copyright 1931 by Oxford University Press. Reprinted by permission of the publisher.

The Personal Element in Poetic Creation

The progress of an artist is a continual self-sacrifice, a continual extinction of personality.

. . .

. . . the more perfect the artist, the more completely separate in him will be the man who suffers and the mind which creates; the more perfectly will the mind digest and transmute the passions which are its material. T. S. ELIOT [1]

On the other hand, without indirect egotism there can be no poetry. There can be no poetry without the personality of the poet, and that, quite simply, is why the definition of poetry has not been found and why, in short, there is none. WALLACE STEVENS [2]

[1] *Selected Essays 1917–1932*, pp. 7, 7–8. Copyright 1932 by Harcourt, Brace and Co., and by Faber and Faber, Ltd. Reprinted by permission of the publishers.

[2] "The Figure of the Youth as Virile Poet," *Sewanee Review*, 52 (Autumn 1944), 513.

The unsophisticated reader is right in his intuitive perception that the poem which moves him is engendered spiritually, the result of personal dynamism and not merely of detached, impersonal mechanical dexterity. D. S. SAVAGE [3]

It is not enough to have thought great things *before* doing the work. The brush stroke at the moment of contact carries inevitably the exact state of being of the artist at that exact moment into the work, and there it is, to be seen and read by those who can read such signs, and to be read later by the artist himself, with perhaps some surprise, as a revelation of himself.

For an artist to be interesting to us he must have been interesting to himself. He must have been capable of intense feeling, and capable of profound contemplation.

He who has contemplated has met with himself, is in a state to see into the realities beyond the surfaces of his subject. Nature reveals to him, and, seeing and feeling intensely, he paints, and whether he wills it or not each brush stroke is an exact record of such as he was at the exact moment the stroke was made. ROBERT HENRI [4]

But a work of art is the expression of a given personality and takes its colour and its life from this personality. "There is one point at which the moral sense and the artistic sense lie very near together; that is in the light of the very obvious truth that the deepest quality of a work of art will always be the quality of the mind of the producer." HERBERT READ [5]

No artist produces great art by a deliberate attempt to express his personality. He expresses his personality indirectly through concentrating upon a task which is a task in the same sense as the

[3] *The Personal Principle*, p. 129. Copyright 1944 by George Routledge and Sons, Ltd. Reprinted by permission of the author and the publisher.

[4] *The Art Spirit*, p. 7. Copyright 1923 and 1930 by the J. B. Lippincott Co. Reprinted by permission of Violet Organ and the publisher.

[5] Quoting Henry James, in *Reason and Romanticism*, p. 219. Copyright 1926 by Faber and Gwyer, Ltd. Reprinted by permission of the publisher.

making of an efficient engine or the turning of a jug or a table-leg. T. S. ELIOT [6]

One thus supposes demonstrated the two truths which precisely are in question, viz the substantial existence of an ego and the analogy between the ego and the work. Nothing entitles us to believe that the work's centre of gravity, so to speak, corresponds necessarily to the author's centre of gravity, *conceived, not as a writer, but as a man.* . . . Words and ideas, the senses and reflexes, serve equally for the building of a work and for the building of a man; agreed; but an experience, or a defect, or a quality, which in the life of a man plays an insignificant part, may become the kernel of a masterpiece, whereas this same man may fail to give an aesthetic form to the things closest to his heart. RAMON FERNANDEZ [7]

But we may remember that the poem [*The Ancient Mariner*] even regarded in this light, is not an attempt merely to present the personal problem but an attempt to transcend the personal problem, to objectify and universalize it. And it is because of the attempt to objectify and universalize, that we can distinguish the themes as inherent in the poem as such from the personal theme or themes which remain irrevocably tied to the man. The personal experience may provide motivations and materials, but in so far as it remains purely personal it does not concern us in the present context. ROBERT PENN WARREN [8]

I have, in early essays, extolled what I called impersonality in art, and it may seem that, in giving as a reason for the superiority of Yeats's later work the greater expression of personality in it, I

[6] *Selected Essays 1917–1932*, p. 96. Copyright 1932 by Harcourt, Brace and Co., and by Faber and Faber, Ltd. Reprinted by permission of the publishers.
[7] *Messages*, pp. 96, 97. Translated from the French by Montgomery Belgion. Copyright 1927 by Harcourt, Brace and Co. Reprinted by permission of the publisher.
[8] Essay, p. 72 in *The Rime of the Ancient Mariner*. Copyright 1946 by Reynal and Hitchcock. Reprinted by permission of Harcourt, Brace and Co.

am contradicting myself. It may be that I expressed myself badly, or that I had only an adolescent grasp of that idea — as I can never bear to re-read my own prose writings, I am willing to leave the point unsettled — but I think now, at least, that the truth of the matter is this. There are two forms of impersonality: that which is natural to the mere skilful craftsman, and that which is more and more achieved by the maturing artist. The first is that of what I have called the "anthology piece," of a lyric by Lovelace or Suckling, or of Campion, a finer poet than either. The second impersonality is that of the poet who, out of intense and personal experience, is able to express a general truth; retaining all the particularity of his experience, to make of it a general symbol. And the strange thing is that Yeats, having been a great craftsman in the first kind, became a great poet in the second. It is not that he became a different man, for, as I have hinted, one feels sure that the intense experience of youth had been lived through — and indeed, without his early experience he could never have attained anything of the wisdom which appears in his later writing. But he had to wait for a late maturity to find expression of early experience; and this makes him, I think, a unique and especially interesting poet. T. S. ELIOT [9]

Keats, at a time when the phrase had not yet been invented, practised the theory of art for art's sake. He is the type not of the poet, but of the artist. He was not a great personality; his work comes to us as a greater thing than his personality. When we read his verse, we think of the verse, not of John Keats. ARTHUR SYMONS [10]

But! but! is it then a poem's relation to the mind that endites which gives it value, or solely its internal organisation? No doubt, the traditional dependence on inspiration is equally misleading. As he [Paul Valéry] well says, rhymes are more proper to suggest

[9] "The Poetry of W. B. Yeats," *Southern Review*, 7 (Winter 1941–42), 446.
[10] *The Romantic Movement in English Poetry*, p. 306. Copyright 1909 by Constable and Co., Ltd. Reprinted by permission of the publisher.

thoughts, than thoughts rhymes; rhythm is hungry for matter, whereas matter may be indifferent to rhythm, or prefer to do without it. What we ask of a poet is not information about his states of mind or about the world, but a beautiful sequence of words and meanings which his skill has not let alone till it was beyond the reach of his imagination to suggest any further improvement. T. STURGE MOORE [11]

Honest criticism and sensitive appreciation are directed not upon the poet but upon the poetry. T. S. ELIOT [12]

The modern poet is to his audience an author, not a man. It is interested in his more generalized emotions, not in his relations with the life and people around him. Yet to himself the poet should be in the first place a man, not an author. He should not be conscious of a distinction between the sensations he gets from his immediate contact with things and the sensations he uses as the material of his art. EDGELL RICKWORD [13]

The Personal Element and the Work of Art

"The author in his work must be like God in the universe, present everywhere and visible nowhere; art being a second nature, the creator of this nature must act by similar methods; in each atom, in every aspect, there must be felt a hidden and infinite impassibility." GUSTAVE FLAUBERT [14]

[11] "A Poet and His Technique," *New Criterion*, 4 (October 1926), 685.
[12] *Selected Essays 1917–1932*, p. 7. Copyright 1932 by Harcourt, Brace and Co., and by Faber and Faber, Ltd. Reprinted by permission of the publishers.
[13] "The Use of 'Negative' Emotions," p. 72 in *Towards Standards of Criticism*, edited by F. R. Leavis. Copyright 1933 by Lawrence and Wishart, Ltd. Reprinted by permission of the publisher. This essay is reprinted in *Critiques and Essays in Criticism*, edited by R. W. Stallman. Copyright 1949 by Ronald Press.
[14] Quoted, p. 81, in *The Novel and the People*, by Ralph Fox. Copyright 1937 by Lawrence and Wishart, Ltd., and by Cobbett Press, Ltd., and 1945 by International Publishers. Reprinted by permission of the publishers.

In lyrical poetry (and by lyrical poetry we shall mean for the present such lyrical poetry as is frankly "about" the poet — Shelley's *Lines written in Dejection* is an example) this process of depersonalization is wrought out. What is poetical in a lyrical poem is not the mere presence of strong emotion and feelings but the imaginative apprehension of them. Hence though we may usefully distinguish different kinds of poetry, lyrical, dramatic, etc., yet all kinds of poetry are poetical for the same reason, that they express imaginative apprehension of an object, whether that object be the poet's own feelings, or someone else's, or a tree, or the moon. The *Lines written in Dejection* are poetry for the same reason that *King Lear* is poetry. The fact that there was once an individual who actually felt as Shelley's poem records is of no poetic importance whatsoever. Our awareness that there was once a person who felt these emotions is as unimportant for our poetic enjoyment as the fact that there never was a person who actually spoke the lines

> To-morrow, and to-morrow, and to-morrow,
> Creeps in this petty pace from day to day.

For poetry, Shelley is no more an historical person than Macbeth; for the poetic consciousness simply is not concerned with history and actual sequence. D. G. JAMES [15]

Let us retreat for a moment on Henry James's notion that as the artist is successful he disappears into his work and there is nothing to say about him as a man; only as he is a failure does he become interesting, does the man cry out for treatment, does his role become heroic and pitiful. R. P. BLACKMUR [16]

Lawrence never succeeded in severing the umbilical cord between himself and his work, and the poems, therefore, instead of achieving wholeness, an organic unity with themselves, point always

[15] *Scepticism and Poetry*, pp. 117–18. Copyright 1937 by Allen and Unwin, Ltd. Reprinted by permission of the publisher.
[16] "Tolstoi's Flight," *Kenyon Review,* 8 (Winter 1946), 141.

outward to an external centre in the history of their author, and this it is which makes them disintegral. D. S. SAVAGE [17]

It is clear that with Auden we are not dealing with a strongly personal poet, projecting in his work a unique vision of experience. The negative personality shown in the weak "I" and the pronounced tendency to write in the second person, and the lack of emotional depth reflected in an absence of verbal power . . . reveal him to be a "social" rather than a personal poet, and this is confirmed by his selection of subject and his attitude toward individuality. Auden's concern throughout is never with his personal experience; he does not deliberately approach life *through* his personal experience, but, leaving his own individuality on one side, he attempts to deal immediately with the larger life *outside* the individual. Throughout his work he is concerned to express a vision of society. D. S. SAVAGE [18]

The personality of the artist also affects the aesthetic "depth" of a creation. Everyone is familiar with the fact that violin tones sound mellow or thin according to the nature of the sound chamber over which the strings are stretched. Now personality in the subjective phase of creation has a role similar to the sound chamber or resonator in tone production. It serves as an amplifier or denudator of undertones and overtones of value. The result is an imaginative structure that is aesthetically subtle and rich or arid and commonplace. . . . The greater wealth of expressive values in the one work reflects a greater depth of value penetration of its creator. It is a product of his "realizations" of the subject and springs from the system of value inclinations and aspirations that he brings to the interpretation of the subject. Thus personality is influential in supplying not only a peculiar idiom and accentual structure to a symbolic system but also an expressive wealth and richness or an expressive bareness and poverty. It may, indeed, mark a difference

[17] *The Personal Principle*, p. 135. Copyright 1944 by George Routledge and Sons, Ltd. Reprinted by permission of the author and the publisher.
[18] *Ibid.*, p. 164. Reprinted by permission of the author and the publisher.

as wide as that between glitter and gold. Two works may brilliantly bespeak in vocabulary and syntax the unmistakable characteristics of the artists. Yet they may be the opposite in expressive density, one meretriculous and thin, the other solid and mellow-toned. D. W. GOTSHALK [19]

The Personal Element in Poetic Appreciation

Literary criticism can be no more than a reasoned account of the feeling produced upon the critic by the book he is criticizing. Criticism can never be a science: it is, in the first place, much too personal, and in the second, it is concerned with values that science ignores. The touchstone is emotion, not reason. We judge a work of art by its effect on our sincere and vital emotion, and nothing else. All the critical twiddle-twaddle about style and form, all this pseudo-scientific classifying and analysing of books in an imitation-botanical fashion, is mere impertinence and mostly dull jargon.

A critic must be able to *feel* the impact of a work of art in all its complexity and its force. To do so, he must be a man of force and complexity himself, which few critics are. A man with a paltry, impudent nature will never write anything but paltry, impudent criticism. And a man who is *emotionally* educated is rare as a phoenix. The more scholastically educated a man is generally, the more he is an emotional boor. D. H. LAWRENCE [20]

Criticism may influence output, correct taste and comment on social and political movements, but it is also in Mr. Murry's words

[19] *Art and the Social Order*, pp. 63–64. Copyright 1947 by the University of Chicago Press. Reprinted by permission of the publisher.
[20] *Phoenix*, p. 539. Copyright 1936 by the Viking Press, and by William Heinemann, Ltd. Reprinted by permission of the publishers.

a 'particular art of literature' and 'a means of self-expression for the critic.' The critic expresses himself through other artists. He must do so without distorting their vision, but he must in fact communicate himself to the reader. And the value of the personality which he communicates is no different from that of many other artists. He possesses a powerful personality and through his meditation on life and art he acquires a peculiar wisdom of his own. Among modern critics Lawrence is a pre-eminent example. His criticism has had far less practical influence than Mr. Eliot's; but *Studies in Classic American Literature* and *Phoenix* are not simply great criticism; they show that Lawrence, with his immense emphasis on life, possessed incomparably the most powerful personality among modern European critics and that from an artistic point of view his criticism is satisfying in a way that Mr. Eliot's is not.

I think that we can assume that in criticism, as in other forms of literature, there are two elements — the eternal and the transitory. We read some critics — Gourmont is an example — because they can still sharpen our own perceptions and because their judgements still seem to be valid, but the personality which they express is neither very attractive nor very impressive. On the other hand, we go on reading the work of certain dead critics long after it has ceased to offer practical assistance and in spite of the apparent wrongness of its judgements because of the personality of the critic. It is for this reason that though Johnson's particular judgements are no longer of great interest to us and his methods are outmoded, *The Lives of the Poets* with their massive common sense remain great criticism and great literature which we continue to read and re-read. MARTIN TURNELL [21]

The end of the enjoyment of poetry is a pure contemplation from which all the accidents of personal emotion are removed; thus we aim to see the object as it really is and find a meaning for the words of Arnold. And without a labour which is largely a labour

[21] "An Essay on Criticism," *Dublin Review*, 444 (Last Quarter 1948), 95.

of the intelligence, we are unable to attain that state of vision *amor intellectualis Dei.* T. S. ELIOT [22]

It follows, then, at least in the crudest and most obvious sense of the words, that the thing presented to us in any poem is not and never can be the personality of the poet. . . . I look with his eyes [the poet's], not at him. He, for the moment, will be precisely what I do not see. . . . The poet is not a man who asks me to look at *him*; he is a man who says "look at that" and points; the more I follow the pointing of his finger the less I can possibly see of *him.* C. S. LEWIS [23]

Now comes the crucial point. While we are reading *The Ancient Mariner* we forget our astronomy and geography and daily ethics. Do we not also forget the author? Does not Samuel Taylor Coleridge, lecturer, opium eater, and dragoon, disappear with the rest of the world of information? We remember him before we begin the poem and after we finish it, but during the poem nothing exists but the poem. Consequently while we read *The Ancient Mariner* a change takes place in it. It becomes anonymous, like the *Ballad of Sir Patrick Spens.* And here is the point I would support: that all literature tends towards a condition of anonymity, and that, so far as words are creative, a signature merely distracts us from their true significance. I do not say literature "ought" not to be signed. . . . It wants not to be signed. That puts my point. It is always tugging in that direction and saying in effect: "I, not my author, exist really." E. M. FORSTER [24]

Housman's poetry needs finally a key, a key which can come only from our knowledge of the poet. This is really an indictment of

[22] *The Sacred Wood*, pp. 14-15. Copyright 1920 and 1928 by Methuen and Co., Ltd., and 1921 and 1930 by Alfred A. Knopf, Inc. Reprinted by permission of the author and the publishers.

[23] *The Personal Heresy*, p. 11. Copyright 1939 by Oxford University Press. Reprinted by permission of the publisher.

[24] *Anonymity: An Enquiry*, pp. 14-15. Copyright 1925 by the Hogarth Press. Reprinted by permission of the publisher.

the poetry, but to Housman it would not have seemed a defect. His own taste in English poetry was plainly a preference for that poetry which might be interpreted as personal statement. His formula, "transfusion of emotion," implies a communication theory of poetry in its most inchoate form. But most of us for whom poetry is a making or a creation, and not a communication, will find flaws in his work arising from the effort to communicate, and what others regard as code or incantation will seem bad workmanship. LAWRENCE LEIGHTON [25]

Where there is no external test of the validity of a writer's work, we fail to distinguish between the truth of his view of life and the personality which makes it plausible; so that in our reading, we may be simply yielding ourselves to one seductive personality after another. The first requisite usually held up by the promoters of personality is that a man should "be himself"; and this "sincerity" is considered more important than that the self in question should, socially and spiritually, be a good or a bad one. This view of personality is merely an assumption on the part of the modern world, and is no more tenable than several other views which have been held at various times and in several places. The personality thus expressed, the personality which fascinates us in the work of philosophy or art, tends naturally to be the *unregenerate* personality, partly self-deceived and partly irresponsible, and because of its freedom, terribly *limited* by prejudice and self-conceit, capable of much good or great mischief according to the natural goodness or impurity of the man: and we are all, naturally, impure. T. S. ELIOT [26]

Poets and critics all down the ages have always had to meet the challenge that poetry must have a rational *use*, and the obvious reply to that is that poetry can and does educate and inspire human nature on the moral plane. As that is a level on which

---

[25] "One View of Housman," *Poetry*, 52 (May 1938), 95.

[26] *After Strange Gods*, pp. 62–63. Copyright 1934 by Faber and Faber, Ltd., and by Harcourt, Brace and Co. Reprinted by permission of the publishers.

everyone can understand poetry, whereas real artistic sensibility is a much rarer quality, the natural result is the instinct to assess the value of poetry in terms of what it *says* rather than in terms of what it *does;* to judge it not by the quality of consciousness it calls into being, but by the quality of rational activity it is likely to promote. The critical standpoint is then shifted from the poem as a work of art to the poem as an illustration of the personality of the poet, and that in turn leads to criticism like that of Dean Inge on Donne: "He was no gentleman, and a very equivocal Christian"; or of Eliot on Shelley: "He was humorless, pedantic, self-centered, and sometimes almost a blackguard." ELIZABETH DREW [27]

"Even the best poetry, when it is at all personal, needs the penumbra of its own time and place and circumstance to make it full and whole." The writer is D. H. Lawrence, in the preface to his *Collected Poems*, and he proceeds: "if we knew a little more of Shakespeare's self and circumstance how much more complete the Sonnets would be to us, how their strange, torn edges would be softened and merged into a whole body!" . . . And yet, should some discovery suddenly place us in possession of the answers — portraits of him and her, the very carcanet from which Shakespeare drew an illustration, the original "great verse" written to the fair friend by the rival poet, the date when the mortal moon endured her eclipse — would the Sonnets mean more? EDMUND BLUNDEN [28]

The great development of biographical criticism, however, came not in England but in France, with Sainte-Beuve's *Causeries du Lundi*, beginning in the middle of the last century. He almost perfectly defined the method with his statement:

[27] In collaboration with John L. Sweeney, *Directions in Modern Poetry*, pp. 176–77. Copyright 1940 by W. W. Norton and Co., Inc. Reprinted by permission of the publisher.
[28] "Behind the Poem," *Times Literary Supplement*, 2173 (September 25, 1943), 462.

Real criticism, as I define it, consists in studying each person, that is, each author, each talent, according to the conditions of his nature, in order to make a vivid and pregnant description of him so that he can later be classified and put in his proper place in the hierarchy of art.

This principle of the identity of the man and his work led Sainte-Beuve into a rather elaborate study of the private lives of the literary, from their physical appearance to the elaborate trivia of their daily routine. From this jumble he produced what few of the literary gossips who have followed his method since ever produced: real insights into the man and his work. On occasion, as in his essay on Gibbon, he pushed the realm of biography into an exhaustive study of the relationship between the author and his time and environment, anticipating the direction the method would later take with his chief disciple, Taine. Taine began as a biographical critic like Sainte-Beuve (and his treatment of Pope largely in terms of his physical infirmities in the *History of English Literature* shows that he never wholly renounced it), but he soon converted the method into an emphasis on *race, moment, milieu*, and thus became chiefly a social determinist critic of literature, in the tradition largely represented by Marxist criticism in our time.

A line of thought essentially German was added to the brew. Goethe had announced that art springs from disease, is a kind of blood-letting. Schopenhauer turned this to an emphasis on the artist's suffering, and Nietzsche added the modification that the art is not only the product of the disease, but a kind of record of it, that every philosophy is a confession, "a species of involuntary and unconscious autobiography." Max Nordau made news of the doctrine that genius is a form of neurosis in his book *Degeneration*, and recently Thomas Mann has been frequently identified with a view of art as produced out of sickness and neurosis, the way the pearl is produced from the oyster, with that art then at once the product of that sickness, its record, and its transcendence. This is, of course, more or less the "wound and the bow" theory that Edmund Wilson has made his own; but with the emphasis taken off disease and neurosis, reduced to a simple determinism of the nature of the life over the works, it is the characteristic assumption of present-day biographical criticism. STANLEY EDGAR HYMAN [29]

[29] *The Armed Vision*, p. 119. Copyright 1948 by Alfred A. Knopf, Inc. Reprinted by permission of the publisher.

VII

The
Problem of
Belief
in Poetry

A man's poetry is a kind of world, and must have in it sun, moon, and stars, as well as plants and animals. He may himself create his greater and lesser lights, but it is a tremendous advantage to him to find them already placed there for him. He has so much the more time to get on with his garden of Eden — and the man, woman, serpent, and fatal tree require no inconsiderable attention.

F. Cudworth Flint, review in *Symposium*, 3 (April 1932), 247.

The Problem Defined

Since poetry, as a way of living, brings the whole personality into activity (in this sense, poetry prevents sentimentality, because it enables the interest to be distributed as widely as possible), we must preserve poetry; we must not endanger it by challenging science on its own ground. We must not go to science to get evidence for the sighing of the grass. We must rely on our own strength to live as poetry enables us to live and believe without belief.

And this independence of poetry from belief refers not only to scientific beliefs. In a passage indicating his awareness of the difficulties in his position, Dr. Richards writes: "A great deal of poetry can, of course, be written for which total independence of all beliefs is an easy matter. But it is never poetry of the more important kind, because the temptation to introduce beliefs is a sign and measure of the importance of the attitudes involved." (*Science and Poetry*, p. 86.) And to-day, he points out, the temptation is strongest to introduce beliefs, not about religion or sexual freedom as formerly, but about political ideology. And yet even in regard to such beliefs, "the necessity for independence is increasing" (p. 86).

In short, poetic utterance, as a fact of mind, recognises no criticism made of it as an utterance about a supposed state of affairs, whether that criticism bases itself on science or on sociology.

In this way Dr. Richards attempts to end through poetry the characteristic difficulties of those held by the bourgeois tradition. We have suggested the importance in the reading of poetry of the reader's identification of himself with the poet and with humanity. Just as the conflict around social solidarity interferes with the enjoyment of poetry, so, on the other hand, the enjoyment of poetry can offer a substitute satisfaction for the impulses of social solidarity which find no other recognised activity. And if the poetry is enjoyed without reference to what the poet is saying about objective reality and to the implications of his attitude in social action, if literature as a whole is regarded as an attitude which cannot be disproved by political ideology and must be maintained independently of it, then one has apparently escaped from the situation which inhibits emotion in actual life. For the source of that inhibition, as we saw, is the inability to make a decision in the issue before society to-day: the individual is aware that the class with which he feels solidarity is working for the destruction of culture; but he cannot identify himself with the class in whom he may see the hope of culture. If he can enjoy the utterance as a fact of mind, irrespective of the utterance to be tested in practice about the state of affairs, then he can identify himself with society through its past cultural activity without having to think or make up his mind about the practical activity of society and his own share in it now.

Thus Dr. Richards' method of escape from all the problems centering around the bourgeois "we" is to make poetry a substitute for social solidarity in action and to isolate it from the practical issues of such action. ALICK WEST [1]

[1] *Crisis and Criticism*, pp. 76–77. Copyright 1937 by Lawrence and Wishart, Ltd. Reprinted by permission of the publisher.

The absence of intellectual belief need not cripple emotional be-lief, though evidently enough in some persons it may. But the habit of attaching emotional belief only to intellectually certified ideas is strong in some people; it is encouraged by some forms of education; it is perhaps becoming, through the increased prestige of science, more common. For those whom it conquers, it means "Good-bye to poetry." I. A. RICHARDS [2]

By distinguishing these two kinds of belief — let me call them *verifiable belief* and *imaginative assent* — I think it is possible to clear up the literary dilemma. If the kind of belief the poet puts into poetry and we must receive from it is verifiable belief, then clearly we can understand very little poetry. On the other hand, if it is imaginative assent that we are talking about, *that* is quite clearly asked for and indeed part and parcel of the understanding of good poetry. And there is in practice nothing to prevent our giving this imaginative assent to all kinds of different views. Only imaginative assent is needed, or, as a rule, possible in reading the poem, and the difficulty in giving it in the cases we are considering seems to come from our habit of treating it as though it were verifiable belief. We have secondary derived attitudes towards veri-fiable beliefs and we take them up with regard to imaginative assents also. Hence, I think, these difficulties; but of course there are many other difficulties in understanding poetry.

The distinction if it is valid appears to have wide bearing and drastic consequences. Imaginative assents, unlike verifiable beliefs, are not subject to the laws of thought. We can easily hold two or more mutually incompatible views together in imaginative as-sent if their incompatibility is merely logical. I think it is relevant to remark here how often religions and philosophies present us with self-contradictions as their central secrets. Imaginative assents are not ordered logically — they have another principle of order based on the compatibilities of movements of the will and the feel-

[2] *Practical Criticism*, p. 278. Copyright 1929 by Harcourt, Brace and Co., and by George Routledge and Sons, Ltd. Reprinted by permission of the publishers.

ings and the desires. This order it is the business of serious poets to explore and follow. But we know, I should say, hardly anything about it as yet in terms of theory; though we know a good deal in terms of practice.

If they are not subject to the laws of thought, it seems doubtful whether they can be said to be either true or false — in the sense in which "true" and "false" apply to verifiable beliefs. A verifiable belief is shown to be false by failure at its juncture with actuality. An imaginative assent cannot be shown to be false in this way. Suppose we define "true" and "false" for verifiable belief as correspondence or non-correspondence with actuality; shall we be able to apply this sense to imaginative assents? The question is very difficult. We do no doubt often feel that the views to which we give imaginative assent or dissent are true or false in this sense, that the picture does represent or misrepresent something which really is so or otherwise. We say to ourselves, "Although I can't prove or disprove this view of the universe or of man in a scientific way, yet it must really be a view, right or wrong, about something, not just an imaginative picture of nothing." And so traditionally these views have nearly always been asserted or denied. I. A. RICHARDS [3]

The name "pseudo-statement," given by Mr. I. A. Richards to such a declaration as "Beauty is Truth," is unfortunate. A "pseudo-statement" sounds a very poor thing — a sham statement. But I find, on consulting Mr. Richards' admirable essay *Science and Poetry*, that this apparently contemptuous nuance in the word is unintentional. Mr. Richards' intention is more clearly given in the following passage from his essay:

A pseudo-statement is "true" if it suits and serves some attitude or links together attitudes which on other grounds are desirable. This kind of truth is so opposed to scientific "truth" that it is a pity to use so similar a word but at present it is difficult to avoid the malpractice. . . . A pseudo-statement is a form of words which

[3] "Belief," *Symposium*, 1 (October 1930), 435-37.

is justified entirely by its effect in releasing or organizing our impulses and attitudes (pp. 58–9).

It is clear from this that Mr. Richards' term "pseudo-statement" is not derogatory in intention, however much it may be in effect. A little later in the same essay, Mr. Richards writes:

On the whole true statements are of more service to us than false statements. None the less we do not and, at present, cannot order our emotions and attitudes by true statements alone. Nor is there any probability that we ever shall contrive to do so. This is one of the great new dangers to which civilization is exposed. Countless pseudo-statements — about God, about the universe, about human nature, the relations of mind to mind, about the soul, its rank and destiny — pseudo-statements which are pivotal points in the organization of the mind, vital to its well-being, have suddenly become, for sincere, honest and informal minds, impossible to believe. For centuries they have been believed; now they are gone irrecoverably; *and the knowledge which has killed them is not of a kind upon which an equally fine organization of the mind can be traced* (p. 60).

Here a "pseudo-statement" is equivalent to a "false statement," an equivalence which is, surely, unwarrantable. For in that case we are involved in the necessity of organizing our emotions and attitudes by statements which we know to be false.

A poetic or metaphorical statement, because it is not "true" in a certain limited sense of correspondence to "fact," is not false. Take Shakespeare's "Ripeness is all." It is an assertion concerning the moral (or as I should say) the metabiological nature of man. Neither logic nor science has any means of checking it. If we paraphrase it into "Maturity is the most necessary achievement of man," most of the unique suggestion is lost; but even in that impoverished form, it is not false. It may perfectly well be true. The assertion that "God is Love" may perfectly well bear, for one who does not believe in the existence of God, a profound meaning; to such a mind it is neither true nor false. It is an inevitably metaphorical expression of something which, for lack of a better phrase, we will provisionally call "spiritual truth." JOHN MIDDLETON MURRY [4]

Here, then, the dualism is seen in all its sharpness: a statement is scientifically true if it corresponds with an outwardly verifiable fact; poetically true — i.e., true as a pseudo-statement — if, regardless of whether or not it corresponds with any outward fact, it successfully organizes some phase of our impulsive and emotional life.

In an article "Between Truth and Truth" [in *Symposium*, April 1931] Dr. Richards elaborated his dualism. Two years earlier, in *Practical Criticism*, he had pursued more fully the question of communication in literature. From that standpoint he now reformulated his position. A poem, he now declared, describes and communicates something, but what? "Two alternatives, and not more I think, are before us, two main senses of 'describe' and 'communicate'. . . . The first sense is that in which a form of words describes or communicates the state of mind or experience of the speaker; the second is that in which it describes or communicates some state of affairs or fact which the speaker is thinking of or knowing (something in all but one case, that of introspection, *other than* the experience which is his thinking of it or knowing it). . . . To take an extreme instance, when a man says 'I'm damned!' he may be saying that eternal judgment has gone against him or showing that he is surprised or annoyed."

Dr. Richards then turns to John Clare's description of the primrose —

> With its crimp and curdled leaf
> And its little brimming eye,

about which, in a previous article, Mr. J. Middleton Murry had remarked that it "is surely an accurate description, but accurate with an accuracy unknown to and unachievable by science." Richards complains: Mr. Murry "does not say explicitly whether he takes it as a description of an object (the primrose) or of the ex-

[4] "Beauty Is Truth," *Symposium*, 1 (October 1930), 495–97.

perience of seeing one." And he adds: "It seems to me not likely that there will be widespread disagreement with the view that the description applies to the experience of seeing or imagining a primrose rather than to actual primroses."

Clearly Dr. Richards has fallen without realizing it into the trap of metaphysics. This is particularly evident in a footnote to the article just mentioned, where he distinguishes the "sensed or imagined primrose" from the "inferred or constructed common or gardener's primrose" on the ground that the former lacks such scientifically determinable characteristics as weight! Now take this in connection with his distinction in *Coleridge on Imagination* (1934) between "utterances as facts of mind" and "the supposed states of affairs which we take them to be utterances about," and Dr. Richards' general presupposition becomes clear. It is the assumption of scientific positivism, in line with Comte and Carnap, that scientifically determinable objects, like the gardener's primrose which can be weighed, are the only objects there are, and the only objects which can significantly be talked about: that when a poet appears to be talking about anything else he is really not talking about anything objective at all; he is merely representing the history of his mind, "his feelings and attitudes in the moment of speaking, and conditions of their governance in the future" (*op. cit.*). To be sure, Dr. Richards regards the poet's total poetic speech act as "a larger and more complex whole" which besides expressing the poet's subjective experiences does also refer to a supposed state of affairs in the actual world; that is to say, the poetry has a referential and denotative as well as an expressive and connotative function. But it is just in this way of stating the double function of poetry that I think Dr. Richards goes astray. For connotations too may be outwardly referential. Naturally I do not deny that poetry does and should express in some sense the poet's feelings, nor that it may and should have for a reader the beneficent and equilibrating effects described in *Principles of Literary Criticism*. All this is important, but it is not, strictly speaking, the business of the literary critic. Every science has its proper object, and this is as true of literary criticism as of any other science. The object of literary criticism is the poem under consideration, and not either the poet's supposed feelings or the reader's expected benefits. The task of a semantics of poetry, then, is to find a language whereby the nature and reference of the poetic statement (which I take to be a more suitable and less misleading term than "pseudo-statement") can be articulated without evasion into a field of discourse peripheral and alien to poetry.

The answer, it seems to me, is this. A poetic statement differs from a literal statement not, as Dr. Richards thinks, in that the one has a merely subjective, the other an objective reference, — at least this is an unnecessary and generally irrelevant difference — but in their manner of asserting. There are differences of what may be called *assertive weight*. A literal statement asserts heavily; it can do so because its terms are solid. A poetic statement on the other hand, consisting as it does in a conjunction or association of plurisigns, has no such solid foundation, and affirms with varying degrees of lightness.

. . .

A poetic statement, then, does not assert its claims so heavily as a proposition; its truth is more fragile. A poem is a complex tension among variously related plurisigns. Some phases of the poetic tension have more of an assertive character than others; and as the assertive character becomes more pronounced a phase of the poetic tension may approximate the character of a literal statement, without ceasing however to be much more. A phase of the poetic tension may contain a literal statement as one of its aspects. PHILIP WHEELWRIGHT [5]

The whole problem turns on the question whether emotional values can be maintained in a scientific universe. Mr. Richards is very well aware — as I know from conversations with him — and I know no one who is more aware — that emotions and sentiments

[5] "On the Semantics of Poetry," *Kenyon Review*, 2 (Summer 1940), 271–74, 275.

appear and disappear in the course of human history, and rapidly too; that certain sentiments of the late Middle Ages, which we should be glad to have if we could, have completely disappeared, like the secrets of the best stained glass or Byzantine enamel-work. It seems quite possible, as Mr. Richards suggests, that a future increase in scientific knowledge may be accompanied by a steady deterioration in "spirituality" (the word is mine, not Mr. Richards'). Mr. Richards thinks that the only thing that can save us from "mental chaos" is poetry, a poetry of the future detached from all belief. What this poetry will be I cannot conceive. If his description of the "poetry of belief" were clearer, we should also have a clearer idea of what he means by the poetry of unbelief. If there is such a distinction as he draws, between the poetry of all the past and the poetry of all the future, then I do not think that he is justified in making exceptions of such poems as *King Lear*. ["We need no beliefs, and indeed we must have none, if we are to read *King Lear*." (*Science and Poetry*, p. 72.)] If he is right, then I think that the chances for the future are not so bright as he hopes. Poetry "is capable of saving us," he says; it is like saying that the wall-paper will save us when the walls have crumbled. It is a revised version of Literature and Dogma. T. S. ELIOT [6]

The theory of poetic belief and understanding here employed for a particular study is similar to that maintained by Mr. I. A. Richards (see his *Practical Criticism*, pp. 179ff. and pp. 271ff.). I say "similar," because my own *general* theory is still embryonic, and Mr. Richards's also is capable of much further development. I cannot therefore tell how far the similarity extends; but for those who are interested in the subject, I should point out one respect in which my view differs from that of Mr. Richards; and then proceed to qualify my own tentative conclusions.

I am in agreement with Mr. Richards's statement on p. 271 *(op. cit.).* I agree for the reason that if you hold any contradictory theory you deny, I believe, the existence of "literature" as well

[6] "Literature, Science, and Dogma," *Dial*, 82 (March 1927), 243.

as of "literary criticism." We may raise the question whether "literature" exists; but for certain purposes, such as the purpose of this essay on Dante, we must assume that there is literature and literary appreciation; we must assume that the reader can obtain the full "literary" or (if you will) "aesthetic" enjoyment without sharing the beliefs of the author. *If* there is "literature," *if* there is "poetry," then it must be possible to have full literary or poetic appreciation without sharing the beliefs of the poet. That is as far as my thesis goes in the present essay. It may be argued whether there is literature, whether there is poetry, and whether there is any meaning in the term "full appreciation." But I have assumed for this essay that these things exist and that these terms are understood.

I deny, in short, that the reader must share the beliefs of the poet in order to enjoy the poetry fully. I have also asserted that we can distinguish between Dante's beliefs as a man and his beliefs as a poet. But we are forced to believe that there is a particular relation between the two, and that the poet "means what he says." If we learned, for instance, that *De Rerum Natura* was a Latin exercise which Dante had composed for relaxation after completing the *Divine Comedy*, and published under the name of one Lucretius, I am sure that our capacity for enjoying either poem would be mutilated. Mr. Richards's statement *(Science and Poetry*, p. 76 footnote) that a certain writer has effected "a complete severance between his poetry and *all* beliefs" is to me incomprehensible.

If you deny the theory that full poetic appreciation is possible without belief in what the poet believed, you deny the existence of "poetry" as well as "criticism"; and if you push this denial to its conclusion, you will be forced to admit that there is very little poetry that you can appreciate, and that your appreciation of it will be a function of your philosophy or theology or something else. . . .

In short, both the view I have taken in this essay, and the view which contradicts it, are, if pushed to the end, what I call heresies (not, of course, in the theological, but in a more general sense). Each is true only within a limited field of discourse, but unless you limit fields of discourse, you can have no discourse at all. Orthodoxy can only be found in such contradictions, though it must be remembered that a pair of contradictions may *both* be false, and that not all pairs of contradictions make up a truth.

And I confess to considerable difficulty in analysing my own feelings, a difficulty which makes me hesitate to accept Mr. Richards's theory of "pseudo-statements." On reading the line which he uses,

Beauty is truth, truth beauty . . .

I am at first inclined to agree with him because this statement of equivalence means nothing to me. But on re-reading the whole Ode, this line strikes me as a serious blemish on a beautiful poem; and the reason must be either that I fail to understand it, or that it is a statement which is untrue. And I suppose that Keats meant something by it, however remote his truth and his beauty may have been from these words in ordinary use. And I am sure that he would have repudiated any explanation of the line which called it a pseudo-statement. On the other hand the line I have often quoted of Shakespeare,

Ripeness is all,

or the line I have quoted of Dante,

La sua voluntade è nostra pace,

strikes very differently on my ear. I observe that the prepositions in these words are very different in kind, not only from that of Keats, but from each other. The statement of Keats seems to me meaningless: or perhaps, the fact that it is grammatically meaningless conceals another meaning from me. The statement of Shakespeare seems to me to have profound emotional meaning, with, at least, no literal fallacy. And the statement of Dante seems to me *literally true.* And I confess that it has more beauty for me now, when my own experience has deepened its meaning, than it did when I first read it. So I can only conclude that I cannot, in practice, wholly separate my poetic appreciation from my personal beliefs. Also that the distinction between a statement and a pseudo-statement is not always, in particular instances, possible to establish. The theory of Mr. Richards is, I believe, incomplete until he defines the species of religious, philosophical, scientific, and other beliefs, as well as that of "everyday" belief.

I have tried to make clear some of the difficulties inhering in my own theory. Actually, one probably has more pleasure in the poetry when one shares the beliefs of the poet. On the other hand there is a distinct pleasure in enjoying poetry as poetry when one does *not* share the beliefs, analogous to the pleasure of "mastering" other men's philosophical systems. It would appear that "literary appreciation" is an abstraction, and pure poetry a phantom; and that both in creation and enjoyment much always enters which is, from the point of view of "Art," irrelevant. T. S. ELIOT [7]

"Beauty is Truth, Truth Beauty": this enigmatic proposition has meaning only in relation to the total intention concretely embodied in the poem itself. The proposition is addressed here to the figures on the urn.* Thus, the meaning of "Truth" is located in the fourth stanza: "Truth" corresponds to "reality."

> What little town by river or sea shore,
> Or mountain-built with peaceful citadel,
>   Is emptied of this folk, this pious morn?
> And, little town, thy streets for evermore
>   Will silent be; and not a soul to tell
>   Why thou art desolate, can e'er return.

That key word "emptied" points to the poet's attitude towards reality, as F. R. Leavis says. In contemplating this scene, since it does not belong to the timeless world of the urn, time intrudes. Here the fantasy world of pure joy, imaged in the beauty of the

[7] *Selected Essays 1917–1932*, pp. 229–31. Copyright 1932 by Harcourt, Brace and Co., and by Faber and Faber, Ltd. Reprinted by permission of the publishers.

timeless urn world, is destroyed by time's painful intrusion in the
image of the emptied town to which

> not a soul to tell
> Why thou art desolate, can e'er return.

The poet's vision of eternity, of which the urn is symbol, we as
observers experience momentarily. The urn itself is "silent form"
and it speaks by "teasing us out of thought." "It is as enigmatic
as eternity is," Cleanth Brooks declares; "for, like eternity, its history is beyond time, outside time, and for this very reason be-
wilders our time-ridden minds: it teases us." The *Ode on a Grecian
Urn* achieves the dictum of its theme.

. . .

Keats' ode, its sculptured figures "motionless in a moment of
vision," *creates* (as Proust defined the experience) "a fragment of
time in its pure state." To experience pure present, that is eternity.
And

> that is all
> Ye know on earth, and all ye need to know.

R. W. STALLMAN [8]

* "For them Beauty *is* Truth because their experience is limited to the
beautiful as depicted on the Urn. . . ." (Letter in the *Times Literary Supplement* for February 5, 1938, by Mr. G. St. Quintin.) He reads the "ye" of the
final line as addressed to the urn figures. This reading — the only possible critical reading — points our interpretation into, rather than out of, the framed
meaning of the poem. Geoffrey Tillotson quotes St. Quintin's letter in his
preface to *Essays in Criticism and Research* (1942), p. xv.

The Problem of Belief in Poetic Creation

It is almost the mark of the poet of genuine merit in our time —
the poet who writes serious works with an intellectual aspect
which are nonetheless poetry — that he performs his work in the

[8] "Keats the Apollinian," *University of Toronto Quarterly*, 16 (January
1947), 156.

light of an insight, a group of ideas, and a faith, with the discipline that flows from them, which taken together form a view of life most readers cannot share, and which, furthermore, most readers feel as repugnant, or sterile, or simply inconsequential.

All this is to say generally . . . that our culture is incomplete with regard to poetry; and the poet has to provide for himself in that quarter where authority and value are derived. It may be that no poet ever found a culture complete for his purpose; it was a welcome and arduous part of his business to make it so. Dante, we may say, completed for poetry the Christian culture of his time, which was itself the completion of centuries. But there was at hand for Dante, and as a rule in the great ages of poetry, a fundamental agreement or convention between the poet and his audience about the validity of the view of life of which the poet deepened the reality and spread the scope. There is no such agreement today. R. P. BLACKMUR [9]

If proof were needed of the confusion and multiplicity of belief in our world verification could be found readily in the wild diversity of poetic styles. Behind the question of multiple styles there is the question of multiple personality.

. . .

The need for belief has not disappeared. The poets, lacking any formulation of ideals or values, attempt to rise out of their unnatural amorality. In one direction they move toward the excesses of D. H. Lawrence — the destruction of *mores* that devitalize man; in another direction they move toward the fantastic. One poet, commenting on belief in our day, said that the modern mind causes worlds to fall neat and steady — "but the mobs march on with Mrs. Eddy." The substitute beliefs of many poets are frequently devoid of philosophical, religious or spiritual value regardless of the sophistication of the minds that have devised them.

Obviously the tap root of the art of Dante, Milton and Blake

[9] *The Expense of Greatness*, pp. 76–77. Copyright 1940 by Arrow Editions. Reprinted by permission of the author.

was their faith. The furious searching after belief exhibited by
our poets is proof that we regard belief as the realm within which
the poet's imagination must be free to play if he would create.
The phenomena are these: The poet finds a belief if he can; fail-
ing this, he constructs a cosmography in which he pretends to
believe. If, as Shapiro says,

> poetry insofar as it depends
> Upon belief succeeds in ratio
> To the success of the belief itself,

the plight of our poets is grave.

. . .

In place of faith, in terms of which the visions of a Dante,
Milton or Blake or the visions of the tragedians were possible, the
contemporary poet has a reverence for *facts*. Lacking a vision of
the universe in which the facts might be subsumed and made
meaningful he frequently falls back upon the neutral theories of
sociology or economics. In this way his insights are tangential,
fragmentary. And to his quest of understanding the facts he
brings his modern's reverence for objectivity. In place of a vision
by which the people of an entire culture might be spiritually en-
riched we have personal creeds and various persuasions. Our poets
are obliged to fall back upon a personal quest for values. WILLIAM
VAN O'CONNOR [10]

Art and Religion are means to similar states of mind. And if
we are licensed to lay aside the science of aesthetics and, going behind our emotion and its object, consider what is in the mind of
the artist, we may say, loosely enough, that art is a manifestation
of the religious sense. If it be an expression of emotion — as I am
persuaded that it is — it is an expression of that emotion which is
the vital force in every religion, or, at any rate, it expresses an
emotion felt for that which is the essence of all. We may say that
both art and religion are manifestations of man's religious sense,

[10] "Shapiro on Rime," *Kenyon Review*, 8 (Winter 1946), 116, 119–20, 120–21.

if by "man's religious sense" we mean his sense of ultimate reality.
CLIVE BELL [11]

But the distinction of art from philosophy (taken widely as including all thinking of the real) brings with it other distinctions,
among which that of art from *myth* occupies the foremost place.
For myth, to him who believes it, presents itself as the revelation
and knowledge of reality as opposed to unreality, — a reality that
drives away other beliefs as illusory or false. It can become art
only for him who no longer believes in it and avails himself of
mythology as a metaphor, of the austere world of the gods as of
a beautiful world, of God as of an image of sublimity. Considered,
then, in its genuine reality, in the soul of the believer and not of
the unbeliever, it is religion and not simple fancy; and religion is
philosophy, philosophy in process of becoming, philosophy more
or less imperfect, but philosophy, as philosophy is religion, more or
less purified and elaborated, in continuous process of elaboration
and purification, but religion or thought of the Absolute or Eternal. Art lacks the thought that is necessary ere it can become myth
and religion, and the faith that is born of thought; the artist
neither believes nor disbelieves in his image: he produces it.
BENEDETTO CROCE [12]

Philosophy may enter the poetic economy in more than one
sense. Most simply, a poem may have for its purpose the communication of independently received or conceived ideas — ideas
that could be formulated accurately enough, though perhaps less
agreeably, in plain logical prose. The poem and its ideas, on that
basis, are distinct essences, strategically united for some reason
extrinsic to the nature of either. Lucretius is proof that this kind
of poetry, or something approximating to it, can rise to mag-
nificence. Nevertheless the Lucretian mode of composition is of

[11] *Art*, p. 92. Copyright 1914 and 1947 by Chatto and Windus, Ltd. Reprinted by permission of the publisher.
[12] "The Breviary of Aesthetic," *Rice Institute Pamphlet*, 2 (December
1915), 237.

ambiguous validity; it plays into the hands of the stubbornly literal interpreter, who in the interests of journalism or pedagogy regards the philosophy of a poem as equivalent to whatever trim propositions can be screened out of it. At bottom this critical misunderstanding rests on what may be called the fallacy of semantic atomism — the willingness to assume that plain open statements are sufficient for all purposes of authentic communication.

In poetry, however, plain statements are less rigid than they seem; a poetic proposition is fringed with its own irony. Its very existence is sometimes a happy accident; Eliot has testified that "a poem, or a passage of a poem, may tend to realize itself first as a particular rhythm before it reaches expression in words." Dionysius skips ahead of Apollo, although it is Apollo who lights the way. Rhythm and ideation, song and vision, collaborate in the poetic act; and their tension motivates — perhaps even is — the poem. To say this is but to reformulate the truism that philosophical and religious ideas are poetically interesting only so far as they are assimilated to the poetic mode of apprehension. PHILIP WHEEL-WRIGHT [13]

There is a kind of sensualism or aestheticism that has decreed in our day that theory is not poetical; as if all the images and emotions that enter a cultivated mind were not saturated with theory. The prevalence of such a sensualism or aestheticism would alone suffice to explain the impotence of the arts. The life of theory is not less human or less emotional than the life of sense; it is more typically human and more keenly emotional. Philosophy is a more intense sort of experience than common life is, just as pure and subtle music, heard in retirement, is something keener and more intense than the howling of storms or the rumble of cities. For this reason philosophy, when a poet is not mindless, enters in-

[13] "Eliot's Philosophical Themes," p. 96 in T. S. Eliot: A Study of His Writings by Several Hands (Focus Three), edited by B. Rajan. Copyright 1947 by Dennis Dobson, Ltd., and by Funk and Wagnalls Co. Reprinted by permission of the publishers.

evitably into his poetry, since it has entered into his life; or rather, the detail of things and the detail of ideas pass equally into his verse, when both alike lie in the path that has led him to his ideal. To object to theory in poetry would be like objecting to words there; for words, too, are symbols without the sensuous character of the things they stand for; and yet it is only by the net of new connexions which words throw over things, in recalling them, that poetry arises at all. Poetry is an attenuation, a rehandling, an echo of crude experience; it is itself a theoretic vision of things heard at arm's length.

Heard philosophies are sweet but those unheard may be sweeter. They may be more unmixed and more profound for being adopted unconsciously, for being lived rather than taught. This is not merely to say what might be said of every work of art and of every natural object, that it could be made the starting-point for a chain of inferences that should reveal the whole universe, like the flower in the crannied wall. It is to say, rather, that the vital straining towards an ideal, definite but latent, when it dominates a whole life, may express that ideal more fully than could the best-chosen words. GEORGE SANTAYANA [14]

Belief in poetry is not the same thing as belief in the propositions of physical science, which is concerned with a primary reality. The imaginative poet, using a concrete language of images, is not trying to prove a proposition or to state facts about the objective world, but to make statements about a secondary reality, the reality of the imagination, which, like religion, is not susceptible to the logic of primary reality. The poet's symbols do not need logical proof, being a matter of appeals, of appositeness. They are not meant to elicit a belief that must be acted on, but rather to arouse a belief that can only be felt. But the good poet does not set out deliberately to arouse a feeling: he simply depicts objects

[14] *Little Essays Drawn from the Writings of George Santayana*, edited by Logan Pearsall Smith, pp. 143-44. Copyright 1920 and 1934 by Charles Scribner's Sons, and by Constable and Co., Ltd. Reprinted by permission of the publishers.

that, if presented properly, discharge a feeling. It must be assumed, then, that the feeling resides in the depiction of the object if not in the object itself. In religious ritual the feeling is prearranged while in the poem it is discovered. But both poem and ritual must convince, must give the impression that the feeling was inevitable and yet alive. If the feeling is very compelling it has what is known as the truth of the imagination, the fact in fiction. JOHN VINCENT HEALY [15]

It is not the absolute, or objective, validity of a belief that vindicates the poetry; it is a gross over-simplification to maintain that a right belief makes a poem good and a wrong belief makes a poem bad. First, beliefs are not so easily sorted out into merely right and merely wrong; secondly, by the time a belief is embodied in a poem, it has suffered a biochemical change, has become blended inextricably with mood, picture, and drama. LOUIS MACNEICE [16]

The relation between belief or attitude and structural quality in poetry is not of course direct and simple. The position is that if a writer has a stable value standard he can more confidently present poetic situations in dialectical patterns than if he has none, for if he has none his symbols can have no certain meaning and therefore their relation to each other will be obscure. It would seem also that in an age of multiple faith, where the symbols become not meaningless but ambivalent, the dialectic can become most brilliant and most subtle. By an age of multiple faith we mean not an age of universal belief but an age where the poet and his public are equally receptive to two or more different sets of beliefs — as was John Donne, for example, for whom difference did not mean mutual exclusiveness as it came to mean in times that were intellectually more settled. There comes a point at which multiple belief can scarcely be distinguished from confused

[15] "Yeats and His Imagination," *Sewanee Review*, 54 (Autumn 1946), 655.
[16] *The Poetry of W. B. Yeats*, p. 231. Copyright 1941 by Oxford University Press. Reprinted by permission of the publisher.

belief: the metaphysical influence on the younger English poets of the 1930's, for example, can be interpreted as arising from the latters' intellectual eclecticism which has something in common with Donne's Janus-faced quality. But multiple belief itself often implies tolerance, and tolerance is often — if unconsciously — based on skepticism, as the case of Sir Thomas Browne will show, so that, paradoxically, skepticism can be the basis of multiple belief as well as of the rejection of all belief. These are difficult questions, but questions very relevant to a discussion of modern poetry. . . .

. . .

Eliot is not content with expressing this theme ["the barrenness and desiccation of modern civilization"] in a simple fable form. He intertwines [in *The Waste Land*] several fables — the story of the grail, primitive vegetation myths, the Christian story of the resurrection, and many others — each of which has the same moral. He switches from one to the other and refers to one while employing the other throughout the poem. Here is tradition with a vengeance: almost all the great myths of the world are called into service. It is thus that Eliot tries to solve the cultural problem of his time.

. . .

If the contemporary world has no generally accepted myth, no common background of belief to hold it together, then Eliot will write in terms of all beliefs, committing himself not to any specific one of them but to a belief in the importance of belief. For Eliot the idea of faith is always more important than any specific faith, the concept of order more important than any given order, the sense of the past more important than any one aspect of the past. So in *The Waste Land* he rolls all previous orders and beliefs into a ball and tosses it into the modern world. Has he solved the problem of being traditional in an age which lacks tradition, or has he simply demonstrated more clearly than ever the existence of the problem? Let the reader decide. DAVID DAICHES [17]

[17] *Poetry and the Modern World*, pp. 103-4, 120, 121. Copyright 1940 by the University of Chicago Press. Reprinted by permission of the publisher.

The Problem of Belief in Poetic Appreciation

Literary criticism of the interpretative kind will only begin to be redeemed from confusion when its exponents realize how unscrupulous a poet may be in his work, how much craft there is in poetry as well as art: for one thing, he may emulate the atheist architect designing an impressive cathedral and write excellent poetry on a religious motive which, in the matter of personal belief, may mean absolutely nothing to him, and furthermore . . . his poetry will inevitably be at odds with whatever prose declarations of belief he may give, since the way a poet "thinks" in poetry is continually being moulded and subtilised and (from the philosopher's point of view) perverted by factors which are comparatively inactive when thought is expressed in prose.* D. J. ENRIGHT [18]

* Cf. a passage from T. S. Eliot's essay on Dante, section 2, which might be useful to students of Eliot's own recent poetry: "We are not to take Dante for Aquinas or Aquinas for Dante. It would be a grievous error in psychology. The *belief attitude* of a man reading the *Summa* must be different from that of a man reading Dante, even when it is the same man, and that man a Catholic." And the *belief attitude* of the man writing the *Divine Comedy* must be different from that of the man writing the *Summa*.

Mr. Eliot's main charge against Shelley is one of intellectual incoherence. Incidentally he reveals a pretty strong distaste for the poet's personality, which is perhaps a logical consequence of the main charge. At the risk of some distortion I must give a summary of the whole indictment. "The ideas of Shelley," Mr. Eliot begins, "seem to me always to be ideas of adolescence. . . . And an enthusiasm for Shelley seems to me also to be an affair of adolescence. . . . I find his ideas repellent; and the difficulty of separating Shelley from his ideas and beliefs is still greater than with Wordsworth. And the biographical interest which Shelley has always excited makes it difficult to read the poetry without remembering the man: and the man was humourless, pedantic,

[18] "Rilke, George and 'Re-integration'," *Scrutiny*, 13 (September 1945), 117–18.

self-centred, and sometimes almost a blackguard. . . ." So far the items in the charge are almost the same as Arnold's, only a little more restrained in formulation. But after a page or so of concessions, Mr. Eliot returns to his main point: "But some of Shelley's views I positively dislike, and that hampers my enjoyment of the poems in which they occur; and others seem to me so puerile that I cannot enjoy the poems in which they occur." This leads to a discussion of the now famous problem of Belief and Poetry, and to the conclusion, in respect of Shelley, that "when the doctrine, theory, belief or 'view of life' presented in a poem is one which the mind of the reader can accept as coherent, mature, and founded on the facts of experience, it interposes no obstacle to the reader's enjoyment, whether it be one that he accept or deny, approve or deprecate. When it is one which the reader rejects as childish or feeble, it may, for a reader of well-developed mind, set up an almost complete check. . . . I can only regret that Shelley did not live to put his poetic gifts, which were certainly of the first order, at the service of more tenable beliefs — which need not have been, for my purposes, beliefs more acceptable to me."

. . .

. . . "We may be permitted to infer," Mr. Eliot says, "in so far as the distaste of a person like myself for Shelley's poetry is not attributable to irrelevant prejudices or to a simple blind spot, but is due to a peculiarity in the poetry and not in the reader, that it is not the presentation of beliefs which I do not hold, or — to put the case as extremely as possible — of beliefs which excite my abhorrence, that makes the difficulty. Still less is it that Shelley is deliberately making use of his poetic gifts to propagate a doctrine; for Dante and Lucretius did the same thing. I suggest that the position is somewhat as follows." And then follows the charge of incoherence, immaturity, childishness, feebleness and shabbiness. But we cannot accept the suggestion (and it is only a suggestion: there is no demonstration). On the contrary, we affirm that Shelley's ideas were no more shabby and incoherent than those of Plato who was their chief inspiration; and that in so far as they were unplatonic, they showed a close parallel to the ideas of Lucretius, whom Mr. Eliot accepts. HERBERT READ [19]

My point is that you cannot afford to *ignore* Dante's philosophical and theological beliefs, or to skip the passages which express them most clearly; but that on the other hand you are not called upon to believe them yourself. It is wrong to think that there are parts of the *Divine Comedy* which are of interest only to Catholics or to mediaevalists. For there is a difference (which here I hardly do more than assert) between philosophical *belief* and poetic *assent*. I am not sure that there is not as great a difference between philosophical belief and scientific belief; but that is a difference only now beginning to appear, and certainly inapposite to the thirteenth century. . . . The vital matter is that Dante's poem is a whole; that you must in the end come to understand every part in order to understand any part.

Furthermore, we can make a distinction between what Dante believes as a poet and what he believed as a man. Practically, it is hardly likely that even so great a poet as Dante could have composed the *Comedy* merely with understanding and without belief; but his private belief becomes a different thing in becoming poetry. It is interesting to hazard the suggestion that this is truer of Dante than of any other philosophical poet. T. S. ELIOT [20]

Richards, furthermore, makes explicit provision for Eliot's "complete check" in the following terms: "The question of belief or disbelief never arises when we are reading well. If unfortunately it does arise, either through the poet's fault or our own, we have for the moment ceased to be readers and have become astronomers, theologians, or moralists [and one may add "or economists"], persons engaged in a quite different type of activity."

. . .

[19] *In Defence of Shelley and Other Essays*, pp. 8–9, 70. Copyright 1936 by William Heinemann, Ltd. Reprinted by permission of the author and the publisher.
[20] *Selected Essays 1917–1932*, pp. 218–19. Copyright 1932 by Harcourt, Brace

We may summarize the position on the question of poetic belief as follows: First, the scientific truth of the doctrine enunciated will not save the poem just as its scientific falsity will not damn it. The poet then must not place an illegitimate dependence in the possible scientific truth of his doctrine. As Tate puts it, the assertions made by the poet must be "a quality of the whole poem" — not "willfully asserted for the purpose of heightening a subject the poet has not implicitly imagined." Second, the doctrine must be one suitable to a poem which is to stand up under "an ironical contemplation." CLEANTH BROOKS [21]

Epipsychidion [by Shelley] raises in an acute form a problem with which Mr. Eliot has been much occupied: I mean the problem of the relation between our judgement on a poem as critics, and our judgement as men on the ethics, metaphysics, or theology presupposed or expressed in the poem. For my own part, I do not believe that the poetic value of any poem is identical with the philosophic; but I think they can differ only to a limited extent, so that every poem whose prosaic or intellectual basis is silly, shallow, perverse, or illiberal, or even radically erroneous, is in some degree crippled by that fact. I am thus obliged to rate *Epipsychidion* rather low, because I consider the thought implied in it a dangerous delusion. C. S. LEWIS [22]

There can be no distinction between a great writer's poetry and what we are pleased to call his "message." It is simply because they were first and foremost great poets that the work of Baudelaire and Rimbaud possesses what for want of a better word can only be called an extra-literary importance. MARTIN TURNELL [23]

and Co., and by Faber and Faber, Ltd. Reprinted by permission of the publishers.
[21] *Modern Poetry and the Tradition*, p. 49. Copyright 1939 by the University of North Carolina Press. Reprinted by permission of the publisher.
[22] *Rehabilitations*, pp. 26–27. Copyright 1939 by Oxford University Press. Reprinted by permission of the publisher.
[23] "The Poet of Revolution," *Scrutiny*, 7 (September 1938), 223.

Hardy failed when he tried to make a direct statement of his beliefs; he succeeded when he used his beliefs to make significant the observations which concerned him. This contrast should suggest that something essential to the nature of poetry may very well be in question. It is a long time since the statement was first made that poetry is more philosophical than history; the example of Hardy provides another instance of how useful and how illuminating the doctrine is. The minute particulars of Hardy's experience might have made a diary, history, or biography; what made them poetry was the functioning of Hardy's beliefs. The function of belief was to generalize his experience into something neither merely particular, which is the historian's concern; nor merely general, which is the philosopher's; but into symbols which possess the qualitative richness, as Mr. Ransom might say, of any particular thing and yet have that generality which makes them significant beyond their moment of existence, or the passing context in which they are located.

. . .

Now there are two ways in which we tend to handle alien beliefs. One of them is to reject those poems which contain beliefs we regard as false. This is an example of judging poetry in terms of its subject, considered in abstraction, and the difficulties are obviously numerous. For one thing, as has been said, we would have to reject most great poetry. Certainly we would have to do without Homer, and without Dante or Shakespeare.

The other alternative, which is in any case preferable to the first, is to judge poetry wholly in terms of its formal character. But this is an act of unjustifiable abstraction also. For it is evident that we enjoy more in a poem, or at least the poem presents more to us, than a refined use of language.

What we need, and what we actually have, I think, is a criterion for the beliefs in a poem which is genuinely a poetic criterion. In reading Hardy when he is successful, in *A Drizzling Easter Morning*, we find that the belief and disbelief operate upon the particular *datum* of the poem to give it a metaphorical significance it would not otherwise have. To repeat, without both belief and disbelief, it is only another rainy morning in the spring. Conversely, in *The Masked Face*, the asserted belief, instead of generalizing the particulars of the poem, merely interferes with them and fails to give them the significance they are intended to have.

In both instances, we are faced with a relationship between the belief in the poem and its other particulars. This is a relationship *internal* to the poem, so to speak. It is not a question of the relationship of the poet's beliefs to the reader's. In *The Masked Face*, for example, the inadequacy proceeds from the relationship between belief that Life is beyond human understanding, and the goose-quill pen which is required to represent the human mind.

It might be objected that this internal relationship between the belief and the rest of the poem is in turn good, or not good, in terms of what the given reader himself believes. Thus it might seem that for a reader who shares Hardy's beliefs, the goose-quill pen was an adequate figure for the human mind. Actually this cannot be so, unless the reader is not interested in poetry but merely in hearing his beliefs stated. If the reader is interested in poetry, the poem itself cannot give him the poetic experience of Life as beyond human understanding, which is its intention. The details of the poem, as presented in the context which the belief and the versification provide, do not do the work in the reader's mind which is done by such an element in *A Drizzling Easter Morning*, as the weary wain, which plods forward, laden heavily. And one reason why they lack that energy is their relationship, within the poem, to the belief the poem asserts. Whether or not the reader shares Hardy's beliefs, even if he shares them completely, the goose-quill pen is an inadequate figure for what it is intended to signify in the context. The belief in the poem fails to make it adequate, and this is a poetic failure, just as, in "The Oxen," the kneeling animals are a poetic success because of the disbelief,

whether the reader himself disbelieves in Christianity or not.
DELMORE SCHWARTZ [24]

What Eliot has said about the use of myth in poetry proves clearly that this too must be a central problem for the critic. In reviewing Joyce's *Ulysses* in 1923 [in *Dial*] Eliot wrote as follows:

In using the myth, in manipulating a continuous parallel between contemporaneity and antiquity, Mr. Joyce is pursuing a method which others must pursue after him. They will not be imitators, any more than the scientist who uses the discoveries of Einstein in pursuing his own, independent, further investigations. It is simply a way of controlling, of ordering, of giving a shape and a significance to the immense panorama of futility and anarchy which is contemporary history. It is a method already cadumbrated by Mr. Yeats, and of the need for which I believe Mr. Yeats to have been the first contemporary to be conscious. Psychology . . . ethnology and *The Golden Bough* have concurred to make possible what was impossible only a few years ago. Instead of the narrative method we may now use the mythical method. It is, I seriously believe, a step toward making the modern world possible for art, toward . . . order and form. . . .

This "mythical method" is of course Eliot's own method in *The Waste Land*, a poem in which we see a "panorama of futility and anarchy" dramatized by the dying-god-and-fertility myth.
RICHARD CHASE [25]

[24] "Poetry and Belief in Thomas Hardy," *Southern Review*, 6 (Summer 1940), 73, 75–77. This essay is reprinted in *Critiques and Essays in Criticism*, edited by R. W. Stallman. Copyright 1949 by Ronald Press.
[25] "The Sense of the Present," *Kenyon Review*, 7 (Spring 1945), 227–28.

VIII

The
Problem of
Intentions

Anything is right only as it answers to the need for which it was ordered. . . .

The ideal artist is he who knows everything, feels everything, experiences everything, and retains his experience in a spirit of wonder and feeds upon it with creative lust. He is therefore best able to select and order the components best suited to fulfill any given desire. The ideal artist is the superman. He uses every possible power, spirit, emotion conscious or unconscious to arrive at his ends.

GEORGE BELLOWS, *The Paintings of George Bellows*. Copyright 1929 by Alfred A. Knopf, Inc. Reprinted by permission of the publisher.

The Problem Defined

In referring to the meaning of a literary work, one should distinguish between (1) the meaning of the work itself, and (2) the meaning that the author intended to express in the work. These two meanings are here called "actual" and "intentional" respectively.

Evidence that the work has a certain actual meaning is derived from a study of the work itself, the words in which it is written and their syntax. Included in the meaning of the words will be their whole history as far as determinable, and all the uses and associations of the words that went to make up their value when the work was produced. The meaning of the work is all that the ideal reader can find in it; and the ideal reader is the one fully aware of the accepted value of the words and least influenced in his interpretation by idiosyncratic associations. Since no reader will ever be ideal and no two readers will ever read the work in exactly the same way, it must be said that the meaning of the work lies within an area of readings, and is, like the pronunciation of language sounds, a norm (*cf.* René Wellek, "The Mode of Existence of a Literary Work of Art," *Southern Review*, 7, 1942). (In the course of years a work may undergo a shift of meaning in some of its words, so that one may have to distinguish between the work "then" and the work "now." It is obvious that in most cases the meanings of words "then" will have more relevance to the total work than the meanings "now.") Of more importance than the idiosyncrasies of the reader are those of the author, the meanings that attach to the words in view of his special share in their history and associations. Biographical study will be part of the total historical study that makes the work fully intelligible. The author must be admitted as a witness to the meaning of his work, and one may even grant special validity to idiosyncratic associations of the author, since at least they will be relevant to the total design. This kind of evidence, however, must be distinguished from the author's "intention." Even though it were known, for example, that a given author intended the word "glory" to mean a "knockdown argument," the word "glory" in his work could not be said to have that meaning in any sense valid for the reader or the work itself. The work after being produced must continue to exist independently of the author's intentions or thoughts about it. The idiosyncrasies of the author must not be repugnant to the norm (but *cf.* Joseph Wood Krutch, *Experience and Art*, 1932, pp. 180–89). W. K. WIMSATT AND M. C. BEARDSLEY [1]

We argue that the design or intention of the author is neither available nor desirable as a standard for judging the success of a work of literary art, and it seems to us that this is a principle which goes deep into some differences in the history of critical attitudes. It is a principle which accepted or rejected points to the polar opposites of classical "imitation" and romantic expression. It entails many specific truths about inspiration, authenticity, biography, literary history and scholarship, and about some trends of contemporary poetry, especially its allusiveness. There is hardly a

[1] "Intention," pp. 326–27 in *Dictionary of World Literature*, edited by Joseph T. Shipley. Copyright 1943 by the Philosophical Library. Reprinted by permission of the publisher.

problem of literary criticism in which the critic's approach will not be qualified by his view of "intention."

"Intention," as we shall use the term, corresponds to *what he intended* in a formula which more or less explicitly has had wide acceptance. "In order to judge the poet's performance, we must know *what he intended*." Intention is design or plan in the author's mind. Intention has obvious affinities for the author's attitude toward his work, the way he felt, what made him write.

We begin our discussion with a series of propositions summarized and abstracted to a degree where they seem to us axiomatic, if not truistic.

1. A poem does not come into existence by accident. The words of a poem, as Professor Stoll has remarked, come out of a head, not out of a hat. Yet to insist on the designing intellect as a *cause* of a poem is not to grant the design or intention as a *standard*.

2. One must ask how a critic expects to get an answer to the question about intention. How is he to find out what the poet tried to do? If the poet succeeded in doing it, then the poem itself shows what he was trying to do. And if the poet did not succeed, then the poem is not adequate evidence, and the critic must go outside the poem — for evidence of an intention that did not become effective in the poem. "Only one *caveat* must be borne in mind," says an eminent intentionalist in a moment when his theory repudiates itself; "the poet's aim must be judged at the moment of the creative act, that is to say, by the art of the poem itself."

3. Judging a poem is like judging a pudding or a machine. One demands that it work. It is only because an artifact works that we infer the intention of an artificer. "A poem should not mean but be." A poem can *be* only through its *meaning* — since its medium is words — yet it *is*, simply *is*, in the sense that we have no excuse for inquiring what part is intended or meant. Poetry is a feat of style by which a complex of meaning is handled all at once. Poetry succeeds because all or most of what is said or implied is relevant; what is irrelevant has been excluded, like lumps from pudding and "bugs" from machinery. In this respect poetry differs from prac-

tical messages, which are successful if and only if we correctly infer the intention. They are more abstract than poetry.

4. The meaning of a poem may certainly be a personal one, in the sense that a poem expresses a personality or state of soul rather than a physical object like an apple. But even a short lyric poem is dramatic, the response of a speaker (no matter how abstractly conceived) to a situation (no matter how universalized). We ought to impute the thoughts and attitudes of the poem immediately to the dramatic *speaker*, and if to the author at all, only by a biographical act of inference.

5. If there is any sense in which an author, by revision, has better achieved his original intention, it is only the very abstract, tautological, sense that he intended to write a better work and now has done it. (In this sense every author's intention is the same.) His former specific intention was not his intention. "He's the man we were in search of, that's true"; says Hardy's rustic constable, "and yet he's not the man we were in search of. For the man we were in search of was not the man we wanted." W. K. WIMSATT AND M. C. BEARDSLEY [2]

But the application of the criterion of internal consistency cannot be made in a vacuum. All sorts of considerations impinge upon the process. And these considerations force on the critic the criterion of external consistency. But consistency in regard to what? First, in regard to the intellectual, the spiritual climate of the age in which the poem was composed. Second, in regard to the over-all pattern of other artistic work by the author in question. Third, in regard to the thought of the author as available from nonartistic sources. Fourth, in regard to the facts of the author's life. These considerations cannot be applied in a mechanical fashion, that is, so as to confuse the material of the poem with the poem itself. If treated mechanically, the first, for example, will give us crude historicism, or the fourth will give us crude psychologism — both

[2] "The Intentional Fallacy," *Sewanee Review*, 54 (Summer 1946), 468. See also R. W. Stallman, "A Note on Intentions," *College English*, 10 (October 1948), 40–41.

of which confound the material with the thing created, both of which deny the creative function of mind, both of which fail to provide any basis for distinguishing the excellent product from the conventional or inept. But treated as conditioning factors, as factors of control in interpretation, the considerations named above provide an invaluable criterion. ROBERT PENN WARREN [3]

Once it leaves the creator's hand, the work of art, be it painting or poem, assumes a life of its own: once Pygmalion's it is now its own — and the public's — Galatea.

If one asks the "meaning" of an artifact, one finds oneself shocked by the ultimate answer. The naïve supposition is that a poem means what its author meant by it; but in that case, what is the meaning of *Hamlet* or *The Exequy*? Shakespeare and King evade consultation; even were they in the realm of mundane existence and amenable to interview, they might well, like Browning and Yeats, be found to have forgotten what they "meant" in the act of composition. Had they provided a prose commentary upon their poems, that would, in turn, require interpretation. As Shakespeare and King have disappeared, we have no means of knowing *their* meaning — which leaves *Hamlet* and *The Exequy* poems evacuated. This position is preposterous; and one must affirm, instead, that the "meaning" about which one is concerned is supplied or evoked for the reader or audience or contemplator — in which case *Hamlet* has as many meanings as readers, in which case, it has no meaning — a conclusion equally absurd.

. . . The search for meaning-as-the-author's leads to historical scholarship; I can never know exactly what Shakespeare meant either by a play or a single line, but I can approximate it; I can, by industry and — let us hope — imagination, build up a context, using the whole corpus of Shakespeare's plays to corroborate my interpretation of a single one; I can read the work of Shakespeare's contemporaries, dramatic and non-dramatic; I can painstakingly acquaint myself with Elizabethan psychology and physics and meta-

---

[3] Essay, pp. 115–16 in *The Rime of the Ancient Mariner*. Copyright 1946 by Reynal and Hitchcock. Reprinted by permission of Harcourt, Brace and Co.

physics, as Craig has done in his *Enchanted Glass;* I can reconstruct the physical instrumentalities of stage and audience and actors with which Shakespeare worked; I can read what books Shakespeare is known to have read, e.g., Plutarch and Ovid and Montaigne. Such an approach, such a circling around the author, assumes that in all respects his emotions and his thoughts must have been "of his age"; if it is possible for a man to escape his age, such a method cannot catch him, or at any rate the part of him that does so "escape."

The second method is that of the critic. Some kinds of interpretation, at least, presuppose scholarship. . . . But there are other kinds of meanings not similarly dependent. One does not need knowledge of the Elizabethan stage and its conventions to judge of Shakespeare's suitability to the current stage, or knowledge of Elizabethan treatises on psychology to judge of Shakespeare's truth to human nature. Shakespeare's remarks anent the rabble have a "meaning for moderns," in a context of Marx and Hitler, as well as for students of English history and readers of Machiavelli. The critic's ultimate concern is, as Arnold used to insist, with *real*, not *historical*, estimates. That Shakespeare should be for "all time" necessitates that he should have immediate significance for many generations. Austin Warren [4]

It is only if we are aware of the reality of the past as past that we can feel it as alive and present. If, for example, we try to make Shakespeare literally contemporaneous, we make him monstrous. He is contemporaneous only if we know how much a man of his own age he was; he is relevant to us only if we see his difference. Or to take a poet closer to us in actual time: Wordsworth's Immortality Ode is acceptable to us only when it is understood to have been written at a certain past moment; if it had appeared much later than it did, if it were offered to us now as a contemporary work, we would not admire it; and the same is true of *The Prelude*, which of all works of the Romantic Movement is closest to our present

[4] "The Criticism of Meaning and the Meaning of Criticism," *Sewanee Review*, 46 (April–June 1938), 219–21.

interest. In the pastness of these works lies the assurance of their validity and relevance.

The question is always arising: What is the real poem? Is it the poem we now perceive? Is it the poem the author consciously intended? Is it the poem the author intended and his first readers read? Well, it is all these things, depending on the state of our knowledge. But in addition the poem is the poem as it has existed in history, as it has lived its life from Then to Now, as it is a thing which submits itself to one kind of perception in one age and another kind of perception in another age, as it exerts in each age a different kind of power. This makes it a thing we can never wholly understand — other things too, of course, help to make it that — and the mystery, the unreachable part of the poem, is one of its aesthetic elements.

To suppose that we can think like men of another time is as much of an illusion as to suppose that we can think in a wholly different way. But it is the first illusion that is exemplified in the attitude of the anti-historical critics. In the admirable poetry textbook of Cleanth Brooks and Robert Penn Warren, the authors disclaim all historical intention. Their purpose being what it is, they are right to do so, but I wonder if they are right in never asking in their aesthetic analysis the question: What effect is created by our knowledge that the language of a particular poem is not such as would be uttered by a poet writing now? To read a poem of even a hundred years ago requires as much translation of its historical circumstances as of its metaphors. This the trained and gifted critic is likely to forget; his own historical sense is often so deeply ingrained that he is not wholly conscious of it, and sometimes, for reasons of his own, he prefers to keep it merely implicit. Yet whether or not it is made conscious and explicit the historical sense is one of the aesthetic and critical faculties. LIONEL TRILLING [5]

A work of art does not exist until it is experienced by an individual mind. It will always be an individual experience; but at the same

[5] *The Liberal Imagination*, pp. 186–87. Copyright 1950 by the Viking Press. Reprinted by permission of the publisher.

time it is an experience given to this individual mind by another mind, and wholly governed by the conditions under which it is given. Thus a play, like any other work of art, consists of a series of three terms: the author, his medium or technique, and the recipient. Of these three terms, the first is the only one that can never change; and the fact that this term is always the same gives us the sense in which it is possible to say, that through all its existences it is always the same play. But the third term, the recipient, changes every time the play comes into existence at all; and it is even possible for changes to occur in the middle term, the technique, provided the change conserves what the author committed to it. Thus a symphony may be transcribed as a pianoforte duet: a remarkable change, but one which, in the case of his own symphonies, Brahms himself carried out. And thus too the medium of *Macbeth* may change from the theatre to the printed page: perhaps an even more remarkable change, but one which it appears Shakespeare himself approved of, and may even to some extent have had in mind. He might very well approve of it, since the printed page merely gave him another way of making essentially the same appeal of imagination. So that, in spite of whatever differences there may be between them, whether we criticize the *Macbeth* we see in the theatre, or the *Macbeth* we read, it is still Shakespeare's *Macbeth* we are criticizing: in that sense, it is in either case the same *Macbeth*.

The existence of a work of art, in fact, is not material at all, but spiritual. It is a continually creative existence, for it exists by continually creating experience. In one sense, this means that it is a continually changing existence; for the experiences it creates must always be individual and therefore unique experiences. Yet in another sense it is always the same; for it always exists in unbroken connexion with its author, who *forms* the experience he gives. It will now appear why liberty of interpretation must necessarily be granted if Shakespeare's plays are regarded as works of art. LASCELLES ABERCROMBIE [6]

[6] "A Plea for the Liberty of Interpreting," pp. 229-30 in *Modern English Essays*, second series. Copyright 1932 by Oxford University Press. Reprinted by permission of the publisher.

The poem, we hear, is the experience of the author. Only in paren-
thesis, we may dismiss the view that the poem is the experience of
the author at any time of his life after the creation of his work when
he rereads it. He then has obviously become simply a reader of his
work and is liable to errors and misinterpretations of his own work
almost as much as any other reader. Many instances of glaring misinterpretations by an author of his own work could be collected: the
old anecdote about Browning professing not to understand his own
poem has probably its element of truth. It happens to all of us that
we misinterpret or do not fully understand what we have written
some time ago. Thus the suggested answer must refer to the experience of the author during the time of creation. By experience
of the author we might mean, however, two different things:
the conscious experience, the intentions which the author wanted to embody in his work, or the total conscious and unconscious experience during the prolonged time of creation. The view
that the genuine poem is to be found in the intentions of the author
is widespread even though it is not always explicitly stated. It justifies much historical research and is at the bottom of many arguments in favor of specific interpretations. However, for most works
of art we have no evidence to reconstruct the intentions of the author except the finished work itself. Even if we are in possession of
contemporary evidence in the form of an explicit profession
of intentions, such a profession need not be binding on a modern
observer. "Intentions" of the author are always *a posteriori* ratioc-
inations, commentaries which certainly must be taken into account but also must be criticized in the light of the finished work
of art. The "intentions" of an author may go far beyond the finished
work of art: they may be merely pronouncements of plans and
ideals, while the performance may be either far below or far aside
the mark. If we could have interviewed Shakespeare he probably
would have expressed his intentions in writing *Hamlet* in a way
which we should find most unsatisfactory. We would still quite
rightly insist on finding meanings in *Hamlet* (and not merely in-

venting them) which were probably far from clearly formulated in Shakespeare's conscious mind.

. . .

The experiences of the author during creation ceased precisely when the poem had begun to exist. If this conception were right, we should never be able to come into direct contact with the work of art itself, but have constantly to make the assumption that our experiences in reading the poem are in some way identical with the long past experiences of the author. Mr. E. M. Tillyard in his book on *Milton* has tried to use the idea that *Paradise Lost* is about the state of the author when he wrote it. . . . That the whole content of a poem was once in contact with the conscious and subconscious mind of Milton is perfectly true, but this state of mind is inaccessible and might have been filled, in those particular moments, with millions of experiences of which we cannot find a trace in the poem itself. Taken literally, this whole solution must lead to absurd speculations about the exact duration of the state of mind of the creator and its exact content, which might include a toothache at the moment of creation. RENÉ WELLEK [7]

The Creative Process

The artist's main business in life, however, is carried on by means of yet a fourth kind of vision, which I will call the creative vision. This, I think, is the furthest perversion of the gifts of nature of which man is guilty. It demands the most complete detachment from any of the meanings and implications of appearances. Almost any turn of the kaleidoscope of nature may set up in the artist this detached and impassioned vision, and, as he contemplates the particular field of vision, the (aesthetically) chaotic and accidental

[7] "The Mode of Existence of a Literary Work of Art," *Southern Review*, 7 (Spring 1942), 742–43, 744. The essay in revised form is reprinted in Austin Warren and René Wellek, *Theory of Literature*. Copyright 1949 by Harcourt, Brace and Co. Reprinted by permission of the publisher.

conjunction of forms and colours begins to crystallise into a harmony; and as this harmony becomes clear to the artist, his actual vision becomes distorted by the emphasis of the rhythm which has been set up within him. Certain relations of directions of line become for him full of meaning; he apprehends them no longer casually or merely curiously, but passionately, and these lines begin to be so stressed and stand out so clearly from the rest that he sees them far more distinctly than he did at first. Similarly colours, which in nature have almost always a certain vagueness and elusiveness, become so definite and clear to him, owing to their now necessary relation to other colours, that if he chooses to paint his vision he can state them positively and definitely. In such a creative vision the objects as such tend to disappear, to lose their separate unities, and to take their places as so many bits in the whole mosaic of vision. ROGER FRY [8]

Let the artist take for stuff and substance of his work whatever is most profound, most exalted and most vile, the moral life of man, the heart of man "hollow and full of filth" — and the rarest passions and the life of the spirit itself, nay, the Gospel and sanctity, everything; but with it all an absolute prohibition, upon pain of committing a sacrilege against art, against pursuing any other end than the pure delight, order, riches, tranquillity and rapture, which the soul ought to savour in the work. This is no longer art *on nothing* as in the theory of gratuitousness in its first form; but art *for* nothing, for nothing but art's sake. JACQUES MARITAIN [9]

First of all, it should be said that the "Cimetière Marin" *as it stands*, is *for me* the result of the *section* of an inner effort by a chance event. One afternoon in the year 1920, our greatly lamented friend, Jacques Rivière, happening to call, found me confronted by

[8] *Vision and Design*, pp. 51–52. Copyright 1920 by Chatto and Windus, Ltd. Reprinted by permission of the publisher.
[9] *Art and Scholasticism*, p. 131. Translated by J. F. Scanlan. Copyright 1943 by Charles Scribner's Sons, and by Geoffrey Bles, Ltd. Reprinted by permission of the publishers.

one of the "states" of this "Cimetière Marin," thinking of doing it over again, omitting, substituting, interposing here and there.

There was no stopping him till he had got it to read; nor till, having read it, he had carried it off with him. Nothing is more decisive than a Review-Editor's mind.

So it was that the form of this work was fixed *by accident*. It was none of my own doing. What is more, as a general thing I am unable to go back over anything I have written without having the thought that I might still make it into something entirely different if some outside interruption or some uncircumstantial circumstance had not broken the spell of my not finishing it. I only care about the work of working; beginnings are tiring and difficult for me, and anything that comes readily I suspect of being perfectible. The spontaneous thing, however excellent, however charming, never seems to me to be quite *mine*. I do not say that my way is "right": I say that this is the way I am . . . No more than that of Author is the conception of the Self a simple one: one added degree of consciousness opposes a new *Same* to a new *Other*.

. . .

This brief venturing upon the difficulties that may arise between "awareness of self" and the custom of writing, will no doubt explain certain *biases* for which I have sometimes been reproached. I have been criticized, for example, for having given out several texts of the same poem, and even contradictory ones. This reproach is not very intelligible to me, as one might expect, after what I have just set forth. On the contrary, I should be tempted (if I followed my feeling in the matter) to urge poets to produce, as musicians do, a number of variants or alternative solutions of the same subject. Nothing could seem to me more in conformity with the idea I cherish most about poets and poetry.

. . .

Every time I ponder the art of writing (whether in verse or in prose), the same "ideal" discloses itself in my mind. The myth of "creation" charms us into wishing to make something out of nothing. And so I fancy that I see my work step by step, starting out from the pure conditions of form, weighed and deliberated upon time and again, brought at last to a degree of precision at which they suggest, or practically impose, a *subject* — or at least, a family of subjects.

Let us note that sharply defined conditions of form are nothing but the expression of our knowledge and consciousness of the *means* at our disposal, and of their range, as well as of their limits and defects. This is why I happen to define a *writer* as the relationship between a certain "mind" and Language. . . .

But I am wholly aware how chimeric my "Ideal" is. The nature of language lends itself least of all to sequential combinations; and besides, the formative influences and habits of the modern reader, whose customary daily bread of incoherence and snap-shot effects makes all refinements of structure imperceptible to him, scarcely encourage his wandering away so far from himself. . . .

Yet the mere thought of constructions of this sort remains for me the most *poetic* of ideas: the idea of composition.

Upon that word I pause . . . It would carry me to indeterminable lengths. To me the most surprising thing about poets is the lack of ingenuity in their composition. In the lyrics of greatest fame, I find hardly more than a purely linear — or . . . feverish — development; that is, a development proceeding from this to that, with no more consecutive organization than is apparent in a trail of gun-powder when a flame leaps along its length. (I say nothing of poems in which a story holds the ascendancy and the chronology of events interposes; these are adulterate works: operas, and not sonatas or symphonies.)

But my astonishment lasts only long enough for me to remember my own experiments and the almost completely discouraging obstacles I have encountered in my attempts at *composition* in the lyric order. For here detail is of essential importance at every moment, and the finest and most skillful intention is obliged to compose with the uncertainty of *trouvailles*. In the lyric universe, each moment must consummate an indefinable alliance of the sensory and the meaningful. It follows that composition is in some way a continuous process, and can hardly be allotted to any other time than that of its execution. There is not one time for "substance" and another time for "form"; and composition of this kind is in opposition not only to disorder or disproportion, but also to *de-composition*. If the sense and the sound (or the substance and the form) can be easily disassociated, the poem *de-composes*.

With this primary consequence: the "ideas" figuring in a poetic work do not play the same part, are not at all the *same kind of values*, as the "ideas" of prose. PAUL VALÉRY [10]

Art begins with intelligence and freedom of choice. The spontaneous gush of images, without which there is no poetry, *precedes and feeds* the operation of the poet; and beyond doubt it is never the effect of premeditation and calculation. This should be insisted on. Normally, however, the mind not only controls but solicits this activity and polarises it. After this it waits results, stops them on their passage, chooses among them, judges. JACQUES MARITAIN [11]

Critical power may be a blight, as the romantics believed, where the original and spontaneous imaginings of an artist are aesthetically weak and the temptation to replace the unconscious with the conscious is, as a consequence, relatively strong. This tendency to an inappropriate use of the conscious and the unconscious is present in all the arts. "There is a good deal, in the writing of poetry, which must be conscious and deliberate," T. S. Eliot declares. "In fact, the bad poet is usually unconscious where he ought to be conscious, and conscious where he ought to be unconscious." *

Generally speaking, then, the creative process involves both the

[10] "Concerning the 'Cimetière Marin'," *Southern Review*, 4 (Summer 1938), 159–60, 163–64. Translated by Florence Codman and Hansell Baugh.

[11] "Poetry and Religion," *New Criterion*, 5 (January 1927), 21. Translated by F. S. Flint.

EDITOR'S NOTE. Contrast with this Edgar Degas' view: "A picture is something which requires as much knavery, trickery, and deceit as the perpetration of a crime. Paint falsely, and then add the accent of nature." *Artists on Art*, edited by Robert Goldwater and Marc Treves (Pantheon Books, 1945), p. 308.

unconscious and the conscious and is, at its best, a combination of genius and taste. DILMAN WALTER GOTSHALK [12]

* T. S. Eliot, *The Sacred Wood* (Methuen and Co., Ltd., 1928), p. 58.

The greatest satisfaction comes, he [Robert Frost] feels, when you can say: "Here is a poem that is a triumphal intention, that bore right through and dismissed itself." The "triumphal intention" is the source of his delight: it is the consummation of "the pure emergence [of the poem] from the logic of the thing." But "the pure emergence" is not necessarily in a straight line; it is more like following stepping-stones across a field in a kind of straight-crookedness. What is memorable in the writing is the "resolved perplexity." There is so much more suspense in perplexity than in preconceived ends. Can he fetch it off? Can he resolve it? "Aye, there's the leverage!"

In the making of form his organic method is diametrically the opposite of Poe's method as illustrated in "The Philosophy of Composition." He considers the prepared and outlined piece of art suspect. "If it is thought out first and expressed last, I dismiss it," he says with finality. He does not write with the end in mind and then attempt to make things fit it. Instead, he proceeds, in Benjamin Franklin's words, "regularly from things known to things unknown, distinctly and clearly without confusion." After the poem finds its direction in the first line, it rides on its own impulse. "Like a piece of ice on a hot stove, the poem must ride on its own melting," he says. He does not try to wrench out the significance of the experience inherent in the poetic impulse; he tries only to release it. REGINALD L. COOK [13]

[12] *Art and the Social Order*, p. 67. Copyright 1947 by the University of Chicago Press. Reprinted by permission of the publisher.

[13] "Robert Frost: A Time to Listen," *College English*, 7 (November 1945), 67–68.

EDITOR'S NOTE. In connection with the first paragraph of this excerpt, compare Henry James' remark in his Preface to *Daisy Miller*: ". . . what longest lives to his backward vision, in the whole business, is not the variable question of the 'success,' but the inveterate romance of the labour." See also his Preface to *The Wings of the Dove*: "Yet one's plan, alas, is one thing and one's result another. . . ." Reprinted in *The Art of the Novel*, pp. 287, 296. Copyright 1941 by Charles Scribner's Sons. Reprinted by permission of the publisher.

Frost's creative challenge consists in the encounter of the form with the spirit and the necessity of commitment. He cites Robert Herrick's *Daffodils* as an example of a poet fulfilling the obligation of his commitment as an artist. He says, "I always marveled how the second stanza is just as perfect as the first." It is otherwise with James Russell Lowell, who was too clever and got out of his commitments too easily. The poet's commitment in the spirit and the form is a very important matter to him. "Sincerity is the relation of the intention to the form. The thing must be genuine, true, and you must have something to be true to." * Nor is it otherwise in other literary forms. "In the short story I like to feel I can still hear the bell ringing from the first word when I finish the story." †

Art serves life by clarifying reality. Every form that fulfills its commitments is to the particular degree of its fulfilment an example of prowess in performance. And this prowess is what Frost has sought. The difference between purity and impurity in poetry would rest with him in whether the poet accepts the commitments and follows through. "Poetry is pure by the way in which it starts, that is, by where it takes its source." Impure poetry starts with the whole subject present; pure poetry doesn't begin with the idea or whole subject present. "A thing thought through before the writer sets pencil to paper is distasteful to me," he says. ‡ Poems written on given subjects or for assignment are impure poetry at its drossiest. REGINALD L. COOK [14]

* Talk at Bread Loaf, July 22, 1946. See also Preface to the Modern Library edition of his poems (1946).
† *Ibid.*
‡ Lecture and Reading, New School for Social Research, Oct. 17, 1935.

The artist sometimes begins with the physical material itself and, so to speak, without an idea in his head. He fools around at the piano, he makes impulsive sketches on paper following the suggestions of the lines and shapes, and slowly, as if from the material itself, an idea is born. The subjective vision is a relatively late arrival

[14] "Robert Frost's Asides on His Poetry," *American Literature*, 19 (January 1948), 354.

upon the scene. Where this is not the case, the material principle remains fertile in formal and expressive suggestions. It is usually far from a merely passive receptacle, as the Crocean account suggests. The material is a creative collaborator, provocative as well as docile, contributing as well as receiving; and the objective phase of creation is sometimes as much a process of discovery in regard to a work's formal and expressive aspects as it is the execution of antecedently formulated ideas. DILMAN WALTER GOTSHALK [15]

The Original Intention of the Artist

I am frequently asked how I can bring myself to violate the original experience that must have informed some poem, by revising it at a later time when my experience must be different. My only answer is that, as a poet, I have never had any experience, and that, as a poet, my concern is the experience that I hope the reader will have in reading the poem. ALLEN TATE [16]

In Rimbaud's poetry we can experience a delectation in our approximate understanding of his vision (and this is all art seeks to do; namely, to cause delight in the contemplation of its beauty). But Rimbaud's experience which caused his poetry to come into existence, continued in mystery and silence after his creative instinct was arrested, and this experience will always be incomprehensible to our minds. Rimbaud understood that he didn't understand. This might have been subject enough for a poet's art. It was, in Baudelaire's case, who modeled and strengthened the "idea" at times with irony, at times with tenderness. WALLACE FOWLIE [17]

---

[15] *Art and the Social Order*, pp. 74–75. Copyright [1947] by the University of Chicago Press. Reprinted by permission of the publisher.

[16] Preface, pp. viii–ix in *Selected Poems*. Copyright 1937 by Charles Scribner's Sons. Reprinted by permission of the publisher.

[17] *Clowns and Angels*, pp. 152–53. Copyright 1943 by Sheed and Ward, Inc. Reprinted by permission of the publisher.

Coleridge's detached, conscious intentions in writing the poem [*The Ancient Mariner*] were no doubt mixed (they certainly included that of defraying the cost of the walking tour on which it was planned). But the achievement, whatever the intention, has unity and coherence. True, the poem is not an allegory. There is no need to think that Coleridge could have paraphrased his theme either before or after writing. . . . All we need suppose is that the fiction Coleridge produced made a special appeal to him and could be handled with special effectiveness because its theme and incidents allowed highly significant though partly unconscious concerns to find expression. This is not to say that he was merely manipulating symbols. The concrete details of the fiction were not *less* but *more* vividly realised because they were charged with something else besides their manifest content. D. W. HARDING [18]

What he [Gauguin] was trying to formulate here of a new approach to meaning in his pictures, he had said earlier in another fashion, directly defending his Boston panel: "If my dream is not communicated, it contains no allegory. It is a musical poem: it does not require a libretto." We must add, if we are to give Gauguin's intention its full significance, that the poetry of these paintings at least is not limited to some definite (abstract) arrangement — harmonious or startling — of lines and colors and shapes, but that these are united with the subject, or perhaps better, that the subject itself evolves under the necessity of the laws of its formal embodiment.

It is therefore not surprising that in this more ambitious painting, executed at a decisive moment in his life, Gauguin should have felt even more acutely his lack of complete control over the creation of his work; that both form and meaning, which as we have seen were inextricably mixed, should have taken shape, as he said,

---

[18] "The Theme of 'The Ancient Mariner'," *Scrutiny*, 9 (March 1941), 342. This essay is reprinted in *The Importance of Scrutiny*, edited by Eric Bentley. Copyright 1949 by George W. Stewart, Inc. Reprinted by permission of the publisher.

"in a dream," a dream whose full import he understood only upon its completion. ROBERT GOLDWATER [19]

Analysis like this may seem perhaps mechanical, and it does not, of course, reproduce the poet's way of constructing the poem. His ways are devious even to himself, and A. E. Housman has specifically said that very little in his poetry was produced by conscious effort. Analysis can only describe in a few obvious aspects the material pattern as finally produced in the poem. And it is certainly true, as Professor Alexander has said, that the poet does not know distinctly what the end-product is to be until it actually *is*. He does not map a pattern and then proceed to fill it out with words. But neither is this pattern a chance or arbitrary one. For its organization is in every detail related to its meaning. . . . Its greatness and perfection do not lie in the fact that the poet could construct this formal pattern representing unity in variety. It lies in the fact that the pattern seems to spring inevitably from the deepest meaning or feeling in the poem [*We'll to the Woods No More*], and that it serves, while being a complete sound pattern in itself, to unite the content with its symbol. For if the symbol were all, if the poem meant no more than that the season for gathering green is over, the poet would not be driven to the extremes of contrast in form and sound, to the reiteration, the intensification, and the enlargement of the form. Just as in life we often know by a man's way of cherishing an object that it is not merely an object but is a symbol of something important to him, so here by Housman's way of cherishing the unimportant idea, he conveys to us without saying it — and indeed causes us to feel — the important meaning beneath. ELISABETH SCHNEIDER [20]

If the difference between tragedy and comedy is a difference between the emotions they express, it is not a difference that can be

---

[19] "The Genesis of a Picture: Theme and Form in Modern Painting," *Critique*, 1 (October 1946), 9.

[20] *Aesthetic Motive*, p. 102. Copyright 1939 by the Macmillan Co. Reprinted by permission of the publisher.

present to the artist's mind when he is beginning his work; if it were, he would know what emotion he was going to express before he had expressed it. No artist, therefore, so far as he is an artist proper, can set out to write a comedy, a tragedy, an elegy, or the like. So far as he is an artist proper, he is just as likely to write any one of these as any other; which is the truth that Socrates was heard expounding towards the dawn, among the sleeping figures in Agathon's dining room. * R. G. COLLINGWOOD [21]

* Plato: *Symposium*, 223 D.

The type of critical analysis which I have just attempted always raises certain questions. I shall state them bluntly and in the terms in which they usually appear:

1. Assuming that certain interpretations can be "drawn out of" or "put into" the poem by an "exercise of ingenuity," how do we know that the poet "intended" them?

2. If the present interpretations are "right," (a) is the poem not obscure, since good and experienced readers of the past have "missed" them, or (b) how is it that such good and experienced readers, having missed the interpretations, have still been deeply affected by the poem?

These questions, it will be readily seen, have to do, in order, with the theory of poetic creation and the theory of poetic appreciation. . . .

I should begin by saying that the questions, *as stated*, are false questions. There are real problems concealed behind these questions, but these are false because they are loaded — they will not permit an answer which does not falsify the nature of the process under discussion.

Let us take the first one.

[21] *The Principles of Art*, p. 116. Copyright 1938 by Clarendon Press. Reprinted by permission of the publisher.

EDITOR'S NOTE. Mr. Collingwood points out that the case is very different with representational art, for "Here the so-called artist knows in advance what kind of emotion he wishes to excite, and will construct works of different kinds according to the different kinds of effect they are to produce." *Ibid.*, p. 116.

The falsity of the first question inheres in the word *intended* as the word is intended in the context. The implication here is that the process of poetic creation is, shall we say, analogous to the process of building a house from a blueprint: the poet has an idea, the blueprint, and according to it, plank by plank and nail by nail, he makes a poem, the house. Actually, the creation of a poem is as much a process of discovery as a process of making. A poem may, in fact, start from an idea — and may involve any number of ideas — but the process for the poet is the process of discovering what the idea "means" to him in the light of his total being and his total experience (in so far as that total experience is available to him for the purpose of poetry — the degree here varies enormously from poet to poet). Or a poem may start from a phrase, a scene, an image, or an incident which has, for the poet, a suggestive quality — what, for him in the light of his total being and total available experience, we may call the symbolic potential. Then the process for the poet is the process of discovering why the item has caught his attention in the first place — which is simply another way of saying that he is trying to develop the symbolic potential. Or the original item may lead by some more or less obscure train of association to another item which will become the true germ of the poem, and whose symbolic potential may supplant that of the first item. However the process starts, it is, of course, enormously complicated. The degree of effort may vary from instance to instance (the poet may dream up his poem in a flash or it may be laboriously accreted like coral), and the degree of self-consciousness may vary from instance to instance (the poet may or may not in the process of creation interlard his symbolical thinking with discursive and critical thinking). As Coleridge said, and as many other poets and even scientists have said, the unconscious may be the genius in the man of genius. But this is not to define the process as an irrational process. What comes unbidden from the depths at the moment of creation may be the result of the most conscious and narrowly rational effort in the past. In any case, the poet always retains the right of rejecting whatever seems to violate his nature and his developing conception

227

of the poem. And the process of rejection and self-criticism may be working continually during the composition of a poem. In the case of *The Ancient Mariner* we have good evidence that the poet was working in terms of a preconceived theme, and we know that the original composition required some months and that the process of revision required years.

Whatever the amount of possible variation from case to case in various respects, we can say that the process is a process of discovery which objectifies itself as a making. What the poet is trying to discover, then, is what kind of poem he can make. And the only thing he, in the ordinary sense, may "intend" is to make a poem. In so far as his process of discovery has been more than a rhetorical exercise, he cannot do otherwise than "intend" what his poem says, any more than he can change his own past as past, but he does not fully know what he "intends" until the poem is fully composed. A purpose "formally conceived" is not, as Wordsworth said, necessary, first to initiate the process of creation, or second, to give the finished poem a meaning ultimately expressive not only of the man but of his "ideas" in a restricted sense. But, he went on to say, "habits of meditation have, I trust, so prompted and regulated my feelings, that my descriptions of such objects as strongly excite those feelings, will be found to carry along with them a *purpose*."

If the poet does not have a blueprint of intention (and if he does happen to have it, we ordinarily have no access to it), on what basis may a poem be interpreted? What kind of evidence is to be admitted? The first piece of evidence is the poem itself. And here, as I have suggested earlier, the criterion is that of internal consistency. If the elements of a poem operate together toward one end, we are entitled to interpret the poem according to that end. Even if the poet himself should rise to contradict us, we could reply that his words do speak louder than his actions. ROBERT PENN WARREN [22]

[22] Essay, pp. 113–15 in *The Rime of the Ancient Mariner*. Copyright 1946 by Reynal and Hitchcock. Reprinted by permission of Harcourt, Brace and Co.

The Actual Intention of the Work of Art

I say that I think it is the business of the poet to express, and to criticise, the culture in which he lives and to which he belongs. But what it is the task of the poet to do, is always something more than, and can be something very different from his conscious purpose. That the purpose of a poet, what he sets out to do and what he thinks he is doing, is relevant to the understanding of his poetry I do not deny; nor do I deny that when he has a conscious purpose, it may be one which can be greatly to the advantage, or alternatively to the detriment of his poetry. I only say that the function of his poetry cannot be judged by his purpose. . . .

. . .

If I am right, then a great deal more goes to the making of poetry than the conscious purpose of the poet; and, if this is so, the poet's social rôle also is more than, and other than, any conscious social purpose of his part. The poet may, or may not, have a deliberate intention to teach or to persuade. It is easy to see that Virgil had a particular attitude towards the Roman people, the Roman City, the Roman Empire, to communicate to his audience in the *Aeneid*; that Dante, and Milton in a different way, were aiming to teach a particular theology, in their more abstract passages, and to make this theology real to their readers, in their descriptions of scenes, events, and characters: and the effect of their poetry upon contemporary readers may be assumed to have been very close to their intentions. But with the passage of time, their poetry reveals new and different significance. And with other poets, also of the first rank, it is not always easy to see what their conscious purpose was, or whether they had any, or whether it matters. Even with the Greek dramatists, did the poet really hope or intend to benefit his audience by precept or example? And did Racine create Roxane in order to warn society against the dangers of uncontrolled passion; or did Shakespeare create Lear as a warning against the self-deception of senile vanity?

It is obvious that any attempt to define the function of poetry in terms of the purpose of the poet, is to involve ourselves in a labyrinth from which there is no extrication. All we can say is that when a poet has had a clear and distinct purpose, this purpose appears to have been a necessary condition of his writing the poetry: his purpose was useful to him. And when he has had such a purpose, we have to take account of it, whether we sympathise with it or not, in order fully to appreciate his poetry; and this is as true when his poem has to do with affairs two thousand years ago as when it deals with affairs contemporary with ourselves. The direct social value of poetry was much in the minds of critics and theorists of the Renaissance, for whom every notable man of antiquity was an example to be imitated or avoided, as the illustration of some virtue or vice described by Aristotle. Later moralists have been less naive, but also more vague. And in recent times, a reason why we have become more cautious in accepting a poet's expressed intention as evidence of what he was really doing, is that we have all become more conscious of the rôle of the unconscious. T. S. ELIOT [23]

Every work of art that lasts long in the world is continually taking on these new colours which the artist neither foresaw nor intended. C. S. LEWIS [24]

It was not until I had written these lines [in *Love and Death*], and read what I had written [the poem as dream-transcript], that I realized I had invented a myth which exactly expressed Freud's theory of the two instincts which control all life — the instincts of Eros and Death. HERBERT READ [25]

[23] "The Social Function of Poetry," *Adelphi*, 21 (July 1945), 154, 155–56. This essay is reprinted in *Critiques and Essays in Criticism*, edited by R. W. Stallman. Copyright 1949 by Ronald Press.

[24] *The Personal Heresy*, p. 16. Copyright 1939 by Oxford University Press. Reprinted by permission of the publisher.

EDITOR'S NOTE. Contrast Pope's dictum:

> In every work regard the writer's End,
> For none can compass more than they intend.
>
> *Essay on Criticism*, II, 255.

[25] *Collected Essays*, p. 114. Copyright 1938 by Faber and Faber, Ltd. Reprinted by permission of the author and the publisher.

In Mr. Empson's poetry there is no scope for vagueness of interpretation, and its "difficulty" arises from this merit. MICHAEL ROBERTS [26]

Mr. Epstein further says: "A work of sculpture or music or painting usually conveys a variety of meanings to people." He is mistaken. For a work of art to do that is not usual. It only does so when it is meaningless. If his groups convey a variety of meanings to people, there is their condemnation. MONTGOMERY BELGION [27]

Expression, to my way of thinking, does not consist of the passion mirrored upon a human face or betrayed by a violent gesture. The whole arrangement of my picture is expressive. The place occupied by figures or objects, the empty spaces around them, the proportions — everything plays a part. Composition is the art of arranging in a decorative manner the various elements at the painter's disposal for the expression of his feelings. In a picture every part will be visible and will play the role conferred upon it, be it principal or secondary. All that is not useful in the picture is detrimental. HENRI-MATISSE [28]

The poet, even when, like Ruskin or De Quincey, he writes in prose, makes the reader pick out the precise particular sense required from an indefinite number of possible senses which a word, phrase or sentence may carry. The means by which he does this are many and varied . . . the way in which he uses them is the poet's own secret, something which cannot be taught. He knows how to do it, but he does not himself know how it is done. I. A. RICHARDS [29]

The best artist constructs his work in such a way as to admit of no interpretation but the single intended one. A work of art has

[26] Preface, p. 12 in *New Signatures*. Copyright 1932 by the Hogarth Press. Reprinted by permission of the publisher.

[27] "Meaning in Art," *Criterion*, 9 (January 1930), 215.

[28] *Notes d'un Peintre*, p. 30. Copyright 1931 by the Museum of Modern Art. Reprinted by permission of the publisher. This essay is reprinted in *Artists on Art*, edited by Robert Goldwater and Marc Treves. Copyright 1945 by Pantheon Books.

[29] *Science and Poetry*, p. 34. Copyright 1926 by W. W. Norton and Co., Inc., and by the Orthological Institute. Reprinted by permission of the publisher.

but a single intention, one total meaning, one composite theme. And all its apparently disparate or conflicting elements — characters, plot, setting, atmosphere, tone, imagery, etc. — all cohere to form that single intention. This principle provides a key for the reader to unlock the meaning of a work. Since each part of the work has been contrived to function as a token or bead strung upon the theme, once we perceive the meaning or function of any single part we have begun our discovery of the composite meaning which forms the work into an intrinsic whole. Knowing that every part is beaded to impart a functional relationship to the whole, the skilful reader perceives the token values of each part, bead by bead, as he reads along to the close. R. W. STALLMAN [30]

He [Hopkins] combines words, breaks them, transposes the parts of speech, forges them anew so that the meaning, if it is to be understood at all, will be understood *his* way. MORRIS U. SCHAPPES [31]

The artist does have an intention, conscious or unconscious, and it is a single intention. That is why, for example, the audience, at the production of one of Racine's tragedies, inquired of the author if they had applauded in the right places. MONTGOMERY BELGION [32]

The Critic as Interpreter of the Original Intention of the Artist (the Intentional Fallacy)

About a work of art there is indeed one question of aesthetic significance which can be asked and answered objectively: does this poem, painting, melody, or whatever it may be, truly express the

---

[30] "The Critical Reader," *College English*, 9 (April 1948), 362. This essay is reprinted in *The Art of Modern Fiction*, by Ray B. West, Jr., and R. W. Stallman. Copyright 1949 by Rinehart and Co., Inc.

[31] Review in *Symposium*, 2 (January 1931), 134.

[32] "What Is Criticism?" *Criterion*, 10 (October 1930), 129.

feeling it was intended to? But the question can be answered only by the artist himself: he alone knows what his intention was. The beauty of the work of art depends upon something wholly different, upon its effect in the observer of it, the "consumer," who makes it the object of aesthetic contemplation. When we expose ourselves, without preconceptions or practical prepossessions, to the effects of an object upon our sensibility, and find those effects agreeable, we call the object beautiful; when we find them disagreeable, we call it ugly. But the effects vary with the individual, and exerted upon the same individual, they vary with time and circumstance. A judgment of beauty is thus wholly relative: *"the particular constitution of the individual critic . . . is the necessary and sufficient ground for all such judgments."* Thus is the spectre of objective control exorcised, and complete freedom established for everyone. LAWRENCE BUERMEYER [33]

From *some* point of view he [the scholar or critic] must learn to deal with the three questions framed by Goethe: "What did the author propose to himself? Is what he proposes reasonable and sensible? And how far has he succeeded in carrying it out?" To answer the first question, he must know how to read; to answer the last, he must have a literary aesthetic; to answer the second, the most difficult question, he must possess at least a tentative "working philosophy," a conception of life developed by experience and reason. NORMAN FOERSTER [34]

It must be admitted, I think, that we have had something like this [i.e., criticism which supposes that a work of art is explained by its source materials] in the interpretation of Shakespeare during the reign of scientific or realistic criticism. And it must surely be admitted, too, that the person who is dealing with certainties

[33] Review of *The Philosophy of Art*, by Curt John Ducasse, in *Symposium*, 1 (April 1930), 272.
[34] "The Study of Letters," p. 25 in *Literary Scholarship*. Copyright 1941 by the University of North Carolina Press. Reprinted by permission of the publisher.

in this business is not the realist but the aesthetic critic. For the one thing certain in a work of art is the effect it has on us. . . . But *judge by results* is the grand principle of aesthetic criticism. The vice of realism — of the interpretation based on the scientific study of conditions — is its noticeable tendency to substitute for that principle some attempt to *judge by intentions*, as if knowledge of the conditions [under which an artist worked] could confer any right to say what was intended. The conditions may be ascertainable fact; but to proceed from them to intentions is to take a blind jump into pure theory. You can never be sure what the intentions of an artist were, whereas you always know what he actually did. And if aesthetic criticism is to take over the invaluable things our scientific criticism has gained for us, it will not be to let *judgement by results*, which are unmistakable, give way to *judgement by intentions*, which can only be speculations, often very vain and impertinent; it will simply be to sharpen and intensify our *judgement by results* by our understanding of the means used to obtain them. LASCELLES ABERCROMBIE [35]

Reference to the artist's "intentions" is usually a sign that the commentator — in so far as he is a commentator rather than a biographer — has lost touch with the essentials of the poetic work. G. WILSON KNIGHT [36]

In all these kinds [of poems] Shelley produces works which, though not perfect, are in one way more satisfactory than any of Dryden's longer pieces: that is to say, they display a harmony between the poet's real and professed intention, they answer the demands of their forms, and they have a unity of spirit. C. S. LEWIS [37]

[35] "A Plea for the Liberty of Interpreting," pp. 205-6 in *Modern English Essays*, second series. Copyright 1932 by Oxford University Press. Reprinted by permission of the publisher.
[36] *The Wheel of Fire*, p. 7. Copyright 1948 by Methuen and Co., Ltd., and 1930 by Oxford University Press. Reprinted by permission of the publishers.
[37] *Rehabilitations*, p. 21. Copyright 1939 by Oxford University Press. Reprinted by permission of the publisher.

What then does Freud believe that the analytical method can do? Two things: explain the "inner meanings" of the work of art and explain the temperament of the artist as man.

A famous example of the method is the attempt to solve the "problem" of *Hamlet* as suggested by Freud and as carried out by Dr. Ernest Jones, his early and distinguished follower. Dr. Jones's monograph is a work of painstaking scholarship and of really masterly ingenuity. The research undertakes not only the clearing up of the mystery of Hamlet's character but also the discovery of "the clue to much of the deeper workings of Shakespeare's mind." Part of the mystery in question is, of course, why Hamlet, after he had so definitely resolved to do so, did not avenge upon his hated uncle his father's death. But there is another mystery to the play — what Freud calls "the mystery of its effect," its magical appeal that draws so much interest toward it. Recalling the many failures to solve the riddle of the play's charm, he wonders if we are to be driven to the conclusion "that its magical appeal rests solely upon the impressive thoughts in it and the splendor of its language." Freud believes that we can find a source of power beyond this.

We remember that Freud has told us that the meaning of a dream is its intention, and we may assume that the meaning of a drama is its intention too. The Jones research undertakes to discover what it was that Shakespeare intended to say about Hamlet. It finds that the intention was wrapped by the author in a dreamlike obscurity because it touched so deeply both his personal life and the moral life of the world; what Shakespeare intended to say is that Hamlet cannot act because he is incapacitated by the guilt he feels at his unconscious attachment to his mother. There is, I think, nothing to be quarreled with in the statement that there is an Oedipus situation in Hamlet; and if psychoanalysis has indeed added a new point of interest to the play, that is to its credit. And, just so, there is no reason to quarrel with Freud's conclusion when he undertakes to give us the meaning of *King Lear* by a tortuous tracing of the mythological implications of the theme of the three caskets, of the relation of the caskets to the Norms, the Fates, and the Graces, of the connection of these triadic females with Lear's daughters, of the transmogrification of the death goddess into the love goddess and the identification of Cordelia with both, all to the conclusion that the meaning of *King Lear* is to be found in the tragic refusal of an old man to "renounce love, choose death, and make friends with the necessity of dying." There is something both beautiful and suggestive in this, but it is not *the* meaning of *King Lear* any more than the Oedipus motive is *the* meaning of *Hamlet*. LIONEL TRILLING [38]

I propose to illustrate from Marvell's *Horatian Ode*. If we follow the orthodox procedure, the obvious way to understand the *Ode* is to ascertain by historical evidence — by letters and documents of all kinds — what Marvell really thought of Cromwell, or, since Marvell apparently thought different things of Cromwell at different times, to ascertain the date of the *Ode*, and then neatly fit it into the particular stage of Marvell's developing opinion of Cromwell. But this yields at best only an approximation of the poem; and there lurk in it some positive perils. For to ascertain what Marvell the man thought of Cromwell, and even to ascertain what Marvell as poet consciously intended to say in his poem, will not prove that the poem actually says this, or all this, or merely this. This last remark, in my opinion, does not imply too metaphysical a notion of the structure of a poem. There is surely a sense in which any one must agree that a poem has a life of its own, and a sense in which it provides in itself the only criterion by which what it says can be judged. CLEANTH BROOKS [39]

Within the urge to artistic production are two distinct impulses. One, possibly the more primitive of the two, is the impulse to

[38] *The Liberal Imagination*, pp. 47–48. Copyright 1950 by the Viking Press. Reprinted by permission of the publisher.
[39] "Criticism and Literary History: Marvell's Horatian Ode," *Sewanee Review*, 55 (Spring 1947), 199–200.

make something. Poetry for the Greeks was a making; and you can trust the Greeks. This impulse to make has come to pass for a desire to express, to communicate. Its existence seems to be what leads Mr. Lewis and Mr. Tillyard [in *The Personal Heresy*] to suppose that a poet, by means of his poems, communicates experience. Indeed, the existence of the impulse to make, and the interpretation of it as a desire to communicate, seem to be what have given rise to the supposition that poems are explicable in terms of the biography and psychology of the poet. If the poet in his poems is communicating something, it is presumably something he has experienced. He has had a mistress, he has seen her in a silk dress. Therefore, if we can only find out enough about the poet himself, we shall come upon his experiences at first hand, and likewise upon his undergoing of them, undistorted by the prism — or whatever it may be — of poetry.

Carried to its logical conclusion, however, this supposition implies the ultimate extinction of poetry. In time psychology and biography, if only they go on being cultivated successfully, may be expected to put us in direct touch with the experiences of a poet and his experiencing of them: the reading of his poems will have become superfluous.

But that is not the only objection. Undeniably there is to be discerned in the urge to artistic production a second impulse in addition to the one I have just spoken of. This second impulse is the impulse to call forth a response from a spectator, auditor, or reader — that is to say, an impulse to play on the feelings of other people. I suggest that this second impulse within the urge to artistic production is the only impulse with which, as regards the poet, readers of poetry, and hence critics also, are really concerned. For, unquestionably, to read a poem is to be affected by it. The poem exacts from us in the reading of it what it is now customary to call a response. It is for the sake of our responses to them that we read poems. And this response, the experience we have whenever we read a poem, is an experience which we have solely in reading poetry. It is a response to words, to their meanings and associations, to their sound and their arrangement. MONT-GOMERY BELGION [40]

The Artist as Interpreter of His Original Intention

But a poet, if he is a real one, judges his own achievements not by those of his contemporaries, but by the standards of his own intention. JOHN MIDDLETON MURRY [41]

The design, your Lordship sees, is good — the colouring transparent, — the drawing not amiss; — or to speak more like a man of science, — and measure my piece in the painter's scale, divided into 20, — I believe, my Lord, the outlines will turn out as 12, — the composition as 9, — the colouring as 6, — the expression 13 and a half, — and the design, — if I may be allowed, my Lord, to understand my own design, and supposing absolute perfection in designing to be as 20, — I think it cannot well fall short of 19. LAURENCE STERNE [42]

Now, there is a rather widespread conception that this [what was the artist trying to do?] is the question one should always ask an artist before beginning to criticize his work. In fairness to the artist, it is said, you should not criticize him for not doing something he was not trying to do. So, you want to know first what he was trying to do, and then you will judge if he did it. This is good advice to inexperienced persons or to critics who are caught in a rut and need some assistance to get out. It calls attention to the possible weakness of the spectator. But if the spectator is not

[40] "The Poet's Name," *Sewanee Review*, 54 (Autumn 1946), 642–43.
[41] *Aspects of Literature*, p. 69. Copyright 1920 by Collins Sons and Co., Ltd. Reprinted by permission of the publisher.
[42] *Tristram Shandy*, p. 17. World's Classics edition, copyright 1931 by Oxford University Press.

weak, there is no reason why the work of art should not explain itself. It can only obtain objectivity of judgment if it does, and, if it is thoroughly integrated, it both explains itself and has an objectivity of value.

So, if you are a man experienced in the potentialities of the materials of an art, and ask the artist what he was trying to do, it amounts to saying that whatever it was he was trying to do he did not succeed in doing it. What you are hoping is that he may have had an idea but lacked the ability to develop it, for then you can give him some assistance perhaps as to what materials to follow through and as to where he failed to answer demands of his materials and the like. When it is necessary to ask an artist what he was trying to do, either the spectator or the artist is weak. It is a question that an honest critic should never be afraid to ask, and that a critic secure in experience would be sure to ask when puzzled, for the most experienced critic has always something to learn about the potentialities of his art. But the question is intrinsically entirely irrelevant to the judgment of the aesthetic worth of an object. The aesthetic value of a work of art as an integration of feeling is as independent of any artist's subjective idea of what he wanted to do when he was making it, as the cognitive value of a scientific description of fact is independent of a scientist's idea of what he wanted to find when he started observing. STEPHEN C. PEPPER [43]

. . . the poet's sources or supposed *intentions* must never be allowed to interrupt or modify our interpretations. G. WILSON KNIGHT [44]

The poet's affection for his brother made it impossible for him to write the last line of this poem [Housman's *1887*] in the spirit of bitter sarcasm which Frank Harris "in all sincerity" found

---

[43] *The Basis of Criticism in the Arts*, pp. 82–83. Copyright 1946 by Harvard University Press. Reprinted by permission of the publisher.

[44] *The Christian Renaissance*, p. 105. Copyright 1933 by the Macmillan Co. of Canada, Ltd. Reprinted by permission of the publisher.

EDITOR'S NOTE. Compare with this D. H. Lawrence's remark, "Never trust the artist. Trust the tale." (See p. 242 of this book.)

there. Harris once told Kipling that he mixed his patriotism with snobbery, but to Housman Harris said: "You have poked fun at the whole thing and made splendid mockery of it." Housman replied sharply: "I never intended to poke fun, as you call it, at patriotism, and I can find nothing in the sentiment to make mockery of. I meant it sincerely. If Englishmen breed as good men as their fathers, then God will save their Queen. I can only reject and resent your — your truculent praise." CARL J. WEBER [45]

The value of a poem consisting in what it does to the readers, all questions about the poet's own attitude to his utterance are irrelevant. The question of his "sincerity" or "disinterestedness" should be forever banished from criticism. C. S. LEWIS [46]

We can never absolutely know that the imaginative experience we obtain from a work of art is identical with that of the artist. In proportion as the artist is a great one, we can be pretty certain that we have only caught his meaning partially and imperfectly. R. G. COLLINGWOOD [47]

A poet can try, of course, to give an honest report of the way in which he himself writes: the result may, if he is a good observer, be illuminating. And in one sense, but a very limited one, he knows better what his poems "mean" than can anyone else; he may know the history of their composition, the material which has gone in and come out in an unrecognisable form, and he knows what he was trying to do and what he was meaning to mean. But what a poem means is as much what it means to others as what it means to the author; and indeed, in the course of time a poet may become merely a reader in respect to his own works, forgetting his

[45] Notes, pp. 108–9 in the Jubilee Edition of *A Shropshire Lad.* Copyright 1946 by the Colby College Press. Reprinted by permission of the editor.

[46] *The Personal Heresy*, p. 120. Copyright 1939 by Oxford University Press. Reprinted by permission of the publisher.

[47] *The Principles of Art*, p. 309. Copyright 1938 by the Clarendon Press. Reprinted by permission of the publisher.

original meaning — or without forgetting, merely changing. So that, when Mr. Richards asserts that *The Waste Land* effects "a complete severance between poetry and all beliefs" I am no better qualified to say No! than is any other reader. T. S. ELIOT [48]

The various foregoing remarks [i.e., Valéry's remarks on the way his poem, *Cimetière Marin*, was conceived] may perhaps offer some idea of an author's reflections in the presence of a commentary on his work. He sees it as it was to have been and as it might have been, much more than as what it is. What, then, could be more interesting for him than the outcome of a scrupulous examination and the impressions of a disinterested scrutiny? It is not within myself that the real unity of a work of mine comes into being. I have written a "score" — but I can hear the thing itself only as it is played by the souls and minds of others.

. . .

As for the matter of the *literal* interpretation, I have already explained my attitude on that point in another place; but one can never insist upon it enough: *there is no true meaning of a text.* No auctorial authority. Whatever the author may have *meant*, he has written what he has written. Once published, a text is like a machine which each person may use as he will and as he can: there is no certainty of the maker's operating it better than another. Moreover, if he knows exactly what he wished to do, that knowledge forever troubles in him the perception of what he has done. PAUL VALÉRY [49]

[48] *The Use of Poetry and the Use of Criticism*, p. 130. Copyright 1933 by Faber and Faber, Ltd., and by Harvard University Press. Reprinted by permission of the publishers.

[49] "Concerning the 'Cimetière Marin'," *Southern Review*, 4 (Summer 1938), 165. Translated by Florence Codman and Hansell Baugh.

EDITOR'S NOTE. Valéry's remarks about the commentary on his work are echoed in a statement by John Malcolm Brinnin which provides further credentials on this critical point: "I can only acknowledge with wonder your almost necromantically exact analysis of my poem *Speech of the Wedding Guest.* You not only brought out conscious intentions, but made subconscious ones manifest; as a result, my reading of the exegesis [in *Poetry: A Critical Supplement*, February 1950], which began as a sort of checking-up, ended as a process of learning." Letter from John Malcolm Brinnin to the Editor.

It is a mistake, therefore, to ask a poet to explain his poems. That is to make the wrong approach to poetry, to knock at the wrong door. This emotional unity [in a poem] which is the *raison d'être* of every poem cannot be measured by the instruments of reason. Otherwise it would be simpler to express it in prose. The poem must be received directly, without questioning, and loved or hated. It has a necessary and external existence; it is impervious to reason, and if it has no discoverable meaning, it has immeasurable power. The poet has created in words an objective equivalence of his emotional experience: the words may not make sense, but they make the emotion — follow the contour of the thought — and reproduce, as nearly as possible, "the mind's internal echo of the imperfect sound." HERBERT READ [50]

The artist usually sets out — or used to — to point a moral and adorn a tale. The tale, however, usually points the other way, as a rule. Two blankly opposing morals, the artist's and the tale's. Never trust the artist. Trust the tale. The proper function of a critic is to save the tale from the artist who created it. D. H. LAWRENCE [51]

From Mr. Crane to the editor:
Your good nature and manifest interest in writing me about the obscurities apparent in my Melville poem ["At Melville's Tomb"] certainly prompt a wish to clarify my intentions in that poem as much as possible. But I realize that my explanations will not be very convincing. For a paraphrase is generally a poor substitute for any organized conception that one has fancied he has put into the more essentialized form of the poem itself.

At any rate, and though I imagine us to have considerable differences of opinion regarding the relationship of poetic metaphor to ordinary logic (I judge this from the angle of approach you use

[50] *Collected Essays*, p. 100. Copyright 1938 by Faber and Faber, Ltd. Reprinted by permission of the author and the publisher.
[51] *Studies in Classic American Literature*, p. 3. Copyright 1923 by Thomas Seltzer, Inc. Reprinted by permission of the Viking Press.

toward portions of the poem), I hope my answers will not be taken as a defense of merely certain faulty lines. I am really much more interested in certain theories of metaphor and technique involved generally in poetics, than I am concerned in vindicating any particular perpetrations of my own.

My poem may well be elliptical and actually obscure in the ordering of its content, but in your criticism of this very possible deficiency you have stated your objections in terms that allow me, at least for the moment, the privilege of claiming your ideas and ideals as theoretically, at least, quite outside the issues of my own aspirations. To put it more plainly, as a poet I may very possibly be more interested in the so-called illogical impingements of the connotations of words on the consciousness (and their combinations and interplay in metaphor on this basis) than I am interested in the preservation of their logically rigid significations at the cost of limiting my subject matter and perceptions involved in the poem.

This may sound as though I merely fancied juggling words and images until I found something novel, or esoteric; but the process is much more predetermined and objectified than that. The nuances of feeling and observation in a poem may well call for certain liberties which you claim the poet has no right to take. I am simply making the claim that the poet does have that authority, and that to deny it is to limit the scope of the medium so considerably as to outlaw some of the richest genius of the past.

. . .

Its paradox, of course, is that its apparent illogic operates so logically in conjunction with its context in the poem as to establish its claim to another logic, quite independent of the original definition of the word or phrase or image thus employed. It implies (this *inflection* of language) a previous or prepared receptivity to its stimulus on the part of the reader. The reader's sensibility simply responds by identifying this inflection of experience with some event in his own history or perceptions — or rejects it altogether. The logic of metaphor is so organically entrenched in pure sensibility that it can't be thoroughly traced or explained outside of historical sciences, like philology and anthropology. This "pseudo-statement," as I. A. Richards calls it in an admirable essay touching our contentions in last July's *Criterion*, demands completely other faculties of recognition than the pure rationalistic associations permit. Much fine poetry may be completely rationalistic in its use of symbols, but there is much great poetry of another order which will yield the reader very little when inspected under the limitation of such arbitrary concerns as are manifested in your judgment of the Melville poem, especially when you constitute such requirements of ordinary logical relationship between word and word as irreducible.

. . .

You ask me how a *portent* can possibly be wound in a *shell*. Without attempting to answer this for the moment, I ask you how Blake could possibly say that "a *sigh* is a *sword* of an Angel King." You ask me how *compass, quadrant and sextant "contrive"* tides. I ask you how Eliot can possibly believe that "Every street *lamp* that I pass *beats* like a fatalistic *drum!*" Both of my metaphors may fall down completely. I'm not defending their actual value in themselves, but your criticism of them in each case was leveled at an illogicality of relationship between symbols, which similar fault you must have either overlooked in case you have ever admired the Blake and Eliot lines, or have there condoned them on account of some more ultimate convictions pressed on you by the impact of the poems in their entirety.

It all comes to the recognition that emotional dynamics are not to be confused with any absolute order of rationalized definitions; ergo, in poetry the *rationale* of metaphor belongs to another order of experience than science, and is not to be limited by a scientific and arbitrary code of relationships either in verbal inflections or concepts.

There are plenty of people who have never accumulated a sufficient series of reflections (and these of a rather special nature) to perceive the relation between a *drum* and a *street lamp* — *via* the *unmentioned* throbbing of the heart and nerves in a distraught man which *tacitly* creates the reason and 'logic' of the Eliot metaphor. They will always have a perfect justification for ignoring those lines and to claim them obscure, excessive, etc., until by some experience of their own the words accumulate the necessary connotations to complete their connection. It is the same with the "patient etherized upon a table," isn't it? Surely that line must lack all eloquence to many people who, for instance, would delight in agreeing that the sky was like a dome of many-colored glass.

If one can't count on some such bases in the reader now and then, I don't see how the poet has any chance to ever get beyond the simplest conceptions of emotion and thought, of sensation and lyrical sequence. If the poet is to be held completely to the already evolved and exploited sequences of imagery and logic — what field of added consciousness and increased perceptions (the actual province of poetry, if not lullabys) can be expected when one has to relatively return to the alphabet every breath or so? In the minds of people who have sensitively read, seen and experienced a great deal, isn't there a terminology something like short-hand as compared to visual description and dialectics, which the artist ought to be right in trusting as a reasonable connective agent toward fresh concepts, more inclusive evaluations? The question is more important to me than it perhaps ought to be; but as long as poetry is written, an audience, however small, is implied, and there remains the question of an active or an inactive imagination as its characteristic.

It is of course understood that a street-lamp simply can't beat with a sound like a drum; but it often happens that images, themselves totally dissociated, when joined in the circuit of a particular emotion located with specific relation to both of them, conduce to great vividness and accuracy of statement in defining that emotion.

Not to rant on forever I'll beg your indulgence and come at once to the explanations you requested on the Melville poem:

> "*The dice of drowned men's bones he saw bequeath*
> *An embassy.*"

Dice bequeath an embassy, in the first place, by being ground (in this connection only, of course) in little cubes from the bones of drowned men by the action of the sea, and are finally thrown up on the sand, having "numbers" but no identification. These being the bones of dead men who never completed their voyage, it seems legitimate to refer to them as the only surviving evidence of certain messages undelivered, mute evidence of certain things, experiences that the dead mariners might have had to deliver. Dice as a symbol of chance and circumstance is also implied.

> "*The calyx of death's bounty giving back,*" etc.

This calyx refers in a double ironic sense both to a cornucopia and the vortex made by a sinking vessel. As soon as the water has closed over a ship this whirlpool sends up broken spars, wreckage, etc., which can be alluded to as *livid hieroglyphs*, making a *scattered chapter* so far as any complete record of the recent ship and her crew is concerned. In fact, about as much definite knowledge might come from all this as anyone might gain from the roar of his own veins, which is easily heard (haven't you ever done it?) by holding a shell close to one's ear.

> "*Frosted eyes lift altars.*"

Refers simply to a conviction that a man, not knowing perhaps a definite god yet being endowed with a reverence for deity — such a man naturally postulates a deity somehow, and the altar of that deity by the very *action* of the eyes *lifted* in searching.

> "*Compass, quadrant and sextant contrive no farther tides.*"

Hasn't it often occurred that instruments originally invented for record and computation have inadvertently so extended the concepts of the entity they were invented to measure (concepts of space, etc.) in the mind and imagination that employed them, that they may metaphorically be said to have extended the original boundaries of the entity measured? This little bit of "relativity" ought not to be discredited in poetry now that scientists are proceeding to measure the universe on principles of pure *ratio*, quite as metaphorical, so far as previous standards of scientific methods extended, as some of the axioms in *Job*.

I may have completely failed to provide any clear interpretation of these symbols in their context. And you will no doubt feel that I have rather heatedly explained them for anyone who professed no claims for their particular value. I hope, at any rate, that I have clarified them enough to suppress any suspicion that their obscurity derives from a lack of definite intentions in the subject-matter of the poem. The execution is another matter, and you must be accorded a superior judgment to mine in that regard. HART CRANE [52]

As some critics have pointed out, we must be wary in accepting Rilke's later explanations of his work. It is quite possible that, carried away by his recognition and the frequent requests for an exposition of his meaning, he may have evolved a prose "philosophy" which is not exactly coincident with the thought-structure of his poetry. Fritz Dehn was very right when he said that the poetry itself has an unconditional precedence over any information the poet might give about its genesis. D. J. ENRIGHT [53]

In general, the greater the degree of a poem's conformity with Poetry, the less the possibility of its being thought in prose without perishing. To summarize a poem, to put it into prose, is simply not to know the essense of an art. Poetic necessity is inseparable from sensory form, and the ideas expressed or suggested by a poem's text are not at all the unique and principal object of the discourse, but *means* which conspire *in equal degree* with the sounds, cadences, beats, and ornaments, to provoke, to sustain a certain tension or exaltation, to beget in us a *world* — or a *modality of being* — that is wholly harmonious.

[52] Quoted, pp. 417–21 in *Hart Crane*, by Brom Weber. Copyright 1948 by the Bodley Press. Reprinted by permission of the publisher.
[53] "A Book on Rilke," *Scrutiny*, 10 (January 1942), 301.

If, therefore, someone questions me; if someone is disturbed (as does happen, and sometimes rather acutely) about what I "meant" in this poem or that, I reply that my meaning was not *to say*, but *to do*, and that it was the intention of *doing* that *made the meaning* of what I *said*. PAUL VALÉRY [54]

The Critic as Interpreter of the Actual Intention of the Work of Art

For my part I approach Mr. Empson's critical work with admiration, and also with caution, because I do not wish to compete with so much learning, taste, and ingenuity. I hesitate only over his sense of proportion, and I mean by that, his sense of the poetic occasion. But perhaps it should be said in justice that he seems to recognize two separate situations with respect to the poet-expositor relation.

The first occurs when Mr. Empson tells us what the poem means to him, and judges that it meant all that to the poet. In most cases, it is certain that other critics will find the poet's meaning not so complex as he represents it. Mr. Empson may urge in modesty that poets, or at least many of them, have had just as ingenious meanings in their heads as he has, and just as many at the same moment. The other critics will probably answer by denying it, which is a soft impeachment of Mr. Empson . . . or they may argue that poets give out what meanings they please, but do not ordinarily take pains to hide them, and do not conceive of poems as charades, or marvels of ratiocination.

The second situation occurs when the poet has not been conscious of all the meanings discovered by the critic for the excellent reason that some of them came out of his unconscious mind; they

[54] "Concerning the 'Cimetière Marin'," *Southern Review*, 4 (Summer 1938), 162.

would not necessarily be for that less willed than the others, nor less important. (This much of their thesis the Freudians have seen carried overwhelmingly.) But here too Mr. Empson will have an argument on his hands, for we know from experience how the Freudians and the less imaginative persons can quarrel as to when a subterranean significance attaches to words and acts that think they are innocent. I must remark in passing that Mr. Empson's kinds of conscious meanings are generally more comprehensive and therefore more sober than the lurid Freudian ones.

It is in this second situation, as I understand Mr. Empson, that he regards his critical elucidation as following a "psychological" method; though I believe he has not made the distinction systematically. The word turns up in his essay on Milton. He fears it may be offensive, since it seems to imply that "Milton wrote in a muddle without knowing his own mind." He offers his feeling that Milton generally understood what he was doing, though there really are places "where there is a muddle whose effect is unsatisfying."

Perhaps the critical method that applies in the other sort of situation, where the poetic effects were fully intended, might rate as "logical." The poem is satisfying if all its effects are logical; which would mean that they are objective, and public or universal, since all men are rational.

And surely there must be effects apparent to certain qualified readers which were concealed from the poet by the disorder in his own mind, the feud between its conscious and unconscious levels. These are effects which would seem to invite the attentions of the sublest critic, who in Mr. Empson's view would be the psychologist. For some years we have been hearing about what psychology is going to do for the study of poetry. Mr. Empson's performance is far the finest fruit this tree has yet borne us. JOHN CROWE RANSOM [55]

Training in aesthetic perception is the cultivation of habits that discriminate details so readily that their meaning, as we call it, is

[55] "Mr. Empson's Muddles," *Southern Review*, 4 (Autumn 1938), 323–24.

read off unconsciously and integrated in the larger but equally determinate effect that we feel as this individual expression of faith or this specifically presented case of dilapidation. *Full* technical aesthetic perception not only apprehends such qualitative character, but discriminates the technical and aesthetic constituents of the effect. And fully adequate aesthetic training would have the result of making us so familiar with the uses of lines and shadings, pigments and brush strokes, washes and masses, color variations and modes of applying varnish, that these would all be discriminated automatically, and viewed not separately but as they have contributed to, and remain integral in, the presented picture, which *feels* expert and subtle and strong, perhaps, as well as effectively desolate or warm or comforting or nobly religious. D. W. PRALL [56]

Henry Purcell [by Hopkins] calls for mention as a curious special case. There can be few readers who have not found it strangely impressive, and few who could have elucidated it without extraneous help. It is not independent of the explanatory note by Hopkins that Bridges prints; yet when one approaches it with the note fresh in mind the intended meaning seems to be sufficiently *in* the poem to allay, at any rate, the dissatisfaction caused by baffled understanding. F. R. LEAVIS [57]

In another of Yeats's best poems, *Among School Children*, there is a passage which becomes, I think, very much better *when it is misunderstood*. Or rather when Yeats's intended meaning is mistaken for another one. DELMORE SCHWARTZ [58]

. . . this quality of transferable or generalized experience might be regarded as the defining quality of lyrical poetry.

What I have just said should make plain the difficulty of com-

[56] *Aesthetic Analysis*, p. 159. Copyright 1936 by Thomas Y. Crowell Co. Reprinted by permission of the publisher.
[57] "Gerard Manley Hopkins," *Scrutiny*, 12 (Spring 1944), 93.
[58] "An Unwritten Book," *Southern Review*, 7 (Winter 1942), 488.

prehending a poem exactly and fully; its total intention may be
very different from its paraphrasable, or purely logical content.
If one take, for example, Mr. Allen Tate's sonnet, *The Subway*,
and translate it into good scholarly prose, using nothing but the
rational content of the poem as reference, one will find the author
saying that as a result of his ideas and of his metropolitan environment, he is going mad. Now as a matter of fact, the poem says
nothing of the sort:

> Dark accurate plunger down the successive knell
> Of arch on arch, where ogives burst a red
> Reverberance of hail upon the dead
> Thunder, like an exploding crucible!
> Harshly articulate, musical steel shell
> Of angry worship, hurled religiously
> Upon your business of humility
> Into the iron forestries of hell!
>
> Till broken in the shift of quieter
> Dense altitudes tangential of your steel,
> I am become geometries — and glut
> Expansions like a blind astronomer
> Dazed, while the worldless heavens bulge and reel
> In the cold revery of an idiot.

The sonnet indicates that the author has faced and defined the
possibility of the madness that I have mentioned (a possibility
from the consideration of which others as well as himself may
have found it impossible to escape) and has arrived at a moral
attitude toward it, an attitude which is at once defined and communicated by the poem. This attitude is defined only by the entire
poem, not by the logical content alone; it is a matter not only of
logical content, but of feeling as well. The feeling is particular
and unparaphrasable, but one may indicate the nature of it briefly
by saying that it is a feeling of dignity and of self-control in the
face of a situation of major difficulty, a difficulty which the poet
fully apprehends. This feeling is inseparable from what we call
poetic form, or unity, for the creation of a form is nothing more
nor less than the act of evaluating and shaping (that is, con-

trolling) a given experience. It should be obvious that any attempt to reduce the rational content of such a poem would tend to confuse or even to eliminate the feeling: the poem consists in the relationship between the two. YVOR WINTERS [59]

[Concerning Yvor Winters' analysis of Allen Tate's "The Subway":]

This is one of the most amazing passages in literary criticism. Its purport is so strange that we cannot at once grasp what is being said. I believe, first, that Winters deceives himself through his phrase, "total intention," at the beginning. The total intention of the poem is something, but not an intention known to the poet at the moment when he begins to work up his logical content into a poem. Total intention is the total meaning of the finished poem, which differs from the original logical content by having acquired a detail which is immaterial to this content, being everywhere specific, or local, or particular, and at any rate unpredictable. And what, precisely, is the poet's intention at the beginning? It is to write a poem, and that is, since he has written poems before, to turn his logical content loose to shift for itself in the world of fortuitous experience; to get out of the world of pure logical content. It is a disrespect to the logic, if you are tremendously interested in the logic. If the given logical content is a moral one, it is a disrespect to morality, if you are devoted to that. It is a disrespect to morality in the degree that it is a respect to something called "poetic" experience. Poetic experience is only to be had by disrespecting whatever kind of logical content we start with. Mathematicians do not care to offer that disrespect to their own logical content, and do not turn it over to poetic composition. Poetic composition would compound their mathematical content with content that was not mathematical at all. And poetic composition will compound an ethical content with what is not

[59] *In Defense of Reason*, pp. 19–21. Copyright 1947 by the Swallow Press, and by William Morrow and Co., Inc. Reprinted by permission of the publishers. Allen Tate's poem, "The Subway," is reprinted by permission of Charles Scribner's Sons.

ethical at all; so that if Mr. Winters is entrusting his morality to poetry he is not a man of greater moral scruple but of less.

Presently Winters quotes a poem comparable with Mr. Tate's, by Mr. Howard Baker, and remarks similarly:

The spiritual control in a poem, then, is simply a manifestation of the spiritual control within the poet, and, as I have already indicated, it may have been an important means by which the poet arrived at a realization of spiritual control.

The idea that the poet is controlling his moral experience, while he puts it through its paces, is hardly consistent with the earlier description of its being free and unpredictable: it becomes free and controlled at once. I should say that he is not controlling so much as relaxing his moral effort, forgetting it; but, and this ought to conciliate the moralist, because he can afford to, because his spiritual control is secure. I should think it a case of spiritual easiness, the aftermath of intense moral experience. And here we are back on familiar ground. This experience is Wordsworth's "emotion recollected in tranquillity." It is described in Coleridge's doctrine of Imagination, when that faculty pierces through the film of "selfish solicitude" and permits us an insight into the real nature of our "familiar objects." It is in the doctrine of psychic distance. JOHN CROWE RANSOM [60]

But of course a critic is still free to say that Keats's good intentions don't come off, that the machine may have been built but still doesn't work. You may well decide that the effect is still "Cockney," like "Oh Attic shape! Fair Attitude With Brede"; that this brash attempt to end with a smart bit of philosophy had not got enough knowledge behind it to justify its claims. I do not feel that myself, but I do not see how to argue about the matter, and much as I dislike a *non possumus* theory in general I am tempted to think that there aren't any arguments. Supposing that I had completely explained how the machine is

[60] *The New Criticism*, pp. 224–26. Copyright 1941 by New Directions. Reprinted by permission of the publisher.

meant to work (of course no doubt I haven't), the question whether it does work is surely a matter of "taste"; it can only be left to the reader to try for himself. WILLIAM EMPSON [61]

But what I have to insist on is that intention in the important sense can only be determined by the tests applied in literary criticism. The analysis and judgment of works of literary art belong to the literary critic, who *is* one in so far as he observes a disciplined relevance in response, comment and determination of significance. He is concerned with the work in front of him as something that should contain within itself the reason why it is so and not otherwise. The more experience — experience of life and literature together — he brings to bear on it the better, of course; and it is true that extraneous information may make him more percipient. But the business of critical intelligence will remain what it was: to ensure relevance of response and to determine what is actually *there* in the work of art. The critic will be especially wary how he uses extraneous knowledge about the writer's intentions. Intentions are nothing in art except as realized and the tests of realization will remain what they were. They are applied in the operation of the critic's sensibility; they are a matter of his sense, derived from his literary experience, of what the living thing feels like — of the difference between that which has been willed and put there, or represents no profound integration, and that which grows from a deep centre of life. These tests may very well reveal that the deep animating intention (if that is the right word) is something very different from the intention the author would declare. F. R. LEAVIS [62]

[61] "Thy Darling in an Urn," *Sewanee Review*, 55 (Autumn 1947), 696-97.
[62] "Henry James and the Function of Criticism," *Scrutiny*, 15 (Spring 1948), 99.

Bibliography 1920-1950

TOPICAL CHECKLISTS OF SELECTED READINGS

I. THE NATURE AND FUNCTION OF CRITICISM

ABERCROMBIE, LASCELLES. *Principles of Literary Criticism.* Gollancz, 1928.

ALEXANDER, SAMUEL. *Beauty and Other Forms of Value.* Macmillan, 1933.

BELGION, MONTGOMERY. *The Human Parrot and Other Essays.* Oxford, 1931.

———. "What Is Criticism?" *Criterion*, 10 (October 1930), 118–37.

BELL, CLIVE. *Art.* Chatto, 1947.

———. "The Critic's Role," *Nation*, 167 (November 20, 1948), 578–80.

BENTLEY, ERIC, editor. *The Importance of Scrutiny.* Stewart, 1948.

BISHOP, J. P. *Collected Essays*, edited by Edmund Wilson. Scribner, 1948.

BLACKMUR, R. P. "A Critic's Job of Work," in *The Double Agent.* Arrow Editions, 1935. Pp. 235, 269–302, and *passim*.

———. *The Expense of Greatness.* Arrow Editions, 1940. Pp. 81, 174ff.

BLUM, MORGAN. "John Crowe Ransom, Critic," *Western Review*, 14 (Winter 1950), 85–102.

BOAS, GEORGE. *A Primer for Critics.* Johns Hopkins University Press, 1937. P. 88.

BROOKS, CLEANTH. "Empson's Criticism," *Accent*, 4 (Summer 1944), 208–16.

BROOKS, VAN WYCK. *The Opinions of Oliver Allston.* Dutton, 1941. Pp. 163–75, 228–46.

BURDETT, OSBERT. *Critical Essays.* Holt, 1927.

BURGUM, E. B., editor. *The New Criticism.* Prentice-Hall, 1930.

BURKE, KENNETH. *A Grammar of Motives.* Prentice-Hall, 1946.

———. "Key Words for Critics," *Kenyon Review*, 4 (Winter 1942), 126–32.

255

———. *The Philosophy of Literary Form.* Louisiana State University Press, 1941.

BUSH, DOUGLAS. "The New Criticism: Some Old-Fashioned Queries," *P.M.L.A.*, 64 (March 1949), 13–21.

CALVERTON, V. F. *The New Grounds of Criticism.* University of Washington Chapbook 34, 1930.

CAZAMIAN, L. F. *Criticism in the Making.* Macmillan, 1929.

———. "The Object of Criticism," *Rice Institute Pamphlet*, 16 (January 1929), 17–31.

COLLINS, SEWARD. "Criticism in America," *Bookman*, 71 (1930), 241–56; 72 (1930), 145–65, 209–28.

COLUM, MARY. *From These Roots.* Scribner, 1937.

COOMARASWAMY, A. K. "What Is the Use of Art Anyway?" *American Review*, 8 (January 1935), 321ff.

"Criticism," in *Encyclopaedia Britannica.* VI, p. 727.

DAICHES, DAVID. "Principles of Literary Criticism," *New Republic*, 98 (March 1, 1939), 8.

———. *A Study of Literature.* Cornell University Press, 1948.

DAY-LEWIS, CECIL. "A Hope for Poetry," in *Collected Poems.* Random House, 1935. P. 199.

Dictionary of World Literature. Edited by Joseph Shipley. Philosophical Library, 1943. Pp. 132–41, 509–11.

DUPEE, F. W. "The Americanism of Van Wyck Brooks," in *Critiques and Essays in Criticism*, edited by R. W. Stallman. Ronald Press, 1949. Pp. 460–71.

———. "Edmund Wilson's Criticism," *Partisan Review*, 4 (May 1938), 48–51.

EASTMAN, MAX. "The Problem of Criticism," in *The Literary Mind.* Scribner, 1935. Pp. 258–71.

ELIOT, T. S. "Donne in Our Time," in *A Garland for John Donne*, edited by Theodore Spencer. Harvard University Press, 1931. P. 7.

———. "The Function of a Literary Review," *Criterion*, 3 (July 1923), 420ff.

———. "The Idea of a Literary Review," *New Criterion*, 4 (January 1926), 752–53.

———. *The Sacred Wood.* Methuen, 1928; Knopf, 1930. Pp. 1–16, 123–24.

———. *Selected Essays 1917–1932.* Harcourt, Faber, 1932. Pp. 4, 13, 18–19, 122.

———. *The Use of Poetry and the Use of Criticism.* Faber, Harvard University Press, 1933. Pp. 16, 56, and *passim*.

ELTON, OLIVER. *The Nature of Literary Criticism.* Manchester University Press, 1935. See also J. Smith, "Evaluations: Croce," *Scrutiny*, 2 (January 1933), 28–44.

FALLS, CYRIL. *The Critic's Armoury.* Cobden Sanderson, 1924.

FEISS, EDWARD. "Edmund Wilson: Art and Ideas," *Antioch Review*, 1 (Fall 1941), 356–67.

FERNANDEZ, RAMON. "Of Philosophic Criticism," in *Messages.* Harcourt, 1927. Pp. 1–58.

FRY, ROGER. *Vision and Design.* Chatto, 1920. Pp. 285–86.

GALLUP, DONALD. *Check-List of the Writings of T. S. Eliot.* Yale University Press, 1947.

GREENE, T. M. "The Nature and Criteria of Criticism," in *The Arts and the Art of Criticism.* Princeton University Press, 1940. Pp. 369–73, 374–76.

HAZLITT, HENRY. *The Anatomy of Criticism, A Trialogue.* Simon and Shuster, 1933.

HEYL, B. C. *New Bearings in Esthetics and Art Criticism.* Yale University Press, 1943.

HICKS, GRANVILLE. "The Intransigence of Edmund Wilson," *Antioch Review*, 6 (Winter 1946–47), 550–62.

HIGGINS, BERTRAM. "The Critical Method of T. S. Eliot," in *Scrutinies*, edited by Edgell Rickword. Lawrence and Wishart, 1931. II, pp. 54–71.

HOWE, IRVING. "James T. Farrell: The Critic Calcified," *Partisan Review*, 14 (September 1947), 545–46, 548, 550, 552.

HUXLEY, ALDOUS. *Music at Night.* Fountain Press, 1931.

JENKINS, IREDELL. "Literary Criticism," in *Encyclopedia of the Arts*, edited by D. D. Runes. Philosophical Library, 1946. Pp. 565–71.

KAZIN, ALFRED. "Criticism at the Poles," *New Republic*, 107 (October 19, 1942), 492–99. Reprinted in *On Native Grounds.* Reynal, 1942.

KNIGHT, G. W. "On the Principles of Shakespeare Interpretation," in *The Wheel of Fire.* Oxford, 1930; Methuen, 1949. P. 1.

KNIGHTS, L. C. "Milton Again," *Scrutiny*, 11 (December 1942), 146.

KRUTCH, J. W. "Beauty's Rose," *Nation*, 145 (July 31, 1937), 132–33.

———. *Experience and Art.* Harrison Smith, 1932.

———. "Half Truth of the Whole Truth," *Nation*, 144 (January 2, 1937), 21–22.

———. "An Open Letter on Critics to Critics," *Nation*, 155 (August 1, 1942), 95.

LAWRENCE, D. H. *Phoenix*, edited by E. McDonald. Viking Press, Heinemann, 1936.

LEAVIS, F. R. "Arnold as Critic," *Scrutiny*, 7 (December 1938), 319–32. Reprinted in *The Importance of Scrutiny*, edited by Eric Bentley. Stewart, 1948. Pp. 88–98.

———. "Coleridge on Criticism," *Scrutiny*, 9 (June 1940), 57–69.

———. "Johnson as Critic," *Scrutiny*, 12 (Summer 1944), 187–204. See also "Doctor Johnson," *Kenyon Review*, 8 (Autumn 1946), 637–57.

———. *Revaluation.* Chatto, 1936; Stewart, 1946. Introduction, pp. 1–3.

———, editor. *Towards Standards of Criticism.* Lawrence and Wishart, 1933. Introduction; p. 60.

Lectures in Criticism. Pantheon Books, 1949.

MACCARTHY, DESMOND. *Criticism.* Putnam, 1932.

MAGNY, C. E. *Les Sandalls d'Empedocle.* Editions de ea Bacomiere, Neuchatel, 1945.

MARSHALL, M., and M. McCARTHY. "Our Critics Right or Wrong," *Nation*, 141 (October 23, 1935), 468–72, 542–44, 595–98, 653–55, 717–19.

MATTHIESSEN, F. O. *The Achievement of T. S. Eliot.* Oxford, 1948.

MEYER, GERARD. "The Direction of Criticism and the Misdirection of Poetry," *New Quarterly of Poetry*, 2 (Summer 1948), 6–12.

MULLER, H. J. "The Function of a Critical Review," *Arizona Quarterly*, 4 (Spring 1948), 5–20.

———. "The Function of Criticism," in *Science and Criticism.* Yale University Press, 1943. Pp. 42–50.

———. "The New Criticism in Poetry," *Southern Review*, 6 (Spring 1941), 811–39.

MUIR, EDWIN. *Transition.* Hogarth Press, Viking, 1926.

MURRY, J. M. "A Critical Credo," in *Countries of the Mind.* Collins, 1922. I, pp. 237–46.

———. "The Function of Criticism," in *Aspects of Literature*. Collins, 1920. Pp. 1–14.

O'CONNOR, W. V. "A Short View of the New Criticism," *College English*, 38 (November 1949), 489–97. See also David Daiches, "Some Qualifications," *College English*, 11 (February 1950), 242–50.

ONG, W. J. "The Meaning of the 'New Criticism'," in *Twentieth Century English*, edited by W. S. Knickerbocker. Philosophical Library, 1946. Pp. 344–83.

ORAGE, A. R. *The Art of Reading*. Farrar, 1930.

PEYRE, HENRI. *Writers and Their Critics*. Cornell University Press, 1944. Bibliography.

PHILLIPS, WILLIAM. "Categories for Criticism," *Symposium*, 4 (January 1933), 31–47.

———, and P. RAHV. "Some Aspects of Literary Criticism," *Science and Society*, 2 (1937), 212–20.

POTTLE, FREDERICK. *The Idiom of Poetry*. Cornell University Press, 1946. Pp. 23–42, 43–57.

POUND, EZRA. *Make It New*. Yale University Press, 1934.

———. *Polite Essays*. Faber, New Directions, 1937. Pp. 138–39.

RADER, M. M., editor. *A Modern Book of Aesthetics*. Holt, 1935.

RAHV, P., and W. PHILLIPS. "Criticism," *Partisan Review*, 2 (April 1935), 16–31.

RANSOM, J. C. Editorial in *Kenyon Review*, 3 (Winter 1941), 96.

———. "Mr. Empson's Muddles," *Southern Review*, 4 (Summer 1938), 322.

———. *The New Criticism*. New Directions, 1941. Pp. 294ff.

READ, HERBERT. "The Attributes of Criticism," in *Reason and Romanticism*. Faber and Gwyer, 1926. Pp. 1–29.

REDMAN, B. R. "Critics in Hobbles and Blinders," *Saturday Review of Literature*, 33 (November 12, 1949), 8–9, 60–62.

RICHARDS, I. A. *Coleridge on Imagination*. Routledge, 1934.

———. *Principles of Literary Criticism*. Harcourt, 1924.

RICKWORD, EDGELL, editor. *Scrutinies*. Lawrence and Wishart, 1931. II, pp. v–viii, 54–71.

ROBBINS, R. H. "The T. S. Eliot Myth," *Science and Society*, 14 (Winter 1949–50), 1–28.

ROBERTSON, J. M. "On Criticism," *New Criterion*, 4 (April 1926), 244–61.

ROUZAUD, MAURICE. *Où va la Critique?* Editions Saint Michel, 1929.

SAVAGE, D. S. "Criticism and Orthodoxy," *Adelphi*, 20 (April 1944), 86–90.

SCHAPPES, MORRIS. "Notes on the Concrete as Method in Criticism," *Symposium*, 2 (July 1931), 315–24.

SCHWARTZ, DELMORE. "The Writing of Edmund Wilson," *Accent*, 2 (1942), 177–86. Reprinted in *Accent Anthology*. Harcourt, 1946.

SCOTT-JAMES, R. A. *The Making of Literature*. Martin Secker, 1928.

SMITH, BERNARD. *Forces in American Criticism*. Harcourt, 1939.

SPARROW, JOHN. *Sense and Poetry*. Yale University Press, 1934.

SPENCER, THEODORE. "The Critic's Function," *Sewanee Review*, 47 (October 1939), 552–58.

———. "How to Criticize a Poem," *New Republic*, 109 (December 6, 1943), 816, 818.

SPINGARN, J. E. "The New Criticism," in *The New Criticism*, edited by E. B. Burgum. Prentice-Hall, 1930. Pp. 3–25.

BIBLIOGRAPHY

STALLMAN, R. W. "Bibliography of Modern Criticism: 1920–1948," in *Critiques and Essays in Criticism*, edited by R. W. Stallman. Ronald Press, 1949. Pp. 519–71.

———. "The New Critics," in *Critiques and Essays in Criticism*, edited by R. W. Stallman. Ronald Press, 1949. Pp. 488–506.

STAUFFER, D. A. "A Letter from the Critical Front," *Kenyon Review*, 4 (Winter 1942), 133.

STOLL, E. E. *Shakespeare and Other Masters*. Harvard University Press, 1940.

SYMONS, ARTHUR. "On Criticism," in *Dramatis Personae*. Bobbs-Merrill, 1923. Pp. 87–95.

TATE, ALLEN. "Poetry and the Absolute," *Sewanee Review*, 35 (January 1927), 41, 51.

———. *Reactionary Essays*. Scribner, 1936. Pp. 53, 86, 211ff.

———. *Reason in Madness*. Putnam, 1941. Pp. 9, 49, 60–61, 64, 105, 110.

THORPE, C., and N. NELSON. "Criticism in the Twentieth Century," *College English*, 8 (May 1947), 395–405.

TILLYARD, E. M. W. *Poetry Direct and Oblique*. Chatto, 1945. Pp. 15, 76.

TREECE, HENRY, editor. *Herbert Read*. Faber, 1944. Pp. 42–59.

TROWBRIDGE, HOYT. "Aristotle and the 'New Criticism'," *Sewanee Review*, 52 (Autumn 1944), 551–52. See also J. C. Ransom, "The Basis of Criticism," *Sewanee Review*, 52 (Autumn 1944), 556–71.

TUCKER, T. G. *The Judgment and Appreciation of Literature*. Melbourne University Press, 1926; Macmillan, 1927.

TURNELL, MARTIN. "An Essay on Criticism," *Dublin Review*, 444 (Last Quarter 1948), 72–95.

VAN DOREN, CARL. "A Fourth Dimension in Criticism," *Nation*, 115 (July 5, 1922), 18.

VAN DOREN, MARK. "Good Critics, Rare and Common," *Nation*, 154 (January 24, 1942), 95–96.

VINES, SHERARD. *Movements in Modern English Poetry and Prose*. Oxford, 1927. Chap. II; pp. 133–241.

VIVAS, ELISEO. "The Esthetic Judgment," *Journal of Philology*, 33 (1936), 57–69.

———. "The Objective Basis of Criticism," *Western Review*, 12 (Summer 1948), 197–210.

WALTON, GEOFFREY. "Art History or Art Criticism?" *Scrutiny*, 9 (September 1940), 181–85.

WANNING, ANDREWS. "Criticism and Principles," *Southern Review*, 6 (Spring 1941), 792, 794.

WARREN, AUSTIN. "The Criticism of Meaning and the Meaning of Criticism," *Sewanee Review*, 46 (June 1938), 213–22.

WELLS, H. W. *The Judgment of Literature*. Norton, 1928.

WEST, ALICK. *Crisis and Criticism*. Lawrence and Wishart, 1937.

WILSON, EDMUND. "Mr. Brooks' Second Phase," *New Republic*, 103 (September 30, 1940), 452–54.

———. "Poe as Literary Critic," *Nation*, 155 (October 31, 1942), 452–53.

———. *The Wound and the Bow*. Houghton, 1941; Oxford, 1947.

WINTERS, YVOR. *In Defense of Reason*. Morrow, 1947.

ZABEL, M. D. "An American Critic," *Poetry*, 50 (September 1937), 330–36.

———. "Towards Standards of Criticism," *Poetry*, 45 (October 1934), 40–46.

———, editor. *Literary Opinion*. Harper, 1937. Pp. xv–liv.

Kinds of Criticism

BURKE, KENNETH. "Kinds of Criticism," *Poetry*, 68 (August 1946), 272–82.

———. "Poetic Categories," in *Attitudes Toward History*. New Republic Books, 1937.

———. "The Problem of the Intrinsic," *Accent*, 3 (Winter 1943), 80–94. Reprinted in *A Grammar of Motives*. Prentice-Hall, 1945. Esp. p. 473.

DOBRÉE, BONAMY. "Criticism," in *Modern Prose Style*. Clarendon Press, 1946. Pp. 157–85.

ELIOT, T. S. "Experiment in Criticism," *Bookman*, 70 (November 1929), 225–33. Reprinted in *Tradition and Experiment*. Oxford, 1929. Pp. 198–215.

GREENE, T. M. *The Arts and the Art of Criticism*. Princeton University Press, 1940.

HYMAN, S. E. *The Armed Vision*. Knopf, 1948.

LEVIN, HARRY. "Literature as an Institution," *Accent*, 6 (1946), 159–68. Reprinted in *Criticism*, edited by Mark Schorer. Harcourt, 1948. Pp. 546–53.

PEPPER, S. C. *The Basis of Criticism in the Arts*. Harvard University Press, 1946. Chap. IV; pp. 50, 74–95, and *passim*.

RANSOM, J. C. "Criticism as Pure Speculation," in *The Intent of the Critic*, edited by D. A. Stauffer. Princeton University Press, 1941. Pp. 91–124.

ROBERTS, MICHAEL. "The Scope of Poetry and Criticism," in *Critique of Poetry*. Jonathan Cape, 1934. Pp. 58ff, 76, 79, 83.

SCHACK, WILLIAM. "A Critique of Art Criticism," *Virginia Quarterly Review*, 18 (Winter 1942), 93–109.

SPENCER, THEODORE. Review in *Hound and Horn*, 2 (July–September 1929), 447.

TROTSKY, LEON. *Literature and Revolution*. International Publishers, 1925.

TURNELL, MARTIN. "Literary Criticism in France," *Scrutiny*, 8 (December 1939), 167–83, 281–98. Reprinted in *Critiques and Essays in Criticism*, edited by R. W. Stallman. Ronald Press, 1949. Pp. 421–48.

WARREN, AUSTIN. "Literature and Society," in *Twentieth Century English*, edited by W. S. Knickerbocker. Philosophical Library, 1946. Pp. 304–5.

WILSON, EDMUND. "Historical Criticism," in *Critiques and Essays in Criticism*, edited by R. W. Stallman. Ronald Press, 1949. Pp. 449–59.

———. *The Triple Thinkers*. Oxford University Press, 1948. Pp. 191–212, 257–70.

The Boundaries of Criticism

AUDEN, W. H. "Criticism in a Mass Society," in *The Intent of the Critic*, edited by D. A. Stauffer. Princeton University Press, 1941. Pp. 127–47.

BATESON, F. W. *English Poetry and the English Language*. Clarendon Press, 1934.

BELGION, MONTGOMERY. "The Poet's Name," *Sewanee Review*, 54 (Autumn 1946), 635–49.

BLACKMUR, R. P. *The Double Agent*. Arrow Editions, 1935. Pp. 277–78.

———. "The Enabling Act of Criticism," in *Critiques and Essays in Criticism*, edited by R. W. Stallman. Ronald Press, 1949. Pp. 412–17.

BOAS, GEORGE. *A Primer for Critics*. Johns Hopkins University Press, 1937.

BURGUM, E. B. "The Humanism of Matthew Arnold," *Symposium*, 2 (January 1931), 85–112.

BURKE, KENNETH. "A Sour Note on Literary Criticism," *New Republic*, 87 (June 24, 1936), 211.

COWLEY, MALCOLM. "Yeats and O'Faolain," *New Republic*, 98 (February 15, 1939), 49–50.

ELIOT, T. S. *Essays Ancient and Modern*. Faber, Harcourt, 1936. P. 92.

———. *Selected Essays 1917–1932*. Harcourt, Faber, 1932. P. 42.

EVANS, B. I. "The Limits of Literary Criticism," in *Essays and Studies*, 18 (1932). Clarendon Press, 1933. Pp. 24–52.

FARRELL, J. T. *A Note on Literary Criticism*. Vanguard, 1936. P. 216.

FOERSTER, NORMAN. "The Aesthetic Judgment and the Ethical Judgment," in *The Intent of the Critic*, edited by D. A. Stauffer. Princeton University Press, 1941. Pp. 64–88.

JAMES, D. G. *Scepticism and Poetry*. G. Allen, 1937. Pp. 242–43.

RANSOM, J. C. "Criticism, Inc.," in *The World's Body*. Scribner, 1938. Pp. 327–50.

READ, HERBERT. *In Defence of Shelley*. Heinemann, 1936. P. 213.

STAUFFER, D. A., editor. *The Intent of the Critic*. Princeton University Press, 1941. P. 57.

WILSON, EDMUND. "Novelist Bites Critic," *Nation*, 142 (June 24, 1935), 808–10.

Scholarship and Literary Criticism

"A Hard Look at Criticism," *Poetry*, 68 (August 1946), 262–89.

ARMS, GEORGE. "The 'More' Middle Ground," *College English*, 3 (1941), 568–74.

BAUGH, A. C. "Graduate Study in English Literature," *English Journal*, 18 (1929), 135–46.

BELGION, MONTGOMERY. "The Poet's Name," *Sewanee Review*, 54 (Autumn 1946), 635–49.

BENNETT, ARNOLD. *Books and Persons*. George H. Doran, 1917. Pp. 41–46, 228–34.

BENTLEY, ERIC. "Education and the Literary Heritage," *Journal of Higher Education*, 2 (February 1948), 67.

———, editor. *The Importance of Scrutiny*. Stewart, 1948. Pp. 12–55.

BERNBAUM, ERNEST. "Graduate Study in English Literature," *English Journal*, 17 (1928), 33–43.

BLACKMUR, R. P. *The Expense of Greatness*. Arrow Editions, 1940. Pp. 277–305.

———. "Notes on Four Categories in Criticism," *Sewanee Review*, 54 (Autumn 1946), 582.

BROOKS, CLEANTH. "Criticism, History, and Critical Relativism," in *The Well Wrought Urn*. Reynal, 1947; Dobson, 1949. Pp. 197–225.

———. "Literary Criticism," in *English Institute Essays* (1946). Columbia University Press, 1947. Pp. 127–58.

———. *Modern Poetry and the Tradition*. University of North Carolina Press, 1939. Preface; Chap. III.

———. "The New Criticism: A Brief for the Defense," *American Scholar*, 13 (Summer 1944), 285–95. See also Darrel Abel, "Intellectual Criticism," *American Scholar*, 13 (Autumn 1943), 414–28.

———. "The New Criticism and Scholarship," in *Twentieth Century English*, edited by W. S. Knickerbocker. Philosophical Library, 1946. Pp. 371–83.

BUSH, DOUGLAS. "The New Criticism: Some Old-Fashioned Queries," *P.M.L.A.*, 64 (March 1949), 13–21.

———. "Scholars, Critics, and Readers," *Virginia Quarterly Review*, 22 (Spring 1946), 242–50.

CANBY, H. S. "What's Wrong with Criticism in America?" *Saturday Review of Literature*, 15 (March 13, 1937), 8.

CARRUTH, HAYDEN. "The University and the Poet," *Poetry*, 75 (December 1949), 89–93. See also "The Poet's Life," *Furioso*, 5 (Spring 1950), 66–69.

CAZAMIAN, L. F. "Eugenius; Or, Everybody His Own Critic," *Rice Institute Pamphlet*, 16 (January 1929), 32–45.

CHAPMAN, R. W. *Portrait of a Scholar*. Clarendon Press, 1922.

CHASE, RICHARD. "The Sense of the Present," *Kenyon Review*, 7 (Spring 1945), 218–31.

COX, R. G. "Academic Scholarship: English and American," *Scrutiny*, 10 (April 1942), 395–97.

CRANE, R. S. "History vs. Criticism in the University Study of Literature," *English Journal*, 24 (October 1935), 645–67.

CROCE, BENEDETTO. "'Aesthetic' and 'Historical' Criticism," *Rice Institute Pamphlet*, 2 (December 1915), 304ff.

Dictionary of World Literature. Edited by Joseph Shipley. Philosophical Library, 1943. P. 443.

EASTMAN, MAX. *The Literary Mind*. Scribner, 1935. Chap. V; pp. 272–94.

EISENSCHIMEL, OTTO. *Reviewers Reviewed: A Challenge to Historical Critics*. Argus Bookstore, 1945.

ELIOT, T. S. "Milton," *Sewanee Review*, 56 (Spring 1948), 186.

———. *The Music of Poetry*. Jackson, 1942.

———. "On a Recent Piece of Criticism," *Purpose*, 10 (1930), 90–94. See also F. R. Leavis, "What's Wrong with Criticism?" *Scrutiny*, 2 (September 1932), 132–40.

———. *The Sacred Wood*. Methuen, 1928; Knopf, 1930. Pp. 96–100, 123–45.

———. *Selected Essays 1917–1932*. Harcourt, Faber, 1932. Pp. 21, 122, and passim.

———. *The Use of Poetry and the Use of Criticism*. Faber, Harvard University Press, 1933. Pp. 32ff.

EVANS, B. I. "The Limits of Literary Criticism," in *Essays and Studies*, 18 (1932). Clarendon Press, 1933. Pp. 24–52.

FARRELL, J. T. *A Note on Literary Criticism*. Vanguard Press, 1936.

FERGUSSON, DELANCEY. "Should Scholars Try to Think?" *American Scholar*, 12 (Spring 1942), 208–19.

FEUILLERAT, ALBERT. "Scholarship and Literary Criticism," *Yale Review*, 14 (1925), 309–24.

FOERSTER, NORMAN. *The American Scholar*. University of North Carolina Press, 1929.

———. "Literary Scholarship and Criticism," *English Journal*, 25 (1936), 224–32.

———. "The Teacher of Great Literature," *Journal of General Education*, 1 1947), 107–13.

FORSTER, E. M. *Aspects of the Novel*. Harcourt, 1927. Pp. 27–28.

GARROD, H. W. "Methods of Criticism in Poetry," in *Poetry and the Criticism of Life*. Harvard University Press, 1931. Pp. 149ff.

———. *The Profession of Poetry*. Harvard University Press, 1929. Pp. 93ff, 163.

———. *Scholarship: Its Meaning and Value*. Cambridge University Press, 1947.

BIBLIOGRAPHY

GORDON, GEORGE P. *The Discipline of Letters*. Clarendon Press, 1946.
——, editor. *On Writing and Writers*, by Sir Walter Raleigh. Arnold, 1926. Preface.
GOSSE, EDMUND. *Questions at Issue*. Heinemann, 1893.
GREENE, T. M. *The Arts and the Art of Criticism*. Princeton University Press, 1940. Pp. 369–76.
GREENLAW, EDWIN. *The Province of Literary History*. Johns Hopkins University Press, 1931.
GRIERSON, H. J. "Criticism and Creation: Their Interaction," in *Essays and Studies*, 29 (1943). Clarendon Press, 1944. Pp. 1–29.
GUERARD, ALBERT, JR. "Criticism and Commodity," *New Republic*, 105 (December 8, 1941), 796, 798, 800.
HEILMAN, R. B. "Footnotes on Literary History," *Southern Review*, 6 (Spring 1941), 759–70.
HYMAN, S. E. *The Armed Vision*. Knopf, 1948.
JARRELL, RANDALL. "Contemporary Poetry Criticism," *New Republic*, 105 (July 21, 1941), 88–90. See also David Daiches, "Academics as Critics," 105 (August 18, 1941), 223.
——. "Critical Scholars," *New Republic*, 105 (October 6, 1940), 439.
JONES, H. M. "Graduate English Study: Its Rational," *Sewanee Review*, 38 (1930), 464–76; 39 (1931), 68–79, 200–6.
——. "The Limits of Contemporary Criticism," *Saturday Review of Literature*, 24 (September 6, 1941), 3–4, 17. See also Editorial, *Southern Review*, 7 (Autumn 1941), iv–xii.
——. "Literary Scholarship and Contemporary Criticism," *English Journal*, 23 (November 1934), 740–57.
——. "Scholarship and Democratic Faith," *University of Kansas City Review*, 8 (Autumn 1942), 12–18.
——. "The Uninfluentials," *Saturday Review of Literature*, 24 (October 21, 1941), 3–4, 20.
JONES, P. M. "A French Critic," *Scrutiny*, 6 (June 1937), 116.
KAIN, RICHARD. "The Reorientation of Literary Scholarship," *College English*, 3 (1941), 361–68.
KAZIN, ALFRED. *On Native Grounds*. Reynal, 1942.
KNIGHTS, L. C. *How Many Children Had Lady Macbeth?* Minority Press, 1933. Reprinted in *Explorations*. Chatto, 1946. Pp. 1–39.
——. "University Teaching of English and History," *Southern Review*, 5 (Winter 1940), 511–23. Reprinted in *Explorations*. Chatto, 1946. Pp. 186–99.
LEAVIS, F. R. "Education and the University," *Scrutiny*, 9 (March 1941), 306–22. See also *Education and the University*. Chatto, 1943; Stewart, 1948. Pp. 68, 85–96.
——. "The Literary Discipline and Liberal Education," *Sewanee Review*, 55 (1947), 586–609.
——. "What's Wrong with Criticism?" *Scrutiny*, 1 (September 1932), 132–46.
——, editor. *Towards Standards of Criticism*. Lawrence and Wishart, 1933. P. 99.
LEAVIS, Q. D. "'The Discipline of Letters': A Sociological Note," *Scrutiny*, 12 (Winter 1943), 12–26.
LEVIN, HARRY, editor. *Perspectives of Criticism*. Harvard University Press, 1950.

LEWIS, C., and E. TILLYARD. *The Personal Heresy*. Oxford University Press, 1939.

Literary History of the United States, edited by R. E. Spiller and others. Macmillan, 1948. III, bibliography.

Literary Scholarship: Its Aims and Methods. University of North Carolina Press, 1941.

"Literature and the Professors," *Southern Review*, 6 (Autumn 1940), 225–69. See also "Literature and the Professors," *Kenyon Review*, 2 (Autumn 1940), 403–42; "The Teaching of Literature," *Sewanee Review*, 55 (Autumn 1947), 569–626.

LOVEJOY, A. O. *Essays in the History of Ideas*. Johns Hopkins University Press, 1948. See also Marius Bewley, "Lovejoy and the History of Ideas," *Scrutiny*, 16 (June 1949), 162–68.

LOWES, J. L. "Humane Scholarship," *P.M.L.A.*, 48 (1933), 1399–1408.

———. *The Road to Xanadu*. Constable, 1927.

LUCAS, F. L. "Criticism," *Life and Letters*, 3 (November 1929), 433–65.

———. "The Criticism of Poetry," Proceedings of the British Academy, 19 (June 1933), 167–93.

———. "English," in *Cambridge University Studies*. Cambridge University Press, 1933.

MACCARTHY, DESMOND. *Leslie Stephen*. Cambridge University Press, 1937. See also Q. D. Leavis, "Leslie Stephen," *Scrutiny*, 7 (March 1939), 404–15.

MACLEISH, ARCHIBALD. *The Irresponsibles*. Duell, Sloan, 1940.

MACNEICE, LOUIS. "Subject in Modern Poetry," in *Essays and Studies*, 22 (1936). Clarendon Press, 1937. P. 144.

MORE, P. E. "Criticism," in *Selected Shelburne Essays*. Oxford, 1935. Pp. 1–24.

PEYRE, HENRI. *Writers and Their Critics*. Cornell University Press, 1944.

POTTER, STEPHEN. *The Muse in Chains*. Jonathan Cape, 1937.

RALEIGH, SIR WALTER. "A Note on Criticism," in *On Writing and Writers*. Arnold, 1926.

RANSOM, J. C. "The Bases of Criticism," *Sewanee Review*, 52 (Autumn 1944), 556–71.

———. "Criticism, Inc.," in *The World's Body*. Scribner, 1938. Pp. 327–50.

———. "Mr. Tate and the Professors," *Kenyon Review*, 2 (Summer 1940), 348–50.

———. *The New Criticism*. New Directions, 1941.

REINHARDT, KURT. "Basic Principles in Literary History and Literary Criticism," *Journal of English and Germanic Philosophy*, 30 (July 1931), 383–91.

RICHARDS, I. A. *Coleridge on Imagination*. Routledge, 1933. Pp. 195–97.

RICKWORD, EDGELL. "Criticism: A Charming Parasite," *Calendar of Modern Letters*, 3 (April 1926), 81–83.

ROBERTS, MICHAEL. "The Critic and the Public," *Southern Review*, 4 (Autumn 1938), 368–81.

SCHUTZE, MARTIN. *Academic Illusions*. University of Chicago Press, 1933.

Scrutiny, edited by F. R. Leavis. 9 (March 1941), 308, 320ff; 10 (April 1942), 396; 12 (Autumn 1944), 294; 12 (Winter 1943), 14.

SHERBURN, GEORGE. "Words that Intimidate," *P.M.L.A.*, 65 (February 1950), 3–12.

SHERMAN, STUART P. *Shaping Men and Women: Essays on Literature and Life*. Peter Smith, 1932; Doubleday, 1928. Pp. 36–86.

SMITH, L. P. *Milton and His Modern Critics*. Oxford, 1940.

SPENCER, THEODORE. "The Central Problem in Literary Criticism," *College English*, 4 (1942), 159–63.

———. "An Ideal for Graduate Education in English Literature," *English Journal*, 27 (1938), 33–43.

SPINGARN, J. E. "Scholarship and Criticism," in *Civilization in the United States*, edited by Harold E. Stearns. Harcourt, 1922.

SPITZER, LEO. "History of Ideas vs. Reading of Poetry," *Southern Review*, 6 (Winter 1941), 584–609.

———. *Linguistics and Literary History*. Princeton University Press, 1948.

———. "A New Program for the Teaching of Literary History," *American Journal of Philology*, 63 (1942), 308–19.

STAUFFER, D. A., editor. *The Intent of the Critic*. Princeton University Press, 1941. Pp. 65–68.

STOLL, E. E. *From Shakespeare to Joyce*. Doubleday, 1944. P. 76.

SUTHERLAND, JAMES. *English in the Universities*. Cambridge University Press, 1945.

TATE, ALLEN. "The Present Function of Criticism," *Southern Review*, 6 (Autumn 1940), 236–46. Reprinted in *Reason in Madness*. Putnam, 1941. Pp. 7–8, 207, 222.

———. "We Read as Writers," *Princeton Alumni Weekly*, 40 (March 8, 1940), 505–6. See also J. C. Ransom, "Mr. Tate and the Professors," *Kenyon Review*, 2 (Summer 1940), 71.

TEETER, LOUIS. "Scholarship and the Art of Criticism," *English Literary History*, 5 (September 1938), 173–94. Cf. Austin Warren, "The Criticism of Meaning," *Sewanee Review*, 46 (June 1938), 213–22.

THORP, WILLARD. "College Teachers of American Literature," *College English*, 8 (April 1947), 360–65.

TILLOTSON, GEOFFREY. *Essays in Criticism and Research*. Cambridge University Press, 1942. Preface.

TINDALL, W. Y. "Scholarship and Contemporary Literature," in *English Institute Annual*, 1940. Columbia University Press, 1941. Pp. 42–60.

TRILLING, LIONEL. *The Liberal Imagination*. Viking Press, 1950.

———. "Literature and Power," *Kenyon Review*, 2 (Autumn 1940), 433–42.

———. "The Sense of the Past," *Partisan Review*, 9 (May 1942), 229–41.

VENTURI, LIONELLO. *Art Criticism Now*. Johns Hopkins University Press, 1941. Preface.

VIGNERON, ROBERT. *Explication de Textes and Its Adaptation to the Teaching of Modern Languages*. University of Chicago Press, 1928.

WARREN, AUSTIN. "The Scholar and the Critic: An Essay in Mediation," *Toronto Quarterly*, 6 (1937), 267–77.

———, and R. WELLEK. *Theory of Literature*. Harcourt, 1949. Bibliography.

WELLEK, RENÉ. "The Decline of Literary-History Writing," *Western Review*, 12 (Autumn 1947), 52–54.

———. "Literary Criticism and Philosophy," *Scrutiny*, 5 (March 1937), 375–83.

———. "The Nature and Scope of Literary History," *Huntington Library Quarterly*, 6 (November 1942), 35–39.

———. *The Rise of English Literary History*. University of North Carolina Press, 1941. Pp. vii, 275.

———. "The Theory of Literary History," *Travaux du Cercle Linguistique de Prague*, 6 (1936), 173–91.

WERNER, W. L. "The Future of Literary Scholarship," *Journal of Higher Education*, 14 (May 1943), 246–48.

WILSON, EDMUND. "The Historical Interpretation of Literature," in *The Triple Thinkers*. Oxford, 1948. Pp. 257–70. Reprinted in *The Intent of the Critic*, Princeton University Press, 1941, pp. 39–62; *Critiques and Essays in Criticism*, edited by R. W. Stallman, Ronald Press, 1949, pp. 449–59.

———. *The Triple Thinkers*. Oxford, 1948. Pp. 3–14, 60–71.

WINTERS, YVOR. "The Significance of 'The Bridge,' by Hart Crane: Or What Are We to Think of Professor X?" in *The Defense of Reason*. Morrow, 1947. Pp. 587–603.

WITTE, W. "The Sociological Approach to Literature," *Modern Language Review*, 36 (1941), 86–94.

WOOLF, VIRGINIA. "How It Strikes a Contemporary," in *The Common Reader*. Harcourt, 1925. Pp. 319–32.

YOUNG, C. M. "The Technique of Criticism: Classical," in *Essays and Studies*, 23 (1938). Clarendon Press, 1939. Pp. 70–78.

ZABEL, M. D. "The Condition of American Criticism: 1939," *English Journal*, 28 (June 1939), 417–28.

II. LIFE AND ART

ADLER, MORTIMER. *How to Read a Book*. Simon and Schuster; Jarrolds, 1940. P. 306.

BELGION, MONTGOMERY. "The Testimony of Fiction," *Southern Review*, 4 (Summer 1938), 152ff.

———. "What Is Criticism?" *Criterion*, 10 (October 1930), 118–37.

BELL, CLIVE. *Art*. Chatto, 1947. Pp. 65–67.

———. "The 'Difference' of Literature," *New Republic*, 33 (November 29, 1922), 18–19.

BLACKMUR, R. P. Introduction to *The Art of the Novel*, by Henry James. Scribner, 1934. Pp. xi, xv, xxxi, xxxviii.

———. *The Double Agent*. Arrow Editions, 1935. Chap. XII; p. 282.

BROOKS, CLEANTH. *The Well Wrought Urn*. Reynal, 1947; Dobson, 1949. Pp. 194–95.

———, and R. P. WARREN. *Understanding Poetry*. Holt, 1938. Pp. 54–58.

BROWN, E. K. "The Revival of E. M. Forster," in *Forms of Modern Fiction*, edited by W. V. O'Connor. University of Minnesota Press, 1948. P. 170.

BURKE, KENNETH. *Counter-Statement*. Harcourt, 1931.

CASSIRER, ERNST. *An Essay on Man*. Yale University Press, 1944. P. 166.

CHURCHILL, R. C. "Dickens, Drama and Tradition," *Scrutiny*, 10 (April 1942), 359.

COLLINGWOOD, R.G. *The Principles of Art*. Clarendon Press, 1938. Pp. 119–21, and *passim*.

DAY-LEWIS, CECIL. "A Hope for Poetry," in *Collected Poems*. Random House, 1935. Pp. 161–256.

DE VOTO, BERNARD. *The Literary Fallacy*. Little, 1944.

Dictionary of World Literature. Edited by Joseph Shipley. Philosophical Library, 1943. Pp. 610–12.

DOBRÉE, BONAMY. *Variety of Ways*. Oxford, 1932. Pp. 2–4, and *passim*.

ELIOT, T. S. "Byron," in *From Anne to Victoria*, edited by Bonamy Dobrée. Cassell, 1937. Pp. 616–17.

———. *Elizabethan Essays*. Faber, 1934.

BIBLIOGRAPHY

——. *The Sacred Wood*. Methuen, 1928; Knopf, 1930. Pp. 43–46, 56, 117, 119, 132.

——. *Selected Essays 1917–1932*. Harcourt, Faber, 1932.

——. *The Use of Poetry and the Use of Criticism*. Faber, Harvard University Press, 1933.

FERNANDEZ, RAMON. *Messages*. Harcourt, 1927.

FORSTER, E. M. *Aspects of the Novel*. Harcourt, 1927. Pp. 71, 96, 98, 100, 102, and *passim*.

FOWLIE, WALLACE. *Jacob's Night*. Sheed and Ward, 1947. Pp. 47, 94.

FOX, RALPH. *The Novel and the People*. Lawrence and Wishart, 1937; International Publishers, 1945. Pp. 29, 79.

FRY, ROGER. *Vision and Design*. Chatto, 1920. Esp. p. 295.

GARROD, H. W. *Poetry and the Criticism of Life*. Harvard University Press, 1931. Pp. 3–21.

GHYKA, MATILA. *The Geometry of Art and Life*. Sheed and Ward, 1946.

GREENE, GRAHAM. "Fielding and Sterne," in *From Anne to Victoria*, edited by Bonamy Dobrée. Cassell, 1937. Pp. 278–79.

GUERARD, ALBERT. *Art for Art's Sake*. Lothrop, 1936.

JAMES, HENRY. *The Art of the Novel*. Scribner, 1941. Pp. 45, 84.

JOYCE, JAMES. "AE," in *Ulysses*. Egoist edition, 1922. P. 177.

KNIGHTS, L. C. *Explorations*. Chatto, 1946. Pp. 2–3, 12–14, 42, 44–45.

LANGER, SUSANNE. *Philosophy in a New Key*. Oxford, 1942.

LEAVIS, F. R. "Arnold as Critic," *Scrutiny*, 7 (December 1938), 324–26.

LEAVIS, Q. D. "Leslie Stephen," *Scrutiny*, 7 (March 1939), 407, 413, 437.

Literary Scholarship: Its Aims and Methods. University of North Carolina Press, 1941. Pp. 138, 143–44.

LUCAS, F. L. *Decline and Fall of the Romantic Ideal*. Macmillan, 1937. Chap. II.

LUKÁCS, GEORGE. "The Intellectual Physiognomy of Literary Characters," *International Literature*, 8 (August 1936), 55–83.

MACCARTHY, DESMOND. *Portraits*. Putnam, 1931. P. 75.

MACKAIL, J. W. "The Study of Poetry," *Rice Institute Pamphlet*, 2 (September 1915), 14, 18–19.

MACNEICE, LOUIS. *The Poetry of W. B. Yeats*. Oxford, 1941. Pp. 3, 22, 88, 227–28.

MATTHIESSEN, F. O. *The Achievement of T. S. Eliot*. Oxford, 1935. Pp. 3ff.

——. *American Renaissance*. Oxford, 1941. Pp. 314, and *passim*.

MAUGHAM, SOMERSET. *The Summing Up*. Doubleday, 1938.

MULLER, H. J. *Modern Fiction*. Funk, 1937. Pp. 71, and *passim*.

MURRY, J. M. *Aspects of Literature*. Collins, 1920.

NUHN, FERNER. *The Wind Blew from the East*. Harper, 1942.

PRAZ, MARIO. *The Romantic Agony*. Oxford, 1933. Pp. 121, 139, and *passim*.

RICHARDS, I. A. *Practical Criticism*. Harcourt, 1929. Pp. 28–29, and *passim*.

——. *Principles of Literary Criticism*. Harcourt, 1925. Pp. 14–18, and *passim*.

——. *Science and Poetry*. Norton, 1926.

RICHARDSON, DOROTHY. "Saintsbury and 'Art for Art's Sake' in England," *P.M.L.A.*, 59 (March 1944), 243–60.

RICKWORD, C. H. "A Note on Fiction," in *Forms of Modern Fiction*, edited by W. V. O'Connor. University of Minnesota Press, 1948. Pp. 294–305.

RICKWORD, EDGELL. Review in *Scrutiny*, 1 (March 1933), 390–91.

RILKE, R. M. *Letters to a Young Poet*. Norton, 1934. P. 18.

267

ROBERTS, MORRIS, editor. *The Art of Fiction*, by Henry James. Oxford, 1948. Pp. 3–23.

SAVAGE, D. S. *The Personal Principle*. Routledge, 1944. Pp. 131–54.

SISSON, C. J. *Mythical Sorrows of Shakespeare*. Oxford, 1934.

SPENDER, STEPHEN. *Life and the Poet*. Secker and Warburg, 1942. Chap. III.

SPINGARN, J. E., editor. *The New Criticism*. Prentice-Hall, 1930. Pp. 153–63, 217–46, 339ff.

"Stage Speech," *Times Literary Supplement*, December 19, 1929.

STALLMAN, R. W. "Life, Art, and 'The Secret Sharer'," in *Forms of Modern Fiction*, edited by W. V. O'Connor. University of Minnesota Press, 1948. Pp. 232–38.

STOLL, E. E. *From Shakespeare to Joyce*. Doubleday, 1944. P. 156.

———. *Shakespeare and Other Masters*. Harvard University Press, 1940.

———. *Shakespeare Studies*. Macmillan, 1927. Chap. VIII; pp. 87–89, 117–214, and *passim*.

TATE, ALLEN. *On the Limits of Poetry*. Morrow, 1948.

———. "Techniques of Fiction," in *Forms of Modern Fiction*, edited by W. V. O'Connor. University of Minnesota Press, 1948. P. 40.

VIVAS, ELISEO. "The Objective Correlative of T. S. Eliot," *American Bookman*, 1 (Winter 1944), 7–18. Reprinted in *Critiques and Essays in Criticism*, edited by R. W. Stallman. Ronald Press, 1949. Pp. 389–400.

WARREN, A., and R. WELLEK. *Theory of Literature*. Harcourt, 1949. Pp. 219, 220–21.

WHARTON, EDITH. "Visibility in Fiction," *Life and Letters*, 11 (April 1929), 263–72.

WILDE, OSCAR. *Intentions*. Brentano, 1912. Pp. 1–56.

WILSON, EDMUND. "The Canons of Poetry," *Atlantic*, 153 (April 1934), 455–62.

———. *The Triple Thinkers*. Oxford, 1948. Pp. 15–30.

WIMSATT, W. K., JR. "Comment on 'Two Essays'," *University Review*, 9 (Winter 1942), 139–43.

WOOLF, VIRGINIA. *The Common Reader*. Harcourt, 1947.

Theories of "Pure Poetry"

BRÉMOND, HENRI. *Prayer and Poetry*. Burns, 1929.

BROOKS, CLEANTH. *Modern Poetry and the Tradition*. University of North Carolina Press, 1939. Pp. 54–68.

CROCE, BENEDETTO. *The Defense of Poetry*. Oxford, 1933. Pp. 22ff.

DE SELINCOURT, E. *Oxford Lectures on Poetry*. Clarendon Press, 1934. Pp. 6ff.

EASTMAN, MAX. *The Literary Mind*. Scribner, 1935. Pp. 79–92.

FRY, ROGER. "Introduction," in *Stéphane Mallarmé: Poems*, edited by Charles Mauron. Chatto, Macmillan, 1938. P. 288.

GARROD, H. W. *The Profession of Poetry*. Oxford, 1929. Pp. 30–48.

HOUSMAN, A. E. *The Name and Nature of Poetry*. Macmillan, 1933.

MacNEICE, LOUIS. *Modern Poetry*. Oxford, 1938.

MARITAIN, JACQUES. *Art and Scholasticism*. Scribner, 1930. Reviewed by P. B. Rice in *Symposium*, 1 (July 1930), 390–92.

MOORE, GEORGE, editor. *An Anthology of Pure Poetry*. Liveright, 1925. Introduction.

MOORE, T. S. "A Poet and His Technique," *Criterion*, 4 (1926), 685.

MORE, P. E. "A Note on Poe's Literary Method," in *American Issues*, edited by W. Thorp, M. Curti, and C. Baker. Lippincott, 1941. II, pp. 731–35.

READ, HERBERT. *Form in Modern Poetry.* Sheed and Ward, 1932.
———. *Reason and Romanticism.* Faber, 1926. Chap. III; pp. 59–66.
RICE, P. B. "Paul Valéry," *Symposium,* 1 (April 1930), 206–20.
SPARROW, JOHN. *Sense and Poetry.* Yale University Press, 1934. Introduction.
WARREN, R. P. "Pure and Impure Poetry," in *Critiques and Essays in Criticism,* edited by R. W. Stallman. Ronald Press, 1949. Pp. 85–104.
YEATS, W. B. *Essays.* Macmillan, 1924.
ZABEL, M. D. "A Mallarmé Primer," *Poetry,* 49 (March 1937), 350–54.

III. FORM

ALEXANDER, SAMUEL. *Beauty and Other Forms of Value.* Macmillan, 1933.
BARZUN, JACQUES. "The Fetish of Form," *Kenyon Review,* 12 (Winter 1950), 86–98.
BELL, CLIVE. *Art.* Chatto, 1947.
BISHOP, J. P. *Collected Essays,* edited by Edmund Wilson. Scribner, 1948. Pp. 175–83.
BLACKMUR, R. P. Introduction to *The Art of the Novel,* by Henry James. Scribner, 1941.
BRADLEY, A. C. *Oxford Lectures on Poetry.* Macmillan, 1909. Pp. 3–34.
BROOKS, CLEANTH. "The Poem as Organism," in *English Institute Essays.* Columbia University Press, 1941. Pp. 20–41.
———. *The Well Wrought Urn.* Reynal, 1947; Dobson, 1949. Pp. 174–75, 199–205.
BURKE, KENNETH. *Counter-Statement.* Harcourt, 1931. Chap. VIII; pp. 38–56, 57ff.
———. *The Philosophy of Literary Form.* Louisiana State University Press, 1941.
CASSIRER, ERNST. *An Essay on Man.* Yale University Press, 1944. Pp. 141–45, and *passim.*
CECIL, DAVID. *Poets and Story-Tellers.* Macmillan, 1949. Pp. 3–24, 141–52.
COLLINGWOOD, R. G. *The Principles of Art.* Clarendon Press, 1938.
CONRAD, JOSEPH. Preface to "The Nigger of the 'Narcissus'," in *The Viking Portable Library,* edited by M. D. Zabel. Viking Press, 1947. Pp. 705–10.
COOK, R. L. "Poet in the Mountains," *Western Review,* 11 (Spring 1947), 175–82.
CROCE, BENEDETTO. "The Breviary of Aesthetic," *Rice Institute Pamphlet,* 2 (December 1915), 247–48.
DAY-LEWIS, CECIL. *The Poetic Image.* Jonathan Cape, 1947. Pp. 122ff.
DEWEY, JOHN. *Art as Experience.* Minton Balch, 1934. Chaps. VI, VII.
Dictionary of World Literature. Edited by Joseph Shipley. Philosophical Library, 1943. P. 253.
DOBRÉE, BONAMY. *Restoration Tragedy.* Clarendon Press, 1929. P. 71.
DUPEE, F. W. *The Question of Henry James.* Holt, 1945. Esp. pp. 92–104.
ELIOT, T. S. *The Music of Poetry.* Jackson, 1942. P. 15.
———. *The Sacred Wood.* Methuen, 1928; Knopf, 1930. Pp. 1, 5, 8, and *passim.*
———. *Selected Essays 1917–1932.* Harcourt, Faber, 1932.
FLORES, ANGEL, editor. *Cervantes Across the Centuries.* Dryden Press, 1947. Pp. 239–45.
FOCILLON, HENRI. *The Life of Forms in Art.* Yale University Press, 1942.
FORSTER, E. M. *Aspects of the Novel.* Harcourt, 1927. Chap. V.

————. "Art for Art's Sake," *Harper's*, 199 (August 1949), 31–34.

FOWLIE, WALLACE. *Rimbaud*. Dobson, 1946. P. 88.

FOX, RALPH. *The Novel and the People*. Lawrence and Wishart, 1937. Pp. 78–79, 83.

FRANK, J. "Spatial Form in Modern Literature," *Sewanee Review*, 53 (1945), 221–40, 433–56, 643–53.

GARDNER, HELEN. *The Art of T. S. Eliot*. Cresset Press, 1949. Chap. II.

GIVENS, SEON, editor. *James Joyce: Two Decades of Criticism*. Vanguard Press, 1949. Esp. pp. 47–94, 203–84.

GOLDWATER, ROBERT. "Theme and Form in Modern Painting," *Critique*, 1 (October 1946), 5–12.

————, and M. TREVES, editors. *Artists on Art*. Pantheon Books, 1945.

GOTSHALK, D. W. *Art and the Social Order*. University of Chicago Press, 1947. Pp. 117–18.

GREENE, T. M. *The Arts and the Art of Criticism*. Princeton University Press, 1940.

GRIERSON, H. J. "Criticism and Creation," *Essays and Studies*, 29 (1943), 27.

HOPKINS, G. M. *The Letters . . . to Robert Bridges*, edited by C. C. Abbott. Oxford, 1935. LIII, p. 66.

HULME, T. E. "Romanticism and Classicism," in *Critiques and Essays in Criticism*, edited by R. W. Stallman. Ronald Press, 1949. P. 15.

KER, W. P. *Form and Style in Poetry*. Macmillan, 1928.

LANGER, S. K. "The Principles of Creation in Art," *Hudson Review*, 2 (Winter 1950), 516.

LEBOWITZ, MARTIN. "Thought and Sensibility," *Kenyon Review*, 5 (Spring 1943), 224–25.

LUBBOCK, PERCY. *The Craft of Fiction*. Jonathan Cape, 1929.

MARCH, HAROLD. *The Two Worlds of Marcel Proust*. University of Pennsylvania Press, 1948. Pp. 135–48, and *passim*.

MELLERS, W. H. Review in *Scrutiny*, 7 (March 1939), 480–81.

MUIR, EDWIN. *The Structure of the Novel*. Hogarth Press, 1928, 1946.

MURRAY, GILBERT. *Classical Tradition in Poetry*. Harvard University Press, 1927. Pp. 147–77.

O'CONNOR, W. V., editor. *Forms of Modern Fiction*. University of Minnesota Press, 1948. Pp. 142, 173, 175–88, 208, 262, 294–305.

OLSON, ELDER. "An Outline of Poetic Theory," in *Critiques and Essays in Criticism*, edited by R. W. Stallman. Ronald Press, 1949. Pp. 264–85.

PARKER, DEWITT. *The Analysis of Art*. Yale University Press, 1926.

PEPPER, S. C. *Aesthetic Quality*. Scribner, 1937. Chaps. VII, VIII, IX.

————. *The Basis of Criticism in the Arts*. Harvard University Press, 1946.

PHILLIPS, WILLIAM. "Categories for Criticism," *Symposium*, 4 (January 1933), 31–47.

PRALL, D. W. *Aesthetic Analysis*. Crowell, 1936.

RADER, M. M., editor. *A Modern Book of Esthetics*. Holt, 1935. Chap. VII.

RANSOM, J. C. *The World's Body*. Scribner, 1938.

READ, HERBERT. *Collected Essays*. Faber, 1937. Pp. 17–20, 57–68.

————. *Form in Modern Poetry*. Sheed and Ward, 1933. Pp. 52–53.

————. "The Later Years," in *A Coat of Many Colours*. Routledge, 1945. Pp. 208–12.

RICHARDS, I. A. *Coleridge on Imagination*. Routledge, 1934. P. 224.

————, C. OGDEN, and J. WOOD. *The Foundations of Aesthetics*. Lear Publishers, 1925. Chap. XII.

ROBERTS, MORRIS, editor. *The Art of Fiction*, by Henry James. Oxford, 1948. P. 13.

SCHNEIDER, ELISABETH. *Aesthetic Motive*. Macmillan, 1939. Pp. 86–104.

SPENGLER, OSWALD. *The Decline of the West*. Knopf, 1926. Two vols.

SPINGARN, J. E., editor. *The New Criticism*. Prentice-Hall, 1930. Pp. 193–215, 259–90, 303–25.

STALLMAN, R. W. Editorial in *Western Review*, 12 (Spring 1948), 130, 191.

STAUFFER, D. A., editor. *The Intent of the Critic*. Princeton University Press, 1941. Pp. 24–25, 109–11.

———. *The Nature of Poetry*. Norton, 1946.

STEIN, LEO. *The A-B-C of Aesthetics*. Liveright, 1927. P. 138.

TATE, ALLEN. "Poetry and the Absolute," *Sewanee Review*, 35 (January 1927), 41–52.

TREECE, HENRY, editor. *Herbert Read*. Faber, 1944. P. 72.

TROWBRIDGE, HOYT. "Aristotle," *Sewanee Review*, 52 (Autumn 1944), 537–55.

TRUEBLOOD, C. K. "The Aesthetics of Gerard Manley Hopkins," *Poetry*, 50 (August 1937), 277ff.

WARREN, A., and R. WELLEK. *Theory of Literature*. Harcourt, 1949. Pp. 140, 154, 224–25, 252, 256ff.

WELLEK, RENÉ. "The Mode of Existence of a Literary Work of Art," in *Critiques and Essays in Criticism*, edited by R. W. Stallman. Ronald Press, 1949. Pp. 210–23.

WEST, ALICK. *Crisis and Criticism*. Lawrence and Wishart, 1937. Chap. XII.

WILSON, EDMUND. *Axel's Castle*. Scribner, 1931. Pp. 139, 146–47, 158.

WIMSATT, W. K., JR. "The Structure of the 'Concrete Universal' in Literature," *P.M.L.A.*, 62 (March 1947), 262–80.

WINTERS, YVOR. *In Defense of Reason*. Morrow, 1947. Pp. 17–29, 30–74, 103–50, and *passim*.

IV. THE PROBLEM OF MEANING

ABERCROMBIE, LASCELLES. *Poetry: Its Music and Meaning*. Oxford, 1932.

ADLER, MORTIMER. *How to Read a Book*. Simon and Schuster, 1940.

BASLER, R. P. *Sex, Symbolism and Psychology in Literature*. Rutgers University Press, 1948.

BEACH, J. W. *The Twentieth Century Novel*. Appleton-Century, 1932.

BELGION, MONTGOMERY. "Meaning in Art," *Symposium*, 1 (January 1930), 209.

BLACKMUR, R. P. "Twelve Poets," *Southern Review*, 7 (Summer 1941), 209.

BROOKS, CLEANTH. "The Language of Paradox," in *The Well Wrought Urn*. Reynal, 1947; Dobson, 1949. Chap. I. Reprinted in *Critiques and Essays in Criticism*, edited by R. W. Stallman. Ronald Press, 1949. Pp. 66–79.

———. "What Does Modern Poetry Communicate?" *American Prefaces*, 6 (Autumn 1940), 18–27.

———, and R. P. WARREN. *Understanding Fiction*. Appleton-Century-Crofts, 1949.

BURGUM, E. B. *The Novel and the World's Dilemma*. Oxford, 1947.

BURKE, KENNETH. *A Grammar of Motives*. Prentice-Hall, 1945.

———. *The Philosophy of Literary Form*. Louisiana State University Press, 1941.

COLLINGWOOD, R. G. *The Principles of Art*. Clarendon Press, 1938. Chap. XIII.

CRANE, R. S. "Two Essays in Practical Criticism," *University of Kansas City Review*, 8 (Spring 1942), 198–219.

DAICHES, DAVID. *The Novel and the Modern World*. University of Chicago Press, 1939.
———. *The Place of Meaning in Poetry*. Oliver and Boyd, 1935.
———. *Poetry and the Modern World*. University of Chicago Press, 1940.
DEUTSCH, BABETTE. *This Modern Poetry*. Faber, 1936.
Dictionary of World Literature. Edited by Joseph Shipley. Philosophical Library, 1943. Pp. 368–69.
DREW, E., and J. SWEENEY. *Directions in Modern Poetry*. Norton, 1940. P. 186.
EASTMAN, MAX. *The Literary Mind*. Scribner, 1931.
ELIOT, T. S. *Elizabethan Essays*. Faber, 1934. P. 56.
———. "Isolated Superiority," *Dial*, 84 (January 1928), 6.
———. *The Music of Poetry*. Jackson, 1942. Pp. 13–15.
———. *The Use of Poetry and the Use of Criticism*. Faber, Harvard University Press, 1933. Pp. 19, 131.
FEIBLEMAN, J. K. *Aesthetics*. Duell, Sloan, 1949.
FERGUSSON, FRANCIS. *The Idea of a Theatre*. Princeton University Press, 1949.
GARDNER, H. L. *The Art of T. S. Eliot*. Cresset Press, 1949.
GARROD, H. W. "Housman: 1939," *Essays and Studies*, 25 (1939), 18–19.
———. *Poetry and the Criticism of Life*. Harvard University Press, 1931. Pp. 38–39.
GORDON, C., and A. TATE. *The House of Fiction*. Scribner, 1950.
GOLDWATER, R., and M. TREVES, editors. *Artists on Art*. Pantheon Books, 1945.
GRAVES, ROBERT. *Poetic Unreason*. Cecil Palmer, 1925. Chaps. I, VI.
———, and A. HODGE. *The Reader Over Your Shoulder*. Jonathan Cape, 1943.
GRUDIN, LOUIS. *A Primer of Aesthetics*. Covici, Friede, 1930.
HEILMAN, R. B. *This Great Stage*. Louisiana University Press, 1948.
HEYL, BERNARD. *New Bearings in Esthetics and Criticism*. Yale University Press, 1944. Bibliography.
HOSPERS, JOHN. *Meaning and Truth in the Arts*. University of North Carolina Press, 1946.
HOUSMAN, A. E. *The Name and Nature of Poetry*. Macmillan, Cambridge University Press, 1933.
HULME, T. S. *Speculations*, edited by Herbert Read. Routledge, 1924; Harcourt, 1936.
JAMES, D. G. *Scepticism and Poetry*. G. Allen, 1937.
KNIGHT, G. W. *The Wheel of Fire*. Methuen, 1949.
LEAVIS, F. R. *The Great Tradition*. Chatto, 1948.
LEWIS, C., and E. TILLYARD. *The Personal Heresy*. Oxford, 1939. Pp. 113–14.
NUHN, FERNER. *The Wind Blew from the East*. Harper, 1942.
OGDEN, C., and I. RICHARDS. *The Meaning of Meaning*. Harcourt, Kegan Paul, 1923.
PEPPER, S. C. *The Basis of Criticism in the Arts*. Harvard University Press, 1946.
POLLOCK, T. C. *The Nature of Literature*. Princeton University Press, 1942.
POTTLE, FREDERICK. *The Idiom of Poetry*. Cornell University Press, 1946.
PRIOR, M. E. *The Language of Tragedy*. Columbia University Press, 1947.
RAHV, PHILLIP. *Image and Idea*. New Directions, 1949.
RANSOM, J. C. "Poetry: The Formal Analysis," *Kenyon Review*, 9 (Summer 1947), 443.
———. *The World's Body*. Scribner, 1938. Pp. 92–94, 111–42, and *passim*.

READ, HERBERT. *Collected Essays.* Faber, 1938. P. 91, and *passim.*
———. "The Form of Modern Poetry," *Symposium,* 1 (July 1930), 308–9.
RICHARDS, I. A. *Coleridge on Imagination.* Routledge, 1934. Chap. IX. Reprinted in *Critiques and Essays in Criticism,* edited by R. W. Stallman. Ronald Press, 1949. Pp. 289–314.
———. *Practical Criticism.* Harcourt, Kegan Paul, 1929. Pp. 181–83.
———. *Principles of Literary Criticism.* Harcourt, 1928. Chaps. IV, XVII, XXXII.
———. *Science and Poetry.* Norton, Orthological Institute, 1926. Chap. II.
SCHNEIDER, ELISABETH. *Aesthetic Motive.* Macmillan, 1939. Pp. 102–3.
SEDGWICK, W. E. *Herman Melville.* Harvard University Press, 1945.
SPARROW, JOHN. *Sense and Poetry.* Yale University Press, 1934. Chap. I.
SPENDER, STEPHEN. "The Making of a Poem," *Partisan Review,* 13 (Summer 1946), 298–99.
STAUFFER, D. A. *The Nature of Poetry.* Norton, 1946. Pp. 155–56, and *passim.*
———. *The Golden Nightingale.* Princeton University Press, 1950.
STEVENS, WALLACE. "The Noble Rider and the Sound of Words," in *The Language of Poetry,* edited by Allen Tate. Princeton University Press, 1942. Pp. 91–125.
TURNELL, MARTIN. *The Classical Moment.* Hamish Hamilton, 1947; New Directions, 1948.
———. "Racine," *Scrutiny,* 6 (March 1938), 453–54.
UNGER, LEONARD, editor. *T. S. Eliot: A Selected Critique.* Rinehart, 1948.
VAN DOREN, MARK. *The Noble Voice.* Harcourt, 1946.
WARREN, A., and R. WELLEK. *Theory of Literature.* Harcourt, 1949. Chap. XV; pp. 190ff, and *passim.*
WEBER, BROM. *Hart Crane.* Bodley Press, 1948.
WEST, R., and R. STALLMAN. *The Art of Modern Fiction.* Rinehart, 1949.
WHEELWRIGHT, PHILIP. "Notes on Meaning," *Symposium,* 1 (July 1930), 381.
WILLIAMS, CHARLES. *Reason and Beauty in the Poetic Mind.* Clarendon Press, 1933.
WIMSATT, W. K., JR. "The Structure of the 'Concrete Universal' in Literature," *P.M.L.A.,* 62 (March 1947), 262–80.
ZABEL, M. D., editor. *Literary Opinion in America.* Harper, 1937. Pp. 25–38.

What the Poem Means: The Language of Poetry

AIKEN, CONRAD. "Notes on Poetic Meaning," *New Republic,* 104 (April 21, 1941), 539–40.
BARFIELD, OWEN. *Poetic Diction: A Study in Meaning.* Faber and Gwyer, 1928.
BENSEN, ALICE. "Problems of Poetic Diction in Twentieth-Century Criticism," *P.M.L.A.,* 60 (March 1945), 271–86.
BLACKMUR, R. P. "Twelve Poets," *Southern Review,* 7 (Summer 1941), 196. 208–9.
BROOKS, CLEANTH. *Modern Poetry and the Tradition.* University of North Carolina Press, 1939.
———. "What Does Modern Poetry Communicate?" *American Prefaces,* 6 (Autumn 1940), 18–27.
———, and R. WARREN. "The Reading of Modern Poetry," *American Review,* 8 (February 1937), 435–49.
CASSIRER, ERNST. *An Essay on Man.* Yale University Press, 1944. Chap. VIII.

DAICHES, DAVID. *A Study of Literature*. Cornell University Press, 1948. Chap. II; pp. 80, 82, 160, 171–95.

DAY-LEWIS, CECIL. *The Poetic Image*. Jonathan Cape, 1947.

DEUTSCH, BABETTE. "The Future of Poetry," *New Republic*, 60 (August 21, 1929), 12–13.

DOUBLEDAY, NEAL. *Studies in Poetry*. Harper, 1949.

DREW, E., and J. SWEENEY. *Directions in Modern Poetry*. Norton, 1940.

ELIOT, T. S. "Byron," in *From Anne to Victoria*, edited by Bonamy Dobrée. Cassell, 1937. P. 611.

———. *The Music of Poetry*. Jackson, 1942. Pp. 17ff.

———. *The Sacred Wood*. Methuen, 1928; Knopf, 1930. Pp. 144–46.

EMPSON, WILLIAM. *Seven Types of Ambiguity*. Chatto, 1930.

———. *Some Versions of Pastoral*. Chatto, 1935.

FRANKENBERG, LLOYD. "Meaning in Modern Poetry," *Saturday Review of Literature*, 39 (March 23, 1946), 5–6, 56–57.

———. *Pleasure Dome*. Houghton, 1950.

GARDNER, W. H. *Gerard Manley Hopkins*. Secker and Warburg: I, 1948; II, 1949. I, Bibliography.

HORREL, JOE. "Notes on Conversion in Poetry," *Southern Review*, 7 (Summer 1941), 117–31.

HOUSMAN, A. E. *The Name and Nature of Poetry*. Macmillan, Cambridge University Press, 1933. See also I. A. Richards, *Coleridge on Imagination*. Routledge, 1934. Pp. 200–13.

JAMES, D. G. *Scepticism and Poetry*. G. Allen, 1937. Pp. 75–108.

KER, W. P. *Form and Style in English Poetry*. Macmillan, 1928.

LEAVIS, F. R. "A Note on Mr. Santayana's 'Tragic Philosophy'," *Scrutiny*, 12 (Autumn 1944), 295.

MILES, Josephine. *Wordsworth and the Vocabulary of Emotion*. University of California Press, 1942.

MIZENER, ARTHUR. "The Structure of Figurative Language in Shakespeare's Sonnets," *Southern Review*, 5 (Summer 1940), 730–48.

MURRY, J. M. *The Problem of Style*. Oxford University Press, 1922.

PETERS, W. A. M. *Gerard Manley Hopkins*. Oxford, 1948. Bibliography.

RYLANDS, GEORGE. *Words and Poetry*. Hogarth Press, 1928.

SPITZER, LEO. *Linguistics and Literary History*. Princeton University Press, 1948.

STAUFFER, D. A. *The Nature of Poetry*. Norton, 1946.

TATE, ALLEN, editor. *The Language of Poetry*. Princeton University Press, 1942.

———. *On the Limits of Poetry*. Morrow, 1948. Parts II, III, IV.

TILLOTSON, GEOFFREY. "Eighteenth Century Poetic Diction," in *Essays in Criticism and Research*. Cambridge University Press, 1942. Pp. 53–85.

UNGER, LEONARD, editor. *T. S. Eliot: A Selected Critique*. Rinehart, 1948.

WALSH, DOROTHY. "The Poetic Use of Language," *Journal of Philosophy*, 35 (1938), 73–81.

WEYAND, NORMAN, editor. *Immortal Diamond*. Sheed and Ward, 1949.

WHEELWRIGHT, PHILIP. "On the Semantics of Poetry," *Kenyon Review*, 2 (1940), 263–83.

WILSON, KATHERINE. *Sound and Meaning in Poetry*. Jonathan Cape, 1931.

WARREN, R. P. "Pure and Impure Poetry," in *Critiques and Essays in Criticism*, edited by R. W. Stallman. Ronald Press, 1949. Pp. 85–104.

What the Poem Means: Obscurity in Poetry

ABEL, DARRELL. "Intellectual Criticism," *American Scholar*, 12 (Autumn 1943), 414–28. See also Cleanth Brooks, "The New Criticism: A Brief for the Defense," *American Scholar*, 12 (Summer 1944), 285–95.

ABRAMS, M. H. "Unconscious Expectations in the Reading of Poetry," *English Literary History*, 9 (1942), 235–44.

AIKEN, CONRAD. "Theme with Variation," *New Republic*, 112 (April 2, 1945), 451–53.

BROOKS, CLEANTH. *Modern Poetry and the Tradition*. University of North Carolina Press, 1939.

———. *The Well Wrought Urn*. Reynal, 1947; Dobson, 1949. Pp. 115–16, 120, 122, 126, 136, 145–46, 160, 179, 203.

———, and R. WARREN. "The Reading of Modern Poetry," *American Review*, 8 (February 1937), 435–49.

DAY-LEWIS, CECIL. "A Hope for Poetry," in *Collected Poems*. Random House, 1935. Pp. 182, 202–3.

EASTMAN, MAX. *The Literary Mind*. Scribner, 1931.

ELIOT, T. S. Preface to *Anabasis: A Poem*, by St. John Perse. Harcourt, 1938.

EMPSON, WILLIAM. *Seven Types of Ambiguity*. Chatto, 1930.

FALLS, CYRIL. *The Critic's Armoury*. Cobden-Sanderson, 1924.

FLINT, F. C. "Metaphor in Contemporary Poetry," *Symposium*, 1 (July 1930), 310–35.

GRAVES, ROBERT. *Another Future of Poetry*. Hogarth Essays XVIII. Woolf Press, 1926.

KORG, JACOB. "The Necessity of Obscurity," *Nation*, 170 (January 28, 1950), 87–88.

KRUTCH, J. W. "On the Difficulty of Modern Poetry," *Nation*, 142 (March 4, 1936), 283–84.

LAZARUS, H. P. "The Poet, the Poem, the Reader," *Nation*, 156 (January 16, 1943), 98–101.

MACNEICE, LOUIS. *Modern Poetry*. Oxford, 1938. Pp. 90, 155.

MATTHIESSEN, F. O. *The Achievement of T. S. Eliot*. Oxford, 1935. Pp. 40, 47–48.

MELLERS, W. H. "Cats in Air-Pumps (or Poets in 1940)," *Scrutiny*, 9 (December 1940), 289–300.

MULLER, H. J. "Surrealism: A Dissenting Opinion," in *New Directions in Prose and Verse*. New Directions, 1940. Pp. 548–62.

"Obscurity in Modern Literature," *American Scholar*, 14 (Summer 1945), 351–55 (W. Y. Tindall), 555–57 (F. W. Dupee), 357–61 (W. V. O'Connor), 362–65 (Marc Friedlander).

O'CONNOR, W. V. *Sense and Sensibility in Modern Poetry*. University of Chicago Press, 1948. Chap. XV.

PEYRE, HENRI. *Writers and Their Critics*. Cornell University Press, 1944. Pp. 183–218.

READ, HERBERT. *Collected Essays*. Faber, 1938. Pp. 91–92.

———. *In Defence of Shelley*. Heinemann, 1936. Pp. 145–63.

———. *The Phases of English Poetry*. Hogarth Press, 1928.

RICHARDS, I. A. "Gerard Hopkins," *Dial*, 81 (September 1926), 195–203.

ROBERTS, MICHAEL. "The Critic and the Public," *Southern Review*, 4 (Autumn 1938), 368–81.

ROSENBERG, HAROLD. Review in *Symposium*, 2 (July 1931), 412–18.

SITWELL, EDITH. *Poetry and Criticism.* Hogarth Essays XI. Woolf Press, 1925.

SPARROW, JOHN. *Sense and Poetry.* Yale University Press, 1934. Chaps. III, IV.

SYMONS, JULIAN. "Obscurity and Dylan Thomas," *Kenyon Review,* 2 (Winter 1940), 61, 65, 69.

WARREN, AUSTIN. "Obscurity and Allegory," *Examiner,* 2 (Spring 1939), 178–83.

WOOLF, LEONARD. *Obscurity.* Hogarth Press Chapbook 40, 1925. Pp. 7–9.

How the Meaning Is Said: Symbolism

BEACH, J. W. *The Twentieth Century Novel.* Appleton, 1932. Pp. 53, 222, 420–21, 487.

BELGION, MONTGOMERY. "Heterodoxy on *Moby Dick?*" *Sewanee Review,* 55 (Winter 1947), 108–25.

BLACKMUR, R. P. "Notes on Four Categories in Criticism," *Sewanee Review,* 54 (Autumn 1946), 589.

BOWRA, C. M. *The Heritage of Symbolism.* Macmillan, 1943.

BROOKS, CLEANTH. *Modern Poetry and the Tradition.* University of North Carolina Press, 1939. Pp. 60–61, 65.

BURKE, KENNETH. *A Grammar of Motives.* Prentice-Hall, 1945. Appendix A; pp. 36, 283–86.

CAMPBELL, J., and H. ROBINSON. *A Skeleton Key to Finnegan's Wake.* Harcourt, 1944.

CAZAMIAN, L. F. "Symbolism and Poetry," *Toronto Quarterly,* 5 (July 1936), 520–43.

CHASE, RICHARD. *Herman Melville.* Macmillan, 1949.

CONRAD, JOSEPH. *Life and Letters,* edited by G. Jean-Aubry. Doubleday, 1927. Pp. 204–5.

DAICHES, DAVID. *The Novel and the Modern World.* University of Chicago Press, 1939. Pp. 39, 65.

FOWLIE, WALLACE. "Mallarmé's Island Voyage," *Modern Philology,* 47 (February 1950), 178–90.

FRY, ROGER. *The Artist and Psycho-Analysis.* Hogarth Press, 1928. P. 296.

GIVENS, SEON, editor. *James Joyce: Two Decades of Criticism.* Vanguard Press, 1949. Esp. pp. 27–46, 132–75.

LANGER, S. K. *Philosophy in a New Key.* Oxford, Harvard University Press, 1942.

LEWIS, C. S. *The Allegory of Love.* Clarendon Press, 1936.

MATTHIESSEN, F. O. *The Achievement of T. S. Eliot.* Oxford, 1935.

———. *American Renaissance.* Oxford, 1941. Pp. 242, 291.

MIZENER, ARTHUR. "Some Notes on the Nature of English Poetry," *Sewanee Review,* 51 (Winter 1943), 27–51.

NEIDER, CHARLES. *The Frozen Sea: A Study of Franz Kafka.* Oxford, 1948.

Poets at Work. Harcourt, 1948.

RICE, P. B. "Thomas Mann and the Religious Revival," *Kenyon Review,* 7 (1945), 374–76.

SALINAS, PEDRO. " 'Don Quixote' and the Novel," *Nation,* 166 (December 20, 1947), 682–83.

SHORT, R. W. "Melville as Symbolist," *University of Kansas City Review,* 15 (Autumn 1948), 38–46.

SPARROW, JOHN. *Sense and Poetry.* Yale University Press, 1934. Chap. II.

STOLL, E. E. "Symbolism in Coleridge," *P.M.L.A.,* 63 (March 1948), 222.

TATE, ALLEN. *On the Limits of Poetry.* Morrow, 1948. Pp. 140–45.
URBAN, W. M. *Language and Reality.* Macmillan, 1939.
WARREN, AUSTIN. *Rage for Order.* University of Chicago Press, 1948.
WARREN, R. P. *The Rime of the Ancient Mariner: An Essay.* Reynal, 1946.
———. "William Faulkner," in *Forms of Modern Fiction*, edited by W. V. O'Connor. University of Minnesota Press, 1948. Pp. 130–33, 135, 143.
WHITEHEAD, A. N. *Symbolism: Its Meaning and Effect.* Macmillan, 1927. Pp. 7–8.
WILSON, EDMUND. *Axel's Castle.* Scribner, 1931. Pp. 1–25, 41, 132ff, 157, 160, 229.
ZABEL, M. D., editor. *Literary Opinion in America.* Harper, 1937. Pp. 359–72.

Poetic Meaning and Reader's Response (the Paraphrase)

BROOKS, CLEANTH. *The Well Wrought Urn.* Reynal, 1947; Dobson, 1949. Pp. 62–73, 152, 176, 179–96, 217–18, 228.
———, and R. WARREN. *Understanding Poetry.* Holt, 1938. P. 497.
COLLINGWOOD, R. G. *The Principles of Art.* Oxford, 1938. Pp. 309–11.
DAICHES, DAVID. *A Study of Literature.* Cornell University Press, 1948. Pp. 165, 167.
Editorial, *Southern Review*, 7 (Autumn 1941), iv–xii.
ELIOT, T. S. "Isolated Superiority," *Dial*, 84 (January 1928), 6.
———. *The Sacred Wood.* Methuen, 1928; Knopf, 1930. Pp. 20, 96, 122.
———. *Selected Essays 1917–1932.* Harcourt, Faber, 1932.
GRAVES, ROBERT. *Poetic Unreason.* Cecil Palmer, 1925. Pp. 78–98.
HENDRICKS, CECILIA. Article in *Explicator*, 1 (May 1943), item 7.
KNIGHT, G. W. *The Imperial Theme.* Oxford, 1931. Pp. 1–31.
LEAVIS, F. R. *Education and the University.* Chatto, 1943. Appendix II; pp. 105–38.
MOORE, T. S. *Armour for Aphrodite.* Grant Richards, 1929. Pp. 49–50, and *passim*.
MULLER, H. J. *Science and Criticism.* Yale University Press, 1943. P. 264.
MURRY, J. M. "Beauty Is Truth," *Symposium*, 1 (October 1930), 466–501. See also I. A. Richards, "Between Truth and Truth," *Symposium*, 2 (April 1931), 233–35.
PEPPER, S. C. *Aesthetic Quality.* Scribner, 1937. Pp. 43–44, 48–52.
RICHARDS, I. A. *Principles of Literary Criticism.* Harcourt, 1928. Chap. XVI.
STAUFFER, D. A. *The Nature of Poetry.* Norton, 1946. P. 175.
WARREN, R. P. *The Rime of the Ancient Mariner: An Essay.* Reynal, 1946. Pp. 69–72, 74, 115–17, 124.
WINTERS, YVOR. *In Defense of Reason.* Morrow, 1947. Pp. 20ff, and *passim*.

V. THE CONCEPT OF THE "OBJECTIVE CORRELATIVE"

BAKER, H. "Hardy's Poetic Certitude," *Southern Review*, 6 (Summer 1940), 51.
BENÉT, W., and N. PEARSON, editors. *The Oxford Anthology of American Literature.* Oxford, 1938. P. 1500.
BLACKMUR, R. P. *The Expense of Greatness.* Arrow Editions, 1940. Pp. 80, 91, 104.
BLOCK, H. M. "The Critical Theory of James Joyce," *Journal of Aesthetics*, 8 (March 1950), 172–84.

BURKE, KENNETH. *Counter-Statement*. Harcourt, 1931. Pp. 250–52.
CHASE, RICHARD. "The Sense of the Present," *Kenyon Review*, 7 (Spring 1945), 221.
COLLINGWOOD, R. G. *The Principles of Art*. Clarendon Press, 1938. Pp. 111, 114.
COLLINS, H. P. *Modern Poetry*. Jonathan Cape, 1925. P. 71.
DAY-LEWIS, CECIL. "A Hope for Poetry," in *Collected Poems*. Random House, 1935. Pp. 250–51.
DEWEY, JOHN. *Art as Experience*. Minton Balch, 1934. Pp. 67, 69.
Dictionary of World Literature. Edited by Joseph Shipley. Philosophical Library, 1943. P. 410.
DOBRÉE, BONAMY. *The Lamp and the Lute*. Clarendon Press, 1929. P. 132.
———. *Modern Prose Style*. Oxford, 1946. P. 159.
———. *Restoration Tragedy*. Clarendon Press, 1929. P. 71.
DREW, E., and J. SWEENEY. *Directions in Modern Poetry*. Norton, 1940. P. 192.
DUCASSE, JOHN. *The Philosophy of Art*. Dial Press, 1930.
ELIOT, T. S. *The Sacred Wood*. Methuen, 1928; Knopf, 1930. P. 100.
———. *Selected Essays 1917–1932*. Harcourt, Faber, 1932. Pp. 100, 115, 124–25, 246, 248, 276, 298–99.
EMPSON, WILLIAM. *Some Versions of Pastoral*. Chatto, 1935.
EVANS, B. I. *Tradition and Romanticism*. Methuen, 1940. Pp. 195–96.
FAIRCHILD, A. H. R. *The Making of Poetry*. Putnam, 1912. Pp. 24–25.
FLORES, ANGEL, editor. *The Kafka Problem*. New Directions, 1946. P. 205.
GREENE, T. M. *The Arts and the Art of Criticism*. Princeton University Press, 1940. Chap. XII; pp. 109–15, 354.
HIGGINS, BERTRAM. "The Critical Method of T. S. Eliot," in *Scrutinies*, edited by Edgell Rickword. Lawrence and Wishart, 1931. II, pp. 63–64.
HOSPERS, JOHN. *Meaning and Truth in the Arts*. University of North Carolina Press, 1946. P. 130.
HOUSMAN, A. E. *The Name and Nature of Poetry*. Macmillan, Cambridge University Press, 1933. Pp. 8, 46–47.
MATTHIESSEN, F. O. *The Achievement of T. S. Eliot*. Oxford, 1935. Chap. III; pp. 55, 60, 66, 71.
McLUHAN, MARSHALL. "Eliot's 'Hippopotamus'," *Explicator*, 2 (May 1944), item 50.
MURRY, J. M. *Aspects of Literature*. Collins, 1920. Pp. 134–35.
O'CONNOR, W. V., editor. *Forms of Modern Fiction*. University of Minnesota Press, 1948. Pp. 43–45, 97, 209.
PHILLIPS, WILLIAM. "Categories for Criticism," *Symposium*, 4 (January 1933), 44–45.
PRAZ, MARIO. "T. S. Eliot and Dante," *Southern Review*, 2 (Winter 1937), 528–31, 539.
RARIG, F. M. "Some Elementary Contributions of Aesthetics to Interpretive Speech," *Quarterly Journal of Speech*, 26 (December 1940).
READ, HERBERT. *Collected Essays*. Faber, 1938. Pp. 44, 90–91, 100.
———. *The Meaning of Art*. Faber, 1931. Pp. 180, 218–20, 222.
———. *Reason and Romanticism*. Faber and Gwyer, 1926. Pp. 68–70.
RICE, P. B. "George Santayana: The Philosopher as Poet," *Kenyon Review*, 5 (Autumn 1940), 465ff.
———. "A Modern Poet's Technique: Guillaume Apollinaire," *Symposium*, 2 (October 1931), 476ff.

RICHARDS, I. A. *Science and Poetry*. Norton, 1926. Chap. II; pp. 23ff.
ROBERTS, MICHAEL. "Aspects of English Poetry," *Poetry*, 46 (January 1937), 212.
——. *Critique of Poetry*. Jonathan Cape, 1934. Pp. 32, 95, 96, 110.
SANTAYANA, GEORGE. *Interpretations in Poetry and Religion*. Scribner, Constable, 1900. Pp. 263–64, 277.
SCHWARTZ, DELMORE. "The Poetry of Allen Tate," *Southern Review*, 5 (Winter 1940), 428.
Scrutiny. Edited by F. R. Leavis. 9 (March 1941), 338, 375; 10 (June 1941), 23–24; 11 (Summer 1943), 295; 13 (Autumn 1945), 204, 206; 13 (Spring 1946), 278, 283.
STALLMAN, R. W. "Annotated Bibliography of A. E. Housman," *P.M.L.A.*, 55 (June 1945), 491–94.
——. "Keats the Apollinian," *University of Toronto Quarterly*, 16 (January 1947), 147–49.
——. "The Poetry of John Peale Bishop," *Western Review*, 11 (Autumn 1946), 9.
——, editor. *Critiques and Essays in Criticism*. Ronald Press, 1949. Pp. 13, 21, 44, 207, 387, 389–400, 497.
STAUFFER, D. A. *The Nature of Poetry*. Norton, 1946. Chap. IV.
TATE, ALLEN. *On the Limits of Poetry*. Morrow, 1948. Pp. 88–90, 144–45, 192, 230.
——. "Poetry and the Absolute," *Sewanee Review*, 35 (1926), 41–52.
——. *Reactionary Essays*. Scribner, 1936. P. 232.
TAUPIN, RENÉ. "The Classicism of T. S. Eliot," *Symposium*, 3 (January 1932), 64–65.
THOMAS, W., and S. BROWN. *Reading Poems*. Oxford, 1941. Pp. 643–46, 650, 655, 662, 674, 745–48.
TREECE, HENRY, editor. *Herbert Read*. Faber, 1944. Pp. 20, 29.
TROY, WILLIAM. "Stendhal," *Partisan Review*, 9 (January 1942), 21.
——. "Virginia Woolf: The Poetic Style," *Symposium*, 3 (April 1932), 161–62.
VALÉRY, PAUL. "A First Course in Poetics," *Southern Review*, 6 (Winter 1940), 405–6.
WALTON, EDA LOU. " 'Not Mine, but Man's'," *Nation*, 143 (November 7, 1936), 552.
WARREN, R. P. "The Blind Poet, Sidney Lanier," *American Review*, 2 (November 1933), 43.
WEISS, TED. "T. S. Eliot and the Courtyard Revolution," *Sewanee Review*, 54 (Spring 1946), 289–307.
WHITEHEAD, A. N. *Symbolism: Its Meaning and Effect*. Macmillan, Cambridge University Press, 1928. Pp. 9, 83–84, 98.
WILLIAMSON, GEORGE. "Donne and the Poetry of Today," in *A Garland for John Donne*, edited by Theodore Spencer. Harvard University Press, 1931. Pp. 175, 176.
WINTERS, YVOR. *In Defense of Reason*. Morrow, 1947. Pp. 466–69.

Art as the Expression of Emotion

ALEXANDER, SAMUEL. *Beauty and Other Forms of Value*. Macmillan, 1933.
BELGION, MONTGOMERY. "The Expression of Emotion," *Southern Review*, 3 (Spring 1938), 783–89.

———. "What Is Criticism?" *Criterion*, 10 (October 1930), 118–37.

BELL, CLIVE. *Art*. Chatto, 1947. Pp. 62–64.

BOAS, GEORGE. *A Primer for Critics*. Johns Hopkins University Press, 1937. Pp. 100–3, 105.

BURKE, KENNETH. *The Philosophy of Literary Form*. Louisiana State University Press, 1941.

CROCE, BENEDETTO. "The Breviary of Aesthetic," *Rice Institute Pamphlet*, 2 (December 1915), 223–310.

———. *The Defence of Poetry*. Clarendon Press, 1933. Pp. 24–25.

DEWEY, JOHN. *Art as Experience*. Minton Balch, 1934. Chaps. IV, V.

FRY, ROGER. *Last Lectures*. Cambridge University Press, 1939.

———. *Vision and Design*. Chatto, 1920. Pp. 37–38, 83–84, 293–302.

GREENE, T. M. *The Arts and the Art of Criticism*. Princeton University Press, 1940. Chaps. XII, XV.

HARDING, R. M. *The Anatomy of Inspiration*. Cambridge University Press, 1940. Pp. 47, 48, 70.

HOUSMAN, A. E. *The Name and Nature of Poetry*. Macmillan, Cambridge University Press, 1933.

JAMES, D. G. *Scepticism and Poetry*. G. Allen, 1937. Pp. 114–15, 119–20.

LAWRENCE, D. H. *Phoenix*. Viking Press, Heinemann, 1936. P. 539.

LEBOWITZ, MARTIN. "Thought and Sensibility," *Kenyon Review*, 5 (Spring 1943), 219–26.

MILES, JOSEPHINE. *Wordsworth and the Vocabulary of Emotion*. University of California Press, 1942.

PEPPER, S. C. *Aesthetic Quality*. Scribner, 1938. Chap. IV.

———. "Emotional Distance in Art," *Journal of Aesthetics*, 4 (June 1946), 235–39.

PRALL, D. W. *Aesthetic Analysis*. Crowell, 1936. Pp. 9, 19, 147, 159.

———. *The Aesthetic Judgment*. Crowell, 1929. Chap. X, sec. 5, and *passim*.

RADER, M. M., editor. *A Modern Book of Esthetics*. Holt, 1935. Chap. III.

RANSOM, J. C. *The New Criticism*. New Directions, 1941. Pp. 153, 155–56.

RICHARDS, I. A. *The Principles of Literary Criticism*. Harcourt, 1925. Pp. 186–89.

RICKWORD, EDGELL. "The Use of 'Negative' Emotions," in *Critiques and Essays in Criticism*, edited by R. W. Stallman. Ronald Press, 1949. Pp. 80–84.

ROBERTS, MICHAEL. *Critique of Poetry*. Jonathan Cape, 1934. Pp. 32, 75, 80, 84, 100, 103, 114, 163, 177–78.

SCHNEIDER, ELISABETH. *Aesthetic Motive*. Macmillan, 1939. Pp. 103–4.

TATE, ALLEN. "The Aesthetic Emotion as Useful," *This Quarter*, 5 (December 1932), 292–303.

VIVAS, ELISEO. "The Aesthetic Transaction," *Naturalism and the Human Spirit*, edited by H. Krikorian. Columbia University Press, 1944. Pp. 111ff.

———. "The Objective Correlative of T. S. Eliot," in *Critiques and Essays in Criticism*, edited by R. W. Stallman. Ronald Press, 1949. Pp. 389–400.

WILLIAMS, CHARLES. *Reason and Beauty in the Poetic Mind*. Clarendon Press, 1933.

WIMSATT, W., and M. BEARDSLEY. "The Affective Fallacy," in *Critiques and Essays in Criticism*, edited by R. W. Stallman. Ronald Press, 1949. Pp. 401–10.

Art as the Expression of "Thought" and "Feeling"

AIKEN, CONRAD. "Poetry, What Direction?" *New Republic*, 104 (May 12, 1941), 670–71.

BATESON, F. W. *English Poetry and the English Language*. Clarendon Press, 1934. Pp. 100, and *passim*.

COLLINGWOOD, R. G. *The Principles of Art*. Clarendon Press, 1938. Chap. VIII; pp. 109–11, 115–17, 121–24.

DOBRÉE, BONAMY. *The Lamp and the Lute*. Clarendon Press, 1929. Pp. 116–18.

EASTMAN, MAX. *The Literary Mind*. Scribner, 1935. Part IV, Chap. I.

ELIOT, T. S. *Elizabethan Essays*. Faber, 1934. Pp. 46 and *passim*.

———. "The Poems of Richard Crashaw," *Dial*, 84 (March 1928), 248–49.

———. *The Sacred Wood*. Methuen, 1928; Knopf, 1930. Pp. 6–7, 54, 63, 106, 110.

———. *Selected Essays 1917–1932*. Harcourt, Faber, 1932. Pp. 8–11, 124–25, 128, 131, 137, 246–47, 258, 273, 298ff.

EMPSON, WILLIAM. "Feelings in Words," *Criterion*, 15 (January 1936), 183–99.

GARY, FRANKLIN. Review in *Symposium*, 3 (October 1932), 528–29.

JAMES, WILLIAM. *The Varieties of Religious Experience*. Random House, 1902. P. 147.

KNIGHTS, L. C. *Explorations*. Chatto, 1946. Pp. 92–111.

LEAVIS, F. R. *Revaluation*. Chatto, 1936.

———. "Shelley," in *Critiques and Essays in Criticism*, edited by R. W. Stallman. Ronald Press, 1949. Pp. 162–80.

———. " 'Thought' and Emotional Quality," *Scrutiny*, 13 (Spring 1945), 53–71.

LEBOWITZ, MARTIN. "Thought and Sensibility," *Kenyon Review*, 5 (Spring 1943), 219–26.

RANSOM, J. C. *The New Criticism*. New Directions, 1941. Pp. 155–56, 163ff.

———. *The World's Body*. Scribner, 1938. Pp. 278–79.

READ, HERBERT. "The Present State of Poetry," *Kenyon Review*, 1 (Autumn 1939), 369.

RICHARDS, I. A. "Emotive Language Still," *Yale Review*, 39 (September 1949), 108ff.

———. *Practical Criticism*. Harcourt, 1929. Pp. 271, 274–78.

SPENCER, THEODORE, editor. *A Garland for John Donne*. Harvard University Press, 1931. Pp. 175–76.

STALLMAN, R. W., editor. *Critiques and Essays in Criticism*. Ronald Press, 1949. Pp. 51, 52, 165–66, 168–69, 176–77, 203, 381–82, 389–400, 500–1.

STAUFFER, D. A., editor. *The Intent of the Critic*. Princeton University Press, 1941. Pp. 96–99.

TATE, ALLEN. *On the Limits of Poetry*. Morrow, 1948. Pp. 91–114.

WINTERS, YVOR. *In Defense of Reason*. Morrow, 1947. Pp. 469–74.

VI. THE PROBLEM OF THE PERSONAL ELEMENT

ABERCROMBIE, LASCELLES. *The Idea of Great Poetry*. Secker and Warburg, 1925.

AUDEN, W. H. "Psychology and Art," in *The Arts To-day*, edited by Geoffrey Grigson. Bodley, 1935. Pp. 1–21.

BAUDOUIN, CHARLES. *Psychoanalysis and Aesthetics*. G. Allen, 1924.

BELGION, MONTGOMERY. "The Poet's Name," *Sewanee Review*, 54 (Autumn 1946), 635–49.

BISHOP, J. P. *Collected Essays*, edited by Edmund Wilson. Scribner, 1948. Pp. 88–89, 135, 141–42.

BLUNDEN, EDMUND. "Behind the Poem," *Times Literary Supplement*, 2173 (September 25, 1943), 462, 466.

BRADBROOK, C. M. *Joseph Conrad*. Cambridge University Press, 1942. Pp. 64, 76.

CHASE, RICHARD. "The Brontës, or, Myth Domesticated," in *Forms of Modern Fiction*, edited by W. V. O'Connor. University of Minnesota Press, 1948. Pp. 102–19.

COWLEY, MALCOLM. "A Plea for Anonymity," *New Republic*, 84 (September 18, 1935), 155–57.

CROCE, BENEDETTO. *Ariosto, Shakespeare, and Corneille*. Holt, 1920. Chap. VII.

DAY-LEWIS, CECIL. "A Hope for Poetry," in *Collected Poems*. Random House, 1935. Pp. 184, 189ff.

Dictionary of World Literature. Edited by Joseph Shipley. Philosophical Library, 1943. P. 431.

DREW, E., and J. SWEENEY. *Directions in Modern Poetry*. Norton, 1940. Pp. 176–77.

EASTMAN, MAX. *The Literary Mind*. Scribner, 1935. Pp. 195–206.

ELIOT, T. S. *After Strange Gods*. Faber, Harcourt, 1934. Pp. 62–63.

———. "The Poetry of W. B. Yeats," *Southern Review*, 7 (Winter 1942), 442–54.

———. *The Sacred Wood*. Methuen, 1928; Knopf, 1930. Pp. 14–15, 47–59, 143.

———. *Selected Essays 1917–1932*. Harcourt, Faber, 1932. Pp. 3–11, 14–15, 96, 124–26.

———. *The Use of Poetry and the Use of Criticism*. Faber, Harvard University Press, 1933. Pp. 33–34.

FERNANDEZ, RAMON. *Messages*. Harcourt, 1927. Pp. 96–97.

FORSTER, E. M. *Anonymity: An Enquiry*. Hogarth Press, 1925. Pp. 14–15.

FRYE, NORTHROP. *Fearful Symmetry: A Study of Blake*. Princeton University Press, 1947. P. 326.

GARROD, H. W. *Poetry and the Criticism of Life*. Oxford, 1931. Pp. 3ff, and *passim*.

———. *The Profession of Poetry*. Clarendon Press, 1929. Pp. 166, 178.

GOLDWATER, R., and M. TREVES, editors. *Artists on Art*. Pantheon Books, 1945.

GOTSHALK, D. W. *Art and the Social Order*. University of Chicago Press, 1947. Pp. 63–64, 120–21.

HALL, J., and M. STEINMANN, editors. *The Permanence of Yeats*. Macmillan, 1950.

HENRI, ROBERT. *The Art Spirit*. Lippincott, 1930. P. 7.

HOFFMAN, F. J. *Freudianism and the Literary Mind*. Louisiana State University Press, 1945.

HYMAN, S. E. *The Armed Vision*. Knopf, 1948. Pp. 118–19.

JAMES, D. G. *Scepticism and Poetry*. G. Allen, 1937. Pp. 117–18.

JONES, ERNEST. *Essays in Applied Psycho-Analysis*. International Psycho-Analytical Press, 1923.

———. *Hamlet: With a Psycho-Analytical Study*. Vision Press, Funk, 1948.

KNIGHTS, L. C. *Explorations*. Chatto, 1946. Pp. 40–65.

LAWRENCE, D. H. *Phoenix*. Viking Press, Heinemann, 1936.

LEAVIS, F. R. "Coleridge on Criticism," *Scrutiny*, 9 (June 1940), 66–67.

———. *Revaluation*. Chatto, 1936. Chap. VII; pp. 208, 244.

LEIGHTON, LAWRENCE. "One View of Housman," *Poetry*, 52 (May 1938), 94–100.

BIBLIOGRAPHY

LEWIS, C., and E. TILLYARD. *The Personal Heresy*. Oxford, 1939. See also review by F. W. Bateson in *Review of English Studies*, 16 (October 1940), 487–89.

MARITAIN, JACQUES. "Poetry and Religion," *Criterion*, 5 (January 1927), 16–17.

MATTHIESSEN, F. O. *The Achievement of T. S. Eliot*. Oxford, 1935. Pp. 71–72, 101–3, 141–42, 145–49.

MIZENER, ARTHUR. "Jude the Obscure as a Tragedy," *Southern Review*, 6 (Summer 1940), 197.

MOORE, T. S. "A Poet and His Technique," *New Criterion*, 4 (October 1926), 685.

MURRY, J. M. *Keats and Shakespeare*. Oxford, 1925.

PORTEUS, H. G. "William Blake," in *From Anne to Victoria*, edited by Bonamy Dobrée. Cassell, 1938. Pp. 465–79.

PORTNOY, JULIUS. *A Psychology of Art Creation*. University of Pennsylvania Press, 1942.

QUILLER-COUCH, SIR ARTHUR. *The Poet as Citizen*. Macmillan, 1935. Pp. 25–43.

RAHV, PHILIP. "The Cult of Experience in American Writing," *Partisan Review*, 7 (November 1940), 412–24.

RANSOM, J. C. *The World's Body*. Scribner, 1938. Pp. 2ff, 79, 231, 233, 257, 259.

READ, HERBERT. *Collected Essays*. Faber, 1938. Pp. 20–40.

———. *The Meaning of Art*. Faber, 1931. Esp. pp. 33ff.

———. *Reason and Romanticism*. Faber and Gwyer, 1926. Pp. 2, 219.

RICHARDS, I. A. *Practical Criticism*. Harcourt, Routledge, 1929. P. 355.

RIDING, L., and R. GRAVES. *A Survey of Modernist Poetry*. Heinemann, 1927. P. 124.

SAVAGE, D. S. *The Personal Principle*. Routledge, 1944.

SCHNEIDER, ELISABETH. *Aesthetic Motive*. Macmillan, 1939. Pp. 103–4.

SCHWARTZ, DELMORE. "The Writing of Edmund Wilson," *Accent*, 2 (Spring 1942), 177–86.

SCOTT-JAMES, R. A. *The Making of Literature*. Secker and Warburg, 1928.

Scrutiny. Edited by F. R. Leavis. 8 (December 1939), 288; 12 (Summer 1944), 179; 13 (Spring 1946), 289, 291; 14 (September 1947), 270.

SISSON, C. J. "The Mythical Sorrows of Shakespeare," *Proceedings of the British Academy*, 20 (1934).

SPARROW, JOHN. *Sense and Poetry*. Yale University Press, 1934. Pp. 108–9.

SPINGARN, J. E. *Creative Criticism*. Harcourt, 1931.

STALLMAN, R. W. "Annotated Bibliography of A. E. Housman," *P.M.L.A.*, 55 (June 1945), 482–85.

———. "Life, Art, and 'The Secret Sharer'," in *Forms of Modern Fiction*, edited by W. V. O'Connor. University of Minnesota Press, 1948. Pp. 229–42.

STAUFFER, D. A. "Critical Principles and a Sonnet," *American Scholar*, 12 (Winter 1943), 52–62.

SWALLOW, ALAN. "Subjectivism as Poetic Method," *New Mexico Quarterly Review*, 13 (Spring 1943), 10–20.

TATE, ALLEN. *Reactionary Essays*. Scribner, 1936. Pp. 40, 53, 213, 231.

———. *Reason in Madness*. Putnam, 1941. Pp. 60, 106–7.

WARREN, A., and R. WELLEK. *Theory of Literature*. Harcourt, 1949.

WARREN, R. P. *The Rime of the Ancient Mariner: An Essay*. Reynal, 1946. Pp. 72, 124.

WEST, R. B., JR. "Ernest Hemingway: The Failure of Sensibility," in *Forms of Modern Fiction*, edited by W. V. O'Connor. University of Minnesota Press, 1948. Pp. 87–101.

Winters, Yvor. "Robert Frost," *Sewanee Review*, 56 (Autumn 1948), 568, 570.

VII. THE PROBLEM OF BELIEF IN POETRY

Abbott, C. C., editor. *The Letters of Gerard Manley Hopkins to Robert Bridges.* Oxford, 1935.

Adler, Mortimer. *Art and Prudence.* Longmans, 1937.

Auden, W. H. "Against Romanticism," *New Republic*, 102 (February 5, 1940), 187.

———. "Criticism in a Mass Society," in *The Intent of the Critic*, edited by D. A. Stauffer. Princeton University Press, 1941. Pp. 125–47.

———. "The Rewards of Patience," *Partisan Review*, 9 (July 1942), 338.

Babbitt, Irving. *The New Laokoon.* Houghton, 1910.

Baker, Howard. "Belief and Dogma," *Hound and Horn*, 12 (July 1933), 608–20.

Belgion, Montgomery. *The Human Parrot and Other Essays.* Oxford, 1931.

Bell, Clive. *Art.* Chatto, 1947.

Bethel, S. L. "A Theory of Value," *Criterion*, 15 (January 1935), 239–50.

Blackmur, R. P. *The Expense of Greatness.* Arrow Editions, 1940. Pp. 76–77.

———. "The Later Poetry of W. B. Yeats," in *Critiques and Essays in Criticism*, edited by R. W. Stallman. Ronald Press, 1949. Pp. 358–76.

Bradley, A. C. *Oxford Lectures on Poetry.* Macmillan, 1909. Pp. 25 and *passim.*

Brémond, Henri. *Prayer and Poetry.* Burns, 1929.

Brooks, Cleanth. *Modern Poetry and the Tradition.* University of North Carolina Press, 1939. Chap. VII; pp. 49, 53, 170.

———. "Poetry and Political Faith," *Poetry*, 50 (August 1937), 280–84.

———. *The Well Wrought Urn.* Reynal, 1947; Dobson, 1949. Pp. 140–41, 226–31.

Brooks, Van Wyck. *The Opinions of Oliver Allston.* Dutton, 1944.

Burke, Kenneth. *Counter-Statement.* Harcourt, 1931.

———. *The Philosophy of Literary Form.* Louisiana State University Press, 1941.

Burnham, James. "On Defining Poetry," *Symposium*, 1 (April 1930), 221–30.

The Case against the Saturday Review of Literature. Modern Poetry Association, 1949.

Connor, F. W. *Cosmic Optimism.* University of Florida Press, 1949.

Croce, Benedetto. *Aesthetics.* Macmillan, 1922.

———. "The Breviary of Aesthetic," *Rice Institute Pamphlet*, 2 (December 1915), 237.

Daiches, David. *The Novel and the Modern World.* University of Chicago Press, 1939. Pp. 7, 13, 164, 219–21.

———. *The Place of Meaning in Poetry.* Oliver and Boyd, 1935.

———. *Poetry and the Modern World.* University of Chicago Press, 1940. Pp. 103–4, 120–21.

———. *A Study of Literature.* Cornell University Press, 1948. Chap. IX.

Davidson, Donald. "The Southern Poet and His Tradition," *Poetry*, 40 (May 1932), 94–103.

Day-Lewis, Cecil. "A Hope for Poetry," in *Collected Poems.* Random House, 1935. Pp. 186–87.

De Voto, Bernard. *The Literary Fallacy.* Little, 1944.

DREW, E., and J. SWEENEY. *Directions in Modern Poetry*. Norton, 1940.

EASTMAN, MAX. *The Literary Mind*. Scribner, 1935.

ELIOT, T. S. *After Strange Gods*. Faber, Harcourt, 1934. Pp. 31–32.

———. *Essays Ancient and Modern*. Faber, 1936.

———. *For Lancelot Andrews*. Faber, Doubleday, 1928.

———. "Isolated Superiority," *Dial*, 84 (January 1928), 7.

———. "Literature, Science, and Dogma," *Dial*, 82 (March 1927), 242–43.

———. "The Mysticism of Blake," *Nation*, 41 (September 17, 1927), 779.

———. "A Note on Belief," *The Enemy*, 1 (January 1927), 15–17.

———. "A Note on Cowley," in *Seventeenth Century Studies Presented to Sir Herbert Grierson*. Clarendon Press, 1938. P. 238.

———. "The Poems of Richard Crashaw," *Dial*, 84 (March 1928), 246.

———. "Poetry and Propaganda," *Bookman*, 70 (February 1930), 595–602.

———. "The Poetry of W. B. Yeats," *Southern Review*, 7 (Winter 1941), 442–54.

———. *The Sacred Wood*. Methuen, 1928; Knopf, 1930. Pp. 51, 116, 118, 160, 170–71.

———. *Selected Essays 1917–1932*. Harcourt, Faber, 1932. Pp. 51, 116–18, 349ff. See also Note to Chap. II.

———. "The Social Function of Poetry," *Adelphi*, 21 (July 1945), 152–61. Reprinted in *Critiques and Essays in Criticism*, edited by R. W. Stallman. Ronald Press, 1949. Pp. 105–16.

———. *The Use of Poetry and the Use of Criticism*. Faber, Harvard University Press, 1933. Pp. 122, 123, 277ff.

EMPSON, WILLIAM. *Some Versions of Pastoral*. Chatto, 1935.

ENRIGHT, D. J. "Rilke, George and 'Re-Integration'," *Scrutiny*, 13 (September 1945), 117–18.

EVANS, W. V. *Belief in Art*. University of Chicago Library, 1939.

FARRELL, J. T. *A Note on Literary Criticism*. Vanguard Press, 1936.

FERNANDEZ, RAMON. *Messages*. Harcourt, 1927. Chap. VI.

FLINT, F. C. "Metaphor in Contemporary Poetry," *Symposium*, 1 (July 1930), 325.

FLORES, ANGEL, editor. *The Kafka Problem*. New Directions, 1946. P. 171.

FRY, ROGER. *Vision and Design*. Chatto, 1920.

GARDNER, W. H. *Gerard Manley Hopkins*. Secker: I, 1944; II, 1949.

———. "The Religious Problem in G. M. Hopkins," *Scrutiny*, 6 (June 1937), 32–42. Reprinted in *Critiques and Essays in Criticism*, edited by R. W. Stallman. Ronald Press, 1949. Pp. 346–57.

GILBY, THOMAS. *Poetic Experience*. Sheed and Ward, 1934.

GREGORY, HORACE. "Beliefs in Poetry," *Nation*, 143 (July 25, 1936), 102–3.

———. *The Shield of Achilles: Essays on Belief in Poetry*. Harcourt, 1944.

———, and M. ZATURENSKA. *A History of American Poetry 1900–1940*. Harcourt, 1946.

GUERARD, ALBERT. *Literature and Society*. Lothrop, 1935.

HALL, J., and M. STEINMANN, editors. *The Permanence of Yeats*. Macmillan, 1950. Bibliography.

HAMILTON, G. R. *Poetry and Contemplation*. Cambridge University Press, 1937.

HEALY, J. V. "Yeats and His Imagination," *Sewanee Review*, 54 (Autumn 1946), 655.

HEYL, B. C. *New Bearings in Aesthetics*. Yale University Press, 1943.

HICKS, GRANVILLE. *The Great Tradition*. Macmillan, 1933.

HONIG, EDWIN. "History, Document and Archibald MacLeish," *Sewanee Review*, 48 (1940), 385–96.

HOSPERS, JOHN. *Meaning and Truth in the Arts*. University of North Carolina Press, 1946.

HOUSE, HUMPHREY, editor. *Notebooks and Papers of Gerard Manley Hopkins*. Oxford, 1937.

HOUSMAN, A. E. *The Name and Nature of Poetry*. Cambridge University Press, 1933. Pp. 33–34.

HULME, T. E. *Speculations*. Kegan Paul, Harcourt, 1924.

JAMES, D. G. *Scepticism and Poetry*. G. Allen, 1937. P. 67, and *passim*.

KNICKERBOCKER, W. S., editor. *Twentieth Century English*. Philosophical Library, 1946. Pp. 23ff.

KRONENBERGER, LOUIS. "A Note on Housman," *Nation*, 145 (December 18, 1937), 690–91.

KRUTCH, J. W. *Experience and Art*. Smith and Haas, 1932. See also Kenneth Burke, "Belief and Art," *Nation*, 135 (November 30, 1932), 536–37.

———. *The Modern Temper: A Study and a Confession*. Harcourt, 1929.

LEAVIS, F. R., editor. *Towards Standards of Criticism*. Lawrence and Wishart, 1933. Pp. 127–39.

LEBOWITZ, MARTIN. "On Tradition, Belief and Culture," *Journal of Philosophy*, 40 (February 1943), 100–5.

LEIGHTON, LAWRENCE. "One View of Housman," *Poetry*, 52 (May 1938), 95.

LEWIS, C. S. *Rehabilitation and Other Essays*. Oxford, 1939. Pp. 18, 21–22, 25–27.

LIND, ROBERT. "The Crisis in Literature: VI," *Sewanee Review*, 48 (April 1940), 198–203.

LUCAS, F. L. *Authors Dead and Living*. Macmillan, 1926. P. 172.

MACLEISH, ARCHIBALD. *The Irresponsibles*. Duell, Sloan, 1940.

———. *A Time to Speak*. Duell, Sloan, 1941.

MACNEICE, LOUIS. *Modern Poetry*. Oxford, 1938.

———. *The Poetry of W. B. Yeats*. Oxford, 1941. P. 231.

MATTHIESSEN, F. O. *The Achievement of T. S. Eliot*. Oxford, 1947. Pp. 90, 108, 110–11, 113.

MARITAIN, JACQUES. *Art and Scholasticism*. Scribner, 1930.

MORE, P. E. *On Being Human*. Princeton University Press, 1936.

———. *Selected Shelburne Essays*. Princeton University Press, Oxford, 1936.

MULLER, H. J. *Modern Fiction*. Funk, 1937.

———. "The New Criticism," *Southern Review*, 6 (Spring 1941), 811–39.

———. *Science and Criticism*. Yale University Press, 1943.

MURRAY, GILBERT. *The Classical Tradition in Poetry*. Harvard University Press, 1927. Pp. 253ff.

MURRY, J. M. *Aspects of Literature*. Collins, 1920. Pp. 133ff.

———. "Beauty Is Truth," *Symposium*, 1 (October 1930), 495–501. See also I. A. Richards, "Between Truth and Truth," *Symposium*, 2 (April 1931).

———. "Literature and Religion," in *The Necessity of Art*, edited by Percy Dearmer. Student Christian Movement, 1924.

———. "Towards a Synthesis," *Criterion*, 5 (May 1927), 294–313.

O'CONNOR, W. V. "Shapiro on Rime," *Kenyon Review*, 8 (Winter 1946), 116, 119–21.

PICK, JOHN. *Gerard Manley Hopkins*. Oxford, 1942.

POTTLE, FREDERICK. *The Idiom of Poetry.* Cornell University Press, 1946.

RANSOM, J. C. "Poetry: A Note on Ontology," in *Critiques and Essays in Criticism,* edited by R. W. Stallman. Ronald Press, 1949. Pp. 30–46.

READ, HERBERT. *Collected Essays.* Faber, 1938. Pp. 333–34, 339.

———. *Form in Modern Poetry.* Sheed and Ward, 1932.

———. *In Defence of Shelley and Other Essays.* Heinemann, 1936. Pp. 8–10, 70, 117ff, 123ff.

———. *The Meaning of Art.* Faber, 1931.

———. *Phases of English Poetry.* Harcourt, 1928.

———. "Poetry and Belief in Gerard M. Hopkins," *New Verse,* 2 (March 1935), 11–15.

———. *Reason and Romanticism.* Faber and Gwyer, 1926.

"Religion and the Intellectuals: A Symposium," *Partisan Review,* 17 (February–March 1950), 103–42, 215–56.

RICE, P. B. "Poets and the Wars," *Nation,* 140 (February 13, 1935), 188–90.

RICHARDS, I. A. "Belief," *Symposium,* 1 (October 1930), 423–39.

———. *Coleridge on Imagination.* Routledge, 1934. Pp. 147, 165.

———. "Lawrence as a Poet," *New Verse,* 2 (March 1933), 15–17.

———. *Mencius on the Mind.* Kegan Paul, 1932. Pp. 111–15.

———. "Poetry and Beliefs," in *Critiques and Essays in Criticism,* edited by R. W. Stallman. Ronald Press, 1949. Pp. 329–33.

———. *Practical Criticism.* Harcourt, Routledge, 1929. Chap. VII; pp. 179ff, 271–78, 300.

———. *Principles of Literary Criticism.* Harcourt, 1925; Kegan Paul, 1924. Chaps. VII, XV, XXXIII, XXXV.

———. *Science and Poetry.* Norton, 1926. Chap. VI.

———. "What Is Belief?" *Nation,* 139 (July 18, 1934), 71–74.

ROBERTS, MICHAEL. *Critique of Poetry.* Jonathan Cape, 1934. Pp. 80, 85, 97, 105, 128, 151, 200.

———. "Psychology and Belief," in *The Modern Mind.* Faber, 1937. Chap. IX.

RODNEY, W. J. *The Problem of 'Poetry and Belief' in Contemporary Criticism.* Catholic University of America Press, 1949.

ROELLINGER, F. X. "Two Theories of Poetry as Knowledge," *Southern Review,* 7 (Spring 1942), 690–705.

SANTAYANA, GEORGE. *Interpretations of Poetry and Religion.* Scribner, 1900.

———. *Little Essays,* edited by L. P. Smith. Scribner, 1934. Pp. 143–44.

SARTRE, JEAN-PAUL. "The Case for Responsible Literature," *Partisan Review,* 12 (1945), 304–8.

SAVAGE, D. S. *The Personal Principle.* Routledge, 1944.

SCHWARTZ, DELMORE. "Poetry and Belief in Thomas Hardy," *Southern Review,* 6 (Summer 1940), 73, 75–76. Reprinted in *Critiques and Essays in Criticism,* edited by R. W. Stallman. Ronald Press, 1949. Pp. 334–45.

SHAPIRO, KARL. *Essay on Rime.* Reynal, 1945.

SPARROW, JOHN. *Sense and Poetry.* Yale University Press, 1934. Chap. I.

SPENDER, STEPHEN. *The Destructive Element.* Jonathan Cape, 1935; Houghton, 1936. See also review by Cleanth Brooks, *Poetry,* 50 (August 1937), 280–84.

———. *Life and the Poet.* Martin Secker, 1942.

———. "Modern Writers in the World of Necessity," *Partisan Review,* 12 (1945), 352–60.

———. "The Year's Poetry: 1940," *Horizon,* 3 (February 1941), 138–48.

SPENCER, THEODORE, editor. *A Garland for John Donne.* Harvard University Press, 1931. Pp. 167–68.

STALLMAN, R. W. "Annotated Bibliography of A. E. Housman," *P.M.L.A.*, 55 (June 1945), 485–90.

——. "The New Critics," in *Critiques and Essays in Criticism*, edited by R. W. Stallman. Ronald Press, 1949. Pp. 502–3.

STAUFFER, D. A. *The Golden Nightingale.* Princeton University Press, 1950.

——. *The Nature of Poetry.* Norton, 1946.

——. "The Search for Beliefs in W. H. Auden's Poetry," *Virginia Quarterly Review*, 22 (Autumn 1946), 570–80.

——, editor. *The Intent of the Critic.* Princeton University Press, 1941.

STEIN, LEO. *The A-B-C of Aesthetics.* Liveright, 1927.

STOLL, E. E. "Symbolism in Coleridge," *P.M.L.A.*, 63 (March 1948), 219.

TATE, ALLEN. "Confusion and Poetry," *Sewanee Review*, 38 (April 1930), 133–49.

——. "Modern Poets and Convention," *American Review*, 8 (February 1937), 427–35.

——. "A New Artist," *New Verse*, 3 (May 1933), 21–23.

——. "A Note on Milton," *New Republic*, 68 (October 21, 1931), 266–68.

——. "Poetry and the Absolute," *Sewanee Review*, 35 (January 1927), 41–52.

——. "The Revolt against Literature," *New Republic*, 49 (February 1927), 329–30.

TOLSTOY, LEO. *What Is Art?* Oxford, 1946.

TURNELL, MARTIN. *Poetry and Crisis.* Paladin Press, 1938.

VAN DOREN, MARK. "Literature and Propaganda," *Virginia Quarterly Review*, 14 (Summer 1938), 203–8.

WATTS, NEVILLE. "The Poetry of A. E. Housman," *Dublin Review*, 200 (January 1937), 117–33.

WEST, ALICK. *Crisis and Criticism.* Lawrence and Wishart, 1937. Chap. VI; pp. 76–77.

WHEELWRIGHT, PHILIP. "Eliot's Philosophical Themes," in *T. S. Eliot (Focus Three)*, edited by B. Rajan. Dobson, Funk, 1947. Pp. 96–97, and *passim*.

——. "On the Semantics of Poetry," *Kenyon Review*, 2 (Summer 1940), 271–72, 275.

——. "Poetry and Logic," *Symposium*, 1 (October 1930), 440–57.

——. "Poetry, Myth, and Reality," in *The Language of Poetry*, edited by Allen Tate. Princeton University Press, 1942. Pp. 3–33.

——. "Toward a Metaphysic of Literary Criticism," *Journal of Philosophy*, 26 (1929), 233–40.

WHITEHEAD, A. N. *Science and the Modern World.* Macmillan, 1928.

WILSON, EDMUND. *Axel's Castle.* Scribner, 1947.

WILDER, AMOS. *The Spiritual Aspects of the New Poetry.* Harper, 1940. See also A. Wanning, "Poetry and Belief," *Kenyon Review*, 3 (Winter 1941), 112–15.

WILLEY, BASIL. *The Seventeenth Century Background.* Chatto, 1934.

WINTERS, YVOR. *The Anatomy of Nonsense.* New Directions, 1943. Pp. 137–42.

——. *In Defense of Reason.* Morrow, 1947. Pp. 475–79.

——. *Maule's Curse.* New Directions, 1938.

——. *Primitivism and Decadence.* Arrow Editions, 1937.

YEATS, W. B. *Autobiography*. Macmillan, 1938.
———. *Essays*. Macmillan, 1924.
———. *Letters to Dorothy Wellesley*. Oxford, 1940.
ZABEL, M. D. "The Poet on Capitol Hill," *Partisan Review*, 8 (January–March 1941), 2–19, 128–45.

Myth and Poetry

BISHOP, J. P. *Collected Essays*, edited by Edmund Wilson. Scribner, 1948.
BLACKMUR, R. P. *The Expense of Greatness*. Arrow Editions, 1940.
BODKIN, MAUD. *Archetypal Patterns in Poetry*. Oxford, 1934.
BOGAN, LOUISE. "This Secular Hell," *Chimaera*, 4 (Spring 1943), 17–20.
BROOKS, CLEANTH. *The Well Wrought Urn*. Reynal, 1947; Dobson, 1949.
CAMPBELL, JOSEPH. *The Hero with a Thousand Faces*. Pantheon Books, 1949.
CASSIRER, ERNST. *An Essay on Man*. Yale University Press, 1944. Chap. VII.
CAUDWELL, CHRISTOPHER. *Illusion and Reality*. Macmillan, 1947. Chap. II.
CHASE, RICHARD. *Herman Melville*. Macmillan, 1950.
———. "Notes on the Study of Myth," *Partisan Review*, 13 (Summer 1946), 338–46.
CHESTERTON, G. K. "The Savage as a Poet," *London Mercury*, 10 (1924), 288–98.
Chimaera, 4 (Spring 1946). "A Special Issue on Myth."
DREW, ELIZABETH. *T. S. Eliot: The Design of His Poetry*. Scribner, 1949.
ELIOT, T. S. "*Ulysses*, Order and Myth," *Dial*, 75 (November 1923), 480–83.
FRYE, NORTHROP. *Fearful Symmetry: A Study of Blake*. Princeton University Press, 1947.
HOOKE, S. H. *Myth and Ritual*. Oxford, 1933.
———, editor. *The Labyrinth*. Macmillan, 1935.
O'DONNELL, G. M. "Faulkner's Mythology," *Kenyon Review*, 1 (1939), 285–99.
PRESCOTT, F. C. *Poetry and Myth*. Macmillan, 1927.
RANSOM, J. C. *God without Thunder*. Harcourt, 1930.
RICHARDS, I. A. *Coleridge on Imagination*. Routledge, 1926.
———. *Science and Poetry*. Norton, Routledge, 1926.
ROSENBERG, HAROLD. "Myth and Poem," *Symposium*, 2 (April 1931), 179–91.
SCHORER, MARK. *William Blake*. Holt, 1946.
TAGGARD, GENEVIEVE. "The Two-Edged Sword," *Nation*, 118 (June 4, 1924), 648–49.
TATE, ALLEN. "A Note on Milton," *New Republic*, 68 (October 21, 1931), 266–68.
———. *On the Limits of Poetry*. Morrow, 1948.
———, editor. *The Language of Poetry*. Princeton University Press, 1942.
TROY, WILLIAM. "Thomas Mann: Myth and Reason," *Partisan Review*, 5 (1938), 51–64.
URBAN, W. M. *Language and Reality*. Macmillan, 1939.
URE, PETER. *Towards a Mythology: Studies in the Poetry of W. B. Yeats*. Hodder and Stoughton, 1946.

VIII. THE PROBLEM OF INTENTIONS

ABERCROMBIE, LASCELLES. "A Plea for the Liberty of Interpreting," in *Modern English Essays*, second series. Oxford, 1932. Pp. 204–6, 213, 221, 229–30.

ALEXANDER, SAMUEL. *Beauty and Other Forms of Value.* Macmillan, 1933. Chaps. IV and V.
BAILEY, RUTH. *A Dialogue on Modern Poetry.* Oxford, 1939. P. 42.
BEATTY, R. C. "The Heritage of Symbolism in Modern Poetry," *Yale Review*, 36 (Spring 1947), 477.
BECK, WARREN. "Conception and Technique," *College English*, 11 (March 1950), 308–17.
BELGION, MONTGOMERY. "The Expression of Emotion," *Southern Review*, 3 (Spring 1938), 784.
———. "The Poet's Name," *Sewanee Review*, 54 (Autumn 1946), 642–43.
———. "What Is Criticism?" *Criterion*, 10 (October 1930), 129.
BLACKMUR, R. P. Introduction to *The Art of the Novel*, by Henry James. Scribner, 1941.
BOAS, GEORGE. *A Primer for Critics.* Johns Hopkins University Press, 1937.
BOWRA, C. M. *The Creative Experiment.* Macmillan, 1949. See also Eliseo Vivas, "The Heresy of Paraphrase," *Poetry*, 75 (January 1950), 217–23.
BRADLEY, A. C. *Oxford Lectures on Poetry.* Macmillan, 1909.
BROOKS, CLEANTH. "Criticism and History," *Sewanee Review*, 55 (Spring 1947), 199.
———. *Modern Poetry and the Tradition.* University of North Carolina Press, 1939. Chap. I.
———. *The Well Wrought Urn.* Reynal, 1947; Dobson, 1949. P. 22.
———, and R. WARREN. *Understanding Poetry.* Holt, 1938. Pp. 42, 44, 477–82, 497.
BUERMEYER, LAWRENCE. Review in *Symposium*, 1 (April 1930), 272.
BURKE, KENNETH. *Counter-Statement.* Harcourt, 1931.
———. *The Philosophy of Literary Form.* Louisiana State University Press, 1941. Pp. 22–23, 93–102.
BUTLER, E. M. *Rainer Maria Rilke.* Cambridge University Press, 1941. See also D. J. Enright's review in *Scrutiny*, 10 (January 1942), 301, 303.
CALAS, Nicholas. *Confound the Wise.* Arrow Editions, 1942.
CASSIRER, ERNST. *An Essay on Man.* Yale University Press, 1944. Pp. 140–44.
CENTANO, AUGUSTO, editor. *The Intent of the Artist.* Princeton University Press, 1941.
CHURCH, R. W. "Art," in *Encyclopedia of the Arts.* Philosophical Library, 1946.
CIARDI, JOHN, editor. *Mid-Century American Poets.* Twayne, 1950.
COLLINGWOOD, R. G. *The Principles of Art.* Clarendon Press, 1938. Pp. 111, 115, 309.
COOK, R. L. "Robert Frost's Asides on His Poetry," *American Literature*, 19 (January 1948), 354.
———. "Robert Frost: A Time to Listen," *College English*, 7 (November 1945), 67–68.
COOMARASWAMY, A. K. "Intention," *American Bookman*, 1 (Winter 1944), 41–48.
CRANE, HART. "A Discussion with Hart Crane," *Poetry*, 25 (October 1926), 34–41. Reprinted in Brom Weber, *Hart Crane.* Bodley Press, 1948. Pp. 416–21.
———. "Two Letters on 'The Bridge'," *Hound and Horn*, 7 (July 1934), 677–82. See also D. S. Savage, *The Personal Principle.* Routledge, 1944. Pp. 117–18.
CROCE, B. *Aesthetics.* Macmillan, 1922. Pp. 20–24, 111–12.
———. *The Defense of Beauty.* Clarendon Press, 1933.

DAY-LEWIS, CECIL. "A Hope for Poetry," in *Collected Poems*. Random House, 1935. P. 241–49.

DEWEY, JOHN. *Art as Experience*. Minton Balch, 1934. Pp. 65, 75, 76.

Dictionary of World Literature. Edited by Joseph Shipley. Philosophical Library, 1943. Pp. 325–29.

DREW, E., and J. SWEENEY. *Directions in Modern Poetry*. Norton, 1940. Pp. 18, 185.

DUPEE, F. W., editor. *The Question of Henry James*. Holt, 1945. Pp. 92–93.

EASTMAN, MAX. *The Literary Mind*. Scribner, 1935. P. 329.

ELIOT, T. S. *Essays Ancient and Modern*. Harcourt, 1936.

———. *The Sacred Wood*. Methuen, 1928; Knopf, 1930. P. 58.

———. *The Music of Poetry*. Jackson, 1942. Pp. 14–16.

———. *Selected Essays 1917–1932*. Harcourt, Faber, 1932. Pp. 125, 129.

———. "The Social Function of Poetry," *Adelphi*, 21 (July 1945), 154–56. Reprinted in *Critiques and Essays in Criticism*, edited by R. W. Stallman. Ronald Press, 1949. Pp. 105–16.

———. *The Use of Poetry and the Use of Criticism*. Faber, Harvard University Press, 1933. P. 130.

———, editor. *A Choice of Kipling's Verse*. Faber, 1941; Scribner, 1943. Introduction.

EMPSON, WILLIAM. *Some Versions of Pastoral*. Chatto, 1935. Pp. 3, 58, 68.

———. "Thy Darling in an Urn," *Sewanee Review*, 55 (Autumn 1947), 696–97.

ENRIGHT, D. J. "A Book on Rilke," *Scrutiny*, 10 (January 1942), 301.

FOWLIE, WALLACE. *Clowns and Angels*. Sheed and Ward, 1943. Pp. 152–53.

FRY, ROGER. *Vision and Design*. Chatto, 1920. Pp. 51–52.

GARNETT, EDWARD, editor. *Conrad's Prefaces to His Works*. Dent, 1937.

GHISELIN, BREWSTER. "The Birth of a Poem," *Poetry*, 69 (October 1946), 30–43.

GOLDWATER, R., and M. TREVES, editors. *Artists on Art*. Pantheon Books, 1945. Pp. 417, 461, 463.

GOTSHALK, D. W. *Art and the Social Order*. University of Chicago Press, 1947. Pp. 67, 74–75.

HALL, J., and M. STEINMANN, editors. *The Permanence of Yeats*. Macmillan, 1950.

HARDING, D. W. "The Theme of 'The Ancient Mariner'," *Scrutiny*, 9 (March 1941), 334–42.

HARDING, R. E. M. *An Anatomy of Inspiration*. Cambridge University Press, 1940; Heffner, 1948.

HEYL, BERNARD. *New Bearings in Esthetics and Art Criticism*. Yale University Press, 1943. P. 10.

HOFFMAN, F. J. *Freudianism and the Literary Mind*. Louisiana State University Press, 1945.

HORTON, PHILIP. *Hart Crane: The Life of an American Poet*. Norton, 1937.

HYMAN, S. E. *The Armed Vision*. Knopf, 1948.

JAMES, HENRY. "The Art of Fiction," in *The Art of Fiction*, edited by Michael Roberts. Oxford, 1948. P. 13.

———. *The Art of the Novel*, edited by R. P. Blackmur. Scribner, 1941. Pp. 287, 296.

KNIGHT, G. W. *Christian Renaissance*. Macmillan, 1933. P. 105.

———. *Shakespeare and Tolstoy*. English Association Pamphlet 88 (April 1934), p. 10.

———. *The Wheel of Fire*. Oxford, 1930; Methuen, 1948. P. 8.

LAWRENCE, D. H. *Studies in Classic American Literature*. Boni, 1923. P. 3.

LEAVIS, F. R. "Gerard Manley Hopkins," *Scrutiny*, 12 (Spring 1944), 93.

———. "Henry James and the Function of Criticism," *Scrutiny*, 15 (Spring 1948), 99.

LEWIS, C. S. *Rehabilitations*. Oxford, 1939. Pp. 7, 21–22, 25.

———, and E. TILLYARD. *The Personal Heresy*. Oxford, 1939. Pp. 16, 120.

Literary Scholarship: Its Aims and Methods. University of North Carolina Press, 1939. P. 25.

LUBBOCK, PERCY. *The Craft of Fiction*. Jonathan Cape, Scribner, 1921; Peter Smith, 1947. Pp. 60, 62.

LUCAS, F. L. *The Decline and Fall of the Romantic Ideal*. Cambridge University Press, 1937. P. 22. See also J. M. Purcell, article in *Explicator*, 3 (1945), item 42.

MACNEICE, LOUIS. *The Poetry of W. B. Yeats*. Oxford, 1941. P. 79.

MARITAIN, JACQUES. *Art and Scholasticism*, Scribner, 1943. P. 131.

MORE, P. E. "On Poe's Literary Method," in *American Issues*, edited by W. Thorp, M. Curti, and C. Baker. Lippincott, 1941. II, pp. 731–35.

MULLER, H. J. *Science and Criticism*. Yale University Press, 1943. P. 48.

MURRY, J. M. *Aspects of Literature*. Collins, 1920. P. 69.

PEPPER, S. C. *The Basis of Criticism in the Arts*. Harvard University Press, 1946. Pp. 82–83.

Poets at Work. Harcourt, 1948.

PRALL, D. W. *Aesthetic Analysis*. Crowell, 1936. P. 159.

RANSOM, J. C. "Mr. Empson's Muddles," *Southern Review*, 4 (Autumn 1938), 323–24.

———. *The New Criticism*. New Directions, 1941. Pp. 224–26.

———. "The Pragmatics of Art," *Kenyon Review*, 2 (Winter 1940), 81ff.

———. *The World's Body*. Scribner, 1938. Pp. 1–28.

READ, HERBERT. *Collected Essays*. Faber, 1938. Pp. 100, 114.

———. "The Form of Modern Poetry," *Symposium*, 1 (July 1930), 295.

RICHARDS, I. A. *Practical Criticism*. Harcourt, Routledge, 1929. Pp. 353–57.

———. *Principles of Literary Criticism*. Kegan Paul, 1924. Chap. XXV.

———. *Science and Poetry*. Norton, 1926. P. 34.

SAVAGE, D. S. *The Personal Principle*. Routledge, 1944. Pp. 114–15, 118.

SCHACK, WILLIAM. "A Critique of Art Criticism," *Virginia Quarterly Review*, 18 (1942), 93–109.

SCHNEIDER, ELISABETH. *Aesthetic Motive*. Macmillan, 1939. Pp. 102, 118.

Scrutiny. Edited by F. R. Leavis. 9 (March 1941), 338, 342, 375; 10 (January 1942), 301; 10 (April 1942), 395–96; 11 (December 1942), 147; 12 (Spring 1944), 29, 33, 93; 13 (September 1945), 99.

SMITH, R. J. "Intention in an Organic Theory of Poetry," *Sewanee Review*, 625–33.

SPENDER, STEPHEN. "The Making of a Poem," *Partisan Review*, 13 (Summer 1946), 294–308. Reprinted in *Critiques and Essays in Criticism*, edited by R. W. Stallman. Ronald Press, 1949. Pp. 17–29.

SPINGARN, J. E. *Creative Criticism*. Harcourt, 1931. Pp. 167–68.

———, editor. *Criticism in America*. Harcourt, 1924. Pp. 24–25, 43, 181.

———, editor. *The New Criticism*. Prentice-Hall, 1930.

STALLMAN, R. W. "The Critical Reader," *College English*, 9 (April 1948), 362. Reprinted in Ray B. West, Jr., and R. W. Stallman, *The Art of Modern Fiction*. Rinehart, 1949. Pp. 443–52.

——. "The Intentional Fallacy," *Quarterly Review of Literature*, 3 (1946), 21.

——. "A Note on Intentions," *College English*, 10 (October 1948), 40–41.

STAUFFER, D. A. *The Nature of Poetry*. Norton, 1946. P. 167.

STEGNER, WALLACE. "A Problem in Fiction," *Pacific Spectator*, 3 (Autumn 1949), 369–75.

STEIN, LEO. *The A-B-C of Aesthetics*. Liveright, 1927. P. 124.

STEVENS, WALLACE. Article in *Explicator*, 7 (November 1948), item 18.

SUTHERLAND, JAMES. *The Medium of Poetry*. Hogarth Press, 1934.

SYMONS, JULIAN. "Obscurity and Dylan Thomas," *Kenyon Review*, 2 (Winter 1940), 66–67.

TATE, ALLEN. "Modern Poets and Convention," *American Review*, 8 (February 1937), 428.

——. "Poetry and the Absolute," *Sewanee Review*, 35 (January 1927), 41–52.

——. *Selected Poems*. Scribner, 1937. Pp. viii–ix.

THOMAS, W., and S. BROWN. *Reading Poems*. Oxford, 1941. P. 657.

TILLOTSON, GEOFFREY. *Essays in Criticism and Research*. Cambridge University Press, 1942. P. xii.

TRILLING, LIONEL. *The Liberal Imagination*. Viking Press, 1950. Pp. 47–48, 186–87.

VALÉRY, PAUL. "Concerning the 'Cimetière Marin'," *Southern Review*, 4 (Summer 1938), 156, 159–60, 165.

——. "Literature," *Hudson Review*, 2 (Winter 1950), 538–58.

WALCUTT, C. C. "Critic's Taste or Artist's Intention?" *University of Kansas City Review*, 12 (Summer 1946), 278–83.

——. "Housman and the Empire," *College English*, 6 (February 1944), 255–58.

WALDOCK, A. J. A. *'Paradise Lost' and Its Critics*. Macmillan, 1947.

WARREN, A., and R. WELLEK. *The Theory of Literature*. Harcourt, 1949.

WARREN, R. P. *The Rime of the Ancient Mariner: An Essay*. Reynal, 1946. Pp. 113–17.

WEBER, BROM. *Hart Crane*. Bodley Press, 1948. Pp. 416–21.

WEBER, C. J., editor. *A Shropshire Lad*. Colby College Library, 1946. Pp. 104–5. See also Cleanth Brooks, "The Whole of Housman," *Kenyon Review*, 3 (1941), 105.

WELLEK, RENÉ. "The Mode of Existence of a Literary Work of Art," *Southern Review*, 7 (Spring 1942), 741–44. Reprinted in *Critiques and Essays in Criticism*, edited by R. W. Stallman. Ronald Press, 1949. Pp. 210–23.

WILSON, T. C. Review in *Decision*, 2 (August 1941), 57–59.

WIMSATT, W. K., JR. "Comment on 'Two Essays'," *University of Kansas City Review*, 9 (Winter 1942), 142.

——, and M. BEARDSLEY. "The Intentional Fallacy," *Sewanee Review*, 54 (Summer 1946), 468–88. See also "Intentions," in *Dictionary of World Literature*, edited by Joseph Shipley. Philosophical Library, 1943. Pp. 325–29.

WINTERS, YVOR. *In Defense of Reason*. Morrow, 1947. Pp. 19–21. See also J. C. Ransom, *The New Criticism*. New Directions, 1941. Pp. 224–26.

YEATS, W. B. *Oxford Book of Modern Verse*. Oxford, 1936. Introduction, p. vii.

Index

INDEX

Donne, John, 33, 72, 74, 75, 156, 157, 157–58, 172, 195, 196: and Eliot, 157: *Air and Angels*, 156; *Canonization*, 75; *First Anniversary*, 156; *Funeral*, 72
Dos Passos, John, 101
Drama, 81–82, 118–19, 211–12, 214, 229: Elizabethan, 157; novel as, 60, 134; poem as, 210; purpose of, 139–40; the "well made" play, 59. See also Tragedy
Dramatic: definition of, 157–58; scene, 142
Dreiser, Theodore, 41
Drew, Elizabeth, and John Sweeney, 88, 110, 124–25, 171–72
Dryden, John, 17, 18, 35, 156, 234
Ducasse, C. J., 232

Eliot, T. S., 5, 7, 8, 17, 18, 20, 21, 22, 24, 28, 30–31, 33, 34, 35, 40, 49–50, 54, 66, 84, 87–88, 89, 92, 105, 119, 121–22, 127, 129–30, 131, 138, 140, 141, 142, 144, 150–51, 151–52, 152–53, 154–55, 156, 157, 161, 162–63, 163–64, 165, 169–70, 171, 172, 184–85, 185–88, 193, 196, 197–99, 200, 203, 220, 229–30, 240–41, 244, 245: and Dante, 127–31: *Ash-Wednesday*, 130; "The Perfect Critic," 140–44; *Sacred Wood*, 24, 40, 129ff; "Tradition and the Individual Talent," 150–51; *Waste Land*, 24, 196, 203, 241
Emerson, R. W., 61
Emotion, 8, 15, 23, 40, 46, 47, 54, 61–62, 63, 82, 86, 92, 107, 111, 112, 116, 119–20, 121–22, 123–24, 126, 127, 128, 131, 132, 133, 137, 138, 139–40, 141, 142, 143, 144–45, 146–49, 150, 152, 153–54, 155, 156, 157, 165, 168, 169, 181, 191, 206, 225–26, 245
Emotion: and feeling, 150, 155, 166 (*see also* Feeling); and form, 62 (*see also* Form); and sensations, 53–54, 99, 117–18, 119, 126 (*see also* Expression); and thought, 152, 212; creative, 156; precise, 61–62, 152; prehension of, 145; transfusion of, 171; "transmuted," 150; "emotion recollected in tranquility," 122, 125, 156, 223, 253
Emotional, 244: complexes, 140;

depth, 167; experience, 142; illusion, 67; states, 89
Emotive language, 50. See also Language
Empson, William, 19, 231, 248–49, 253–54
Enright, D. J., 197, 247
Epstein, Jacob, 231
Euripides, 67
Evaluation, 18, 112. See also Judgment
Evans, B. I., 8–9
Expression, 117–18, 119, 121, 123, 124, 140, 142–43, 143–44, 145, 154, 164, 193, 224, 231, 247, 250: of emotion, 139–51, 191, 225–26; self-expression, 145

Fairchild, A. H. R., 118
Fallacy, see Affective fallacy
Farrell, J. T., 20–21
Faustian, 126
Feeling, 30, 81, 86, 91, 95, 99–100, 105–6, 107, 111, 112, 117, 118, 122, 124, 139–40, 142, 147–48, 149, 154, 183–84, 187, 194, 195, 225, 228, 231, 237, 243, 249, 250, 251, 252, 254: aesthetic, 124 (*see also* Aesthetic); and emotion, 150, 155, 166; and form, 62; and thought, 44, 49, 61, 127, 130, 137, 145, 151–58, 162, 197; as tone, 84, 85; in criticism, 13, 15, 168; in language, 89–90, 92, 93–94
Feibleman, James, 96–97
Fernandez, Ramon, 163
Fiction, 140. See also Novel and novelists
Fielding, Henry, 38, 46, 66–67
Flaubert, Gustave, 38, 52, 53, 69–70, 134–35, 165
Flint, F. C., 71–73, 176
Foerster, Norman, 23–24, 233
Form, 9, 19, 38, 42, 46, 52, 54–55, 86, 88, 91–92, 118, 119, 123, 124, 145, 146, 152–53, 156, 164–65, 199, 203, 217, 218, 219, 220, 221, 222, 224, 225, 231, 234. See also Pattern, Structure
Form: aesthetic, 163 (*see also* Aesthetic); and content, 23, 27, 45, 65, 66, 143, 252–53; and creation, 19; and language, 95; and meaning, 45; and "scenario content," 112; and style, 168; and symbol, 225 (*see also* Symbol); and theme, 63, 189 (*see also*

250–52. *See also* Intentions, Obliquity, Paraphrase, Sense

Meaning: abstract, 82, 86; and form, 65 (*see also* Form); place of in poem, 88, 145, 151–52, 153–54; poet's intention, 186; points of reference, 59; problem of, 80–114; "total," 86, 232 (*see also* Intentions)

Metaphysical poets and poetry, 131, 156–57, 157–58. *See also* Donne, John; Marvell, Andrew

Method, 22–23, 25, 28, 82, 106, 128, 203, 212: aesthetic, 27; analytical, 235; biographical, 172–73; contrast and comparison, 28, 35; empirical, 7; historical, 27–28, 28–29; "mythical," 203; narrative, 203; organic, 221; poetic, 63, 64, 71–73, 126–27, 128, 129; problem of, 10; psychological, 72f, 249; scientific, 247 (*see also* Science); symbolic, 96–97, 97–98, 98–99, 100; theoretical, 6–7. *See also* Criticism, Technique

Milton, John, 3, 15, 21, 22, 29, 128, 156, 190, 191, 216, 229: *Paradise Lost,* 3, 15, 216

Montaigne, 212

Moore, T. S., 152, 164–65

Morgan, Charles, 66

More, P. E., 31

Muller, H. J., 41–42, 44–45, 100–1

Murray, Gilbert, 40

Murry, J. M., 19, 54–55, 125, 126–27, 169–70, 180–82, 238, 243, 244

Musicalization, *see* Language

Myers, W. L., 42

Myth, 97, 98, 101f, 192, 196, 203; mythological, 236

Nashe, Thomas, 71

Naturalism, 25; positivistic movement, 25

Nietzsche, 44, 173

Novel and novelists, 50, 51, 70, 71, 101, 116: point of view of, 52–53

O'Connor, W. V., 189–90

Objective correlative, 7, 100, 118, 152: concept of, 116–58; echoes and parallelisms, 116–20; threefold aspects of the concept, 120–38; objective equivalence, 124, 132, 242

Objectivity, 11, 239. *See also* Judgment

Obliquity, 63, 81, 82, 83, 91, 104f, 106–10. *See also* Meaning

Obscurity, 96, 132, 147, 226, 243, 246–47, 250

Oedipus motive, 236; situation, 235

Olson, Elder, 90–91

Ong, W. J., 85–86

Organic, *see* Form, Method

Originality, 121–22

Ovid, 212

Paraphrase, 83–84, 86–87, 104–14, 124, 242–47, 251–52; paraphrastic heresy, 111f (*see also* Meaning). *See also* Analysis

Parrington, V. L., 26

Pater, Walter, 43

Pattern, 60, 95, 97, 110, 132, 210, 225: as design, 148, 149; as form, 65, 66; dialectical, 195; sound-patterns, 93. *See also* Form

Pepper, S. C., 238–39

Personal element, 27, 30, 54–55, 82, 117–18, 119–20, 120–21, 121–22, 123, 133, 145, 155, 170, 177, 183, 186, 189–90, 190–91, 197–98, 199, 270; anonymity, 170; emotion, 142

Problem of the personal element, 159–74: in poetic creation, 160–65 (*see also* Creation); in the work of art, 165–68; in poetic appreciation, 168–74

Philology, 32

Philosophy, 23, 233: and art, 192–93, 193–94 (*see also* Art, Science); and attitude, 27 (*see also* Attitude); and poetry, 125, 197, 199, 200, 247, 253

Plato, 17, 59, 91, 198f, 226

Plot, 48, 50–51, 82–83, 85, 232: organic, 51; "suspense of plot," 66–67

Plutarch, 212

Poe, E. A., 104, 221

Poet: and philosopher, 197; in relation to poem, 207–8, 208–10, 215–16, 242; in relation to public, 190, 245; philosophical, 199, 200

Poetry: definition of, 137–38, 250–51; function of, 229–30; message in, 171, 200, 210; method of, 129; nature of, 8, 74, 104, 105, 213, 236–37; of feelings, 154; physiological theory of,